Sharon Trammell
Eat Off the Land

A Wild Foraging and Survival
Cookbook Featuring Mushrooms,
Plants, Fish, and Game from the
Pacific Northwest and Beyond

(Forage and Thrive Series Book One)

Printed in the United States of America

ISBN 979-8-9912848-6-8 (sc)

Contents

Dedication

This is my first outdoor genre book. I am lovingly dedicating it to my friends at NOWA. I joined as a new writer, with plenty of talent, but little knowledge of how the field of outdoor writing works. As I have birthed this project, the support received from many of you, who I now call colleagues and friends, really helped my work take root and continue to grow. Especially I want to thank Gary, George, Keith, and Brad. Having people believe in me while I was still learning to believe in myself has really shaped the trajectory of my writing career.

With deep gratitude,

Sharon

Preface

When I was in the process of writing this cookbook, it dawned on me how many of the other prepper cookbooks focus specifically on eating only staples: stockpiling beans, rice, flour, salt, and sugar. That appears to be the name of the game for many "survival" chefs. I wrote this to propose a different way. We don't have to live like the pioneers and eat only the well-known survival staples, regulating what meager supplies we have just to get by. Instead, we could be like traditional Native Americans and eat off the land! That's right! In this book, my goal is to teach you how to recognize, harvest, preserve, and prepare delicious wild foods! In this way, we are shifting the mindset from a fear-based one, where we focus on rationing grain, like farmers feeding their livestock for survival, to realizing the abundance that exists around us in the natural world! From an energetic standpoint, this takes us from scarcity to an abundant lifestyle! You will learn how to identify mushrooms, plants, and berries, where to search for them, and once you get them home, how to cook them in a simple, yet delicious way! You will also learn the secrets to delicious wild meats—how to remove the gamey flavor but retain the wild accent and the juicy texture, so you feel like you are eating meals fit for a king—you won't even know they are wild meat, except, of course, for the exceptional quality—free of preservatives, growth hormones, and feedlot mentality (because, yes, that energy transfers from the animal to YOU when you buy poor quality meat from the supermarket). So, let's get started! No grocery store, no problem!

Note: This book was written based on PNW plants. Therefore, much of the identification guide is focused on how these plants appear in the Pacific Northwest: Alaska, Oregon, Washington, California, Idaho, and Montana. However, the wild food mentioned in this book is not distinct to the Pacific Northwest. Most of the items can be found throughout various regions of the world.

Author's Note

I grew up surrounded by outdoorsmen and women. Some of my fondest memories come from elk camp in Western Washington, early morning trout fishing trips with my grandfather to high mountain lakes full of mosquitoes, and long plant walks with my mother down our secluded forest road. I learned plenty about hunting, fishing, and which plants to avoid —but we rarely talked about sustainability.

It wasn't until my time studying at Oregon State University—diving into Native American philosophy and fisheries management—that I began to see wild harvest through a different lens. I came to understand that, while we're meant to gather plants, fungi, fish, and big game, we must do it responsibly, with respect for the land and the species we rely on.

Years in the PNW fishing and foraging scene have shown me the good, the bad, and the careless. I've seen greed push people to take more than they need, without thinking about tomorrow. But I've also learned from spiritual and Indigenous perspectives that value balance, gratitude, and true stewardship. Throughout this book, you'll find traditional Indigenous practices, wisdom, and recipes woven alongside modern survival skills—reminders that abundance and respect can exist together.

If we can shift our mindset from short-term gain to long-term abundance, we can harvest plenty *and* leave plenty. It's not hunting or fishing that threatens our wild places—it's disrespect for the systems that keep them thriving. By learning sustainable practices and giving back to the land, we keep this way of life alive for our families and the generations to come.

Stay wild, stay ready, and never forget: the land will always provide—if you know how to listen.

—Sharon Trammell

Safety Notice

Sharon Trammell is not responsible for what the reader decides to consume. Foraging for wild edibles is a personal choice that the individual takes at their own risk. Please do your research regarding what plants are edible and understanding poisonous look-alikes. Although this guide offers identification diagrams, it is a good idea to check it against a second identification book if you are new to foraging. Double and triple check before consuming any plant you harvest. No one should EVER ingest anything unless they have positively identified it. See resources at the end of this book for plant identification guides.

Cooking First: As a general rule, wild mushrooms (and some wild plants) should not be ingested without prior cooking.

Allergy Test: For anyone who is trying new wild foods for the first time, make sure to try a small amount to test for allergies. Orally, this can look like eating one small bite of any edible plant or edible mushroom (after a positive identification; this is not to test if its edible). Topically, rub a small leaf or piece against your back or arm and look for an allergic reaction.

Medical Disclaimer: Information provided in this guide is not designed to diagnose, prescribe, or treat any illness or injury. Always consult a health care professional or medical doctor when suffering from any health ailment, disease, illness, or injury, before attempting a holistic remedy.

When using natural remedies for beauty products or hygiene purposes, it is always best to consult a doctor prior to the first use. If you are pregnant, breastfeeding, or have any medication you are taking or any medical condition, don't use without the consultation of a professional.

Pollution and Spraying: If you are harvesting from urban areas, be aware of potential for pollution because of spraying or weed control. Also think about pollution due to human population living in areas such as city parks, when harvesting from these types of areas.

General Regulations

There are many laws relating to foraging and even more when it comes to hunting and fishing. While I cannot list all of them here, it is imperative that you familiarize yourself with your local laws before doing any hunter-gatherer activities. To hunt or fish, even for things like crab or clams, you need, generally, a license, and for hunting or fish like steelhead and salmon, a tag. For mushroom hunting, there are often different laws depending on where you are geographically. For instance, National Parks prohibit collecting, while National Forests and State Forests often allow limited personal-use foraging. To commercially harvest, you often need a permit from the forest service; you may need a permit even if you are harvesting for personal uses if you take over a certain amount (example: 5 gallons). Familiarize yourself with these laws before going out to harvest!

Understanding Best Practices in Foraging

One common argument in foraging is whether or not to pull up the entire fungus. While many have debated this, believing that pulling kills the mycelium, the research points to the fact that spores are embedded in the ground, and taking the entire mushroom won't remove the spores from the area. So, while it is up to you whether you cut or pull your mushrooms, one thing that you could do to ensure future harvests on most fungi is to spread the spores. Yes, they are already in the ground, but I have noticed patch improvements by spreading the spores in my own patches. I do this by picking up a few of the ones that are past their prime, and breaking them up to spread around the area. Another great way to spread the spores is to use a mesh bag, or even a crate with slats in the bottom. In this way, you are spreading spores not only in the direct area you are harvesting, but also on your hike back to your vehicle. Finally, if you do pull the entire mushroom up, you can trim the mushroom ends and spread these throughout the area.

Ethics in Harvesting Fish and Game

Some are called to hunt and fish, others are not. Not everyone can take a life to nourish their own. Whether or not you feel that you can is of no consequence. There should be no judgment for yourself for being a hunter, or for consuming only plants. What is important is how you harvest. If you kill fish or big game, be thankful. Do a gratitude ritual. Thank the universe for blessing you with fresh meat. Thank the spirit of the animal for giving itself up for you. Remember that this was a choice; this animal allowed itself to be harvested, because he knew that he was fulfilling his purpose on this Earth in doing so. Always follow ethical guidelines suggested for any hunt you are doing. Be a good steward, the universe always watches, feels your energy, and will reward you as such.

Finally, the most important thing, whether you are big game hunting, or harvesting the readily available horsetail for hair or skin benefit, is to be present. Immerse yourself in nature. Breathe deeply. Look at how blue the sky is. Place your hand on a fir tree and feel the texture of its bark. Take off your shoes when you cross a creek and let your toes feel the silty bottom. Wear only enough sunscreen to be protected, but let that glorious, God-given light into your skin. It is there to heal you, to nurture you. Enjoy the stillness. Happy gathering!

ACORNS

If you are contemplating off grid living or simply want to know a good replacement for traditional wheat flour, harvested straight from the wild, acorn flour may be your flour of choice. **Acorns**, the nuts of oak trees (*Quercus* spp.), have been a staple food for Indigenous peoples across North America for thousands of years. High in complex carbs, fiber, minerals like potassium and magnesium, and healthy fats, acorns can be turned into a nutrient-dense flour—perfect for survival cooking. With proper preparation to remove their natural bitterness (and harmful tannins), they become a versatile, storable, and sustainable food source straight from the wild. Acorns are found across most of North America, especially in temperate forests. Look for them in regions with native oak species like:

White Oak (Quercus alba) – Eastern U.S.
Black Oak, Red Oak – Eastern & Central U.S.
Valley Oak, Live Oak – West Coast & California
Gambel Oak – Rocky Mountain region
Bur Oak – Midwest plains

Did You Know?

Some Indigenous peoples leached acorns in cold running streams for days to remove bitter tannins—a simple but smart survival type method that turns these nuts into a nutritious flour for breads and porridges!

Oak Tree
(Quercus garryana and related sp.)

Leaves

Oak leaves are usually lobed, with rounded (white oak group) or pointed (red oak group) tips

Acorns

Oval or round, usually with textured cap ("hat") covering the top

White oak acorns are sweeter and less bitter than red oak acorns, which are high in tannins.

Bark

Varies by species; often deeply ridged or scaly in mature trees

Foraging Guide

Habitat

Oak trees thrive in many areas—from dry, rocky hillsides to moist forests and river valleys. In the Pacific Northwest, you'll often find native oaks like the Garry oak (Oregon white oak) in dry grasslands, open woodlands, and mixed conifer forests. In other regions, oaks grow in deciduous forests, along forest edges, and even in urban parks—anywhere there's well-drained soil and good sun. If you harvest from urban areas, check for spraying or other pollution.

Season

- September--November

Note: Look for firm, brown acorns without cracks or holes. Picking off the tree too early can be dangerous because green nuts have higher levels of tannins. Additionally, it should be noted that white oak acorns have the lowest level of tannins and therefore, require less leaching—making them a better fit for survival flour.

Toxic Look-Alikes and Cautions

1. **Horse Chestnuts (Aesculus spp., also known as Buckeyes)**
   – These nuts fall around the same time, but their distinct spiky shell makes them easy to tell apart
   – **Toxic to humans if eaten raw**—they contain aesculin, which can cause severe digestive upset
2. **Beech Nuts (*Fagus spp.*)**
   – Sometimes confused with small acorns—but they're generally easy to tell apart because beech nuts are three-sided and come in a prickly burr
   – **Edible in small amounts** when fully ripe and cooked; raw nuts may contain small amounts of saponins and tannins which can cause mild stomach upset in large quantities

Key tip: True acorns always grow on oak trees and have a signature cap ("cupule") that covers the top of the nut. If you're unsure—check the tree's leaves. Oak leaves have distinctive lobed shapes.

Avoid: Acorns with pinholes (sign of bugs), mold, or spots

A Word of Caution on Tannins

Tannins, found in most raw acorns, can be toxic in large amounts, irritating the digestive tract and interfering with nutrient absorption. Even after leaching, it's best to eat acorn-based foods in moderation. Never skip the tannin removal step, no matter how "sweet" the acorn may taste.

Cleaning, Drying, & Removing Tannins

Clean

Rinse acorns to remove dirt and debris. Discard the ones that float—they're usually rotten or bug-infested. Crack open shells using a rock, hammer, or nutcracker.

Remove Tannins (Leaching)

Two survival-friendly methods:
1. **Cold Water Leach (Best for Flour):**
   - Place shelled acorn meat in a cloth bag or jar of cold water.
   - Change water 2–3 times a day until the water runs clear and acorns taste mild (3–7 days).
   - Keep in a cool place or stream during process.
2. **Boiling Method (Faster, but changes the makeup of the starch):**
   - Boil acorns in water, then discard the water.
   - Repeat several times until water is no longer brown and acorns are mild.
   - Alternate pots of boiling water to prevent the tannins from binding.

Making Acorn Flour

Dry:
- Once tannins are removed, dry the acorn bits thoroughly—sun-dry, air-dry, or use a dehydrator. In a dehydrator, it might take 12-14 hours and you should use the lowest possible heat setting. You will know they are dry when they crack like dried nuts instead of bending.

Grind:
- Use a mortar & pestle, hand grinder, or food processor to grind into fine flour.
- Store in a sealed container in a cool, dry place.

Use:
- Survival breads, thickening agent for soups/stews, pancakes, and wild pie crusts.
- Mix with wheat or other flour if desired for better binding.

Survival Tips
- Always test a small batch first to make sure tannins are fully removed.
- Acorn flour can be stored long-term if dried well—ideal for caching or winter prep.
- Consider roasting small pieces of leached acorn for trail snacks or campfire meals.

Flavor Profile

Acorns have a mildly nutty, earthy flavor with a hint of sweetness, similar to chestnuts when properly leached.

Where to Buy

Online retailers including Amazon (easiest to buy as flour unless you prefer to make your own for learning purposes). Farmers markets.

Wild Boil-in-a-Bag Campfire Cake (with Tallow)

A survivalist-style steamed dessert using foraged ingredients, cooked over the fire—no oven needed.

Time to Make: 45 minutes

Makes: 2–3 servings

Ingredients

Dry Mix (prep ahead or mix in camp):
- ¾ cup flour + ¼ cup acorn flour
- 1 tsp baking powder
- ¼ tsp salt
- 2 Tbsp brown sugar, maple sugar, or crushed dried wild apples
- ½ tsp cinnamon or dried spicebush (optional)

Wet Mix:
- 1 egg
- ¼ cup water or milk (or water + 1 Tbsp powdered milk)

Optional: chopped **Oregon oxalis** stems for tang

Optional: drizzle of wild honey or spoonful of berry jam inside the bag

- 2 Tbsp rendered **tallow**, melted

Foraged Add-ins:
- ¼–½ cup wild edibles such as:
  - **Huckleberries**
  - **Salmonberries**
  - **Thimbleberries**
  - **Wild strawberries**
  - **Fireweed blossoms**

Directions

1. **Mix:**
   - In a heavy-duty freezer bag or silicone boil-safe pouch, combine dry ingredients.
   - Add egg, water, and melted tallow. Mix until smooth.
   - Gently fold in your foraged berries or flowers.
   - Squeeze out excess air and seal the bag tightly.
2. **Boil:**
   - Bring a pot of water to a boil and reduce to a simmer.
   - Place a cloth or flat rock at the bottom of the pot to prevent scorching.
   - Submerge the sealed bag (upright if possible).
   - Simmer gently for **30–45 minutes**, rotating occasionally if needed.
3. **Serve:**
   - Let cool slightly before opening.
   - Eat straight from the bag or slice and top with fresh berries, wild jam, or foraged flower petals.

Survivalist Tip: Tallow adds richness and keeps this cake fuel-dense for the backwoods or off grid type situations. Pre-mix dry ingredients into zip bags at home, and pack a small tin of rendered tallow to scoop and melt as needed.

Acorn Flour Pancakes

Nutty, filling, and with a rustic flavor—acorn pancakes are high in fiber and protein. Acorn flour is said to have an average of 7 grams protein per cup—adding egg and milk can help make this even more filling and nutritious!

Makes: 8 pancakes

Time to Make: 20 minutes

Ingredients

- 1 cup leached, dried, and ground acorn flour
- 1 cup all-purpose or oat flour
- 1½ tsp baking powder
- ¼ tsp salt

- 1½ cups milk (or plant milk)
- 2 eggs
- 2 Tbsp melted butter, tallow, or oil
- 1 Tbsp granulated sugar

Directions

1. **Mix** dry ingredients in one bowl, wet ingredients in another.
2. **Combine** and stir until just mixed—do not overbeat.
3. **Heat** a greased skillet over medium heat (or the edge of the campfire).
4. **Cook** pancakes 2–3 minutes per side until golden—look for bubbles throughout before flipping. If the pan is smoking too much, they are likely to burn. Turn the heat down and monitor them closely.
5. **Serve** with fir tip syrup or wild berry preserves.

Acorn Bannock Campfire Flatbread

A simple, pan-fried bread made with wild acorn flour—no yeast, no rising, just hearty nutrition from the forest to the table!

Makes: 3-4 flatbreads

Time to Make: 20 minutes

Ingredients

1 cup acorn flour (leached & dried)
1 cup all-purpose or other flour (for binding)
1 tsp salt

1 tsp baking powder
¾ cup water (adjust as needed)
2 Tbsp oil or melted rendered tallow

Directions

1. **Mix dry** ingredients in a bowl.
2. **Slowly** add water and oil, stirring until a thick dough forms. It should be moist but not sticky.
3. **Knead** briefly, then divide into 2–4 patties.
4. **Fry in** a floured or lightly greased skillet over a campfire or stovetop for 3–4 minutes per side, until browned and cooked through.

Survival Tips:

- Add other foraged flours (like cattail or pine bark) if desired.
- Serve warm with thimbleberry jam (see thimbleberry section), honey, or vegetable barley soup (see lobster mushroom section for recipe).
- Can also be baked on a hot rock or wrapped around a stick over fire.

BLACKBERRIES

The Pacific Northwest (PNW)—including western Washington, Oregon, and parts of British Columbia—is a prime region for blackberry (*Rubus sp.*) growth due to its wet, temperate climate. However, they grow widely across subtropical regions, including North America, Europe, parts of Asia, South America, and Australia. Beyond their culinary appeal, blackberries are rich in antioxidants, especially vitamin C and anthocyanins, which support immune health and reduce inflammation. They're high in fiber, promoting healthy digestion, and high levels of vitamins K and A in blackberries support bone and skin health. **Blackberries** also contain brain-boosting compounds and may even help regulate blood sugar levels.

Did you know?

In Cherokee tradition, blackberry root was brewed into tea to treat stomach ailments.
In European folklore, blackberries were avoided after late September—said to be cursed by the devil.

Types of Blackberries in the PNW and Identification Guide

The third type is evergreen blackberries, not included in the diagram.

Himalayan Blackberry
(*Rubus armeniacus*)
Invasive but most common prolific.

- **Thorns** Thick, curved, sharp
- **Stems Large,** arching, reddish-purple with 5 ridges
- **Leaves** Five leaflets; large, oval and toothed
- **Berries** Large, plump, shiny black when ripe; sweet and juicy
- **Growth Pattern** Aggressive thickets climbs over other plants

Trailing Blackberry
(*Rubus ursinus*)
Native species and favored by wildlife.

- **Thorns** Fine and sparse
- **Stems** Slender, trailing along the ground
- **Berries** Smaller, often elongated, dark purple-black; more complex flavor
- **Growth Pattern** Less dense; low to the ground, often hidden in underbrush

Foraging Guide

Habitat

- Roadsides and trails
- Abandoned lots and fields
- Forest edges and clearings
- Urban green spaces and parks
- Riversides and ditches

Blackberries thrive in disturbed soil and full to partial sunlight. You'll often find them forming dense thickets. In fact, they are considered an invasive species in many parts of the world, including the Pacific Northwest, where they often take over vacant lots, backyards, and even fields.

Season

- **Evergreen Blackberry** – August to September
- **Himalayan Blackberry** – Mid-July to September
- **Trailing Blackberry** – June to August

Toxic Look-Alikes and Cautions

1. **Deadly Nightshade** (*Atropa belladonna*): Its shiny black berries can look similar from a distance but grow alone or in small clusters on herbaceous plants, not thorny brambles. **Extremely toxic—never eat.**
2. **Pokeweed Berries** (*Phytolacca americana*): These dark purple-black berries grow in large drooping clusters on tall, non-woody stems with red-purple stalks. **All parts of pokeweed are poisonous if not properly prepared—avoid!**

Other Cautions:

- Wear gloves and long sleeves—thorns can scratch and irritate.
- Watch for bees and wasps—they're often nearby.
- Avoid polluted areas—don't pick near roadsides with heavy traffic or industrial zones.

Cleaning

Blackberries can be washed gently in a colander or strainer using a spray nozzle in the kitchen sink. Do this in small batches and gently stir them with your hand to remove bugs, petals, or leaf parts.

Storage

Blackberries keep in the fridge for up to 5 days. For best shelf-life, store them unwashed in a berry carton with slats to prevent trapped moisture.

Freezing

Wash berries as described above. Lay them in a single layer on a baking sheet. Freeze for about 4 hours or until completely frozen. Transfer to Ziploc bags for long-term storage.

They'll last in the freezer for up to two years—if freezer burn (or hungry children) doesn't get to them.

Note: Drying is not recommended; you'll mostly be left with seeds once the moisture is removed. However, see **salal berry section** for a fruit leather recipe you can use for blackberries if you want to dry them.

Flavor Profile

Wild blackberries deliver a bold, complex flavor that balances tartness with deep sweetness. Their juicy flesh offers subtle notes of red wine, forest herbs, and a touch of earthy bitterness from the seeds. Aromatic and slightly floral, they shine in both sweet and savory dishes. Perfect with citrus, honey, dark chocolate, or game meats.

Where to Buy

Commercially grown blackberries can be found in the frozen section of most grocery stores. However, for the best flavor, buy directly from a farm or farmers' market during the season and freeze them yourself. The taste of farm-fresh blackberries far exceeds that of store-bought—even in baked goods!

Wild Blackberry Jam (Low-Sugar)

Makes: 4-5 pint jars

Time to Make: 1 hour

Ingredients

- 4 cups fresh wild blackberries (washed, stems removed)
- 2 cups granulated sugar (or adjust to taste—you can use less with this pectin)
- 1 packet Ball RealFruit Low or No-Sugar Needed Pectin
- 2 Tbsp fresh lemon juice

Directions

1. **Mash the Berries:** In a large pot, gently mash the blackberries to release their juices.
2. **Add Pectin:** In a small bowl, mix the pectin powder with about ¼ cup of the measured sugar. Add this mixture to the berries and stir well.
3. **Cook the Jam:** Bring the berry mixture to a full rolling boil over medium-high heat, stirring constantly.
4. **Add Remaining Sugar:** Stir in the remaining sugar and return to a full rolling boil. Boil hard for 1 minute, stirring constantly. Remove from heat.
5. **Place** a towel on the counter. Place clean jars on the towel.
6. **Place** the Mason jar flat lids (not the rings) in very hot water to get them ready.
7. **Fill** your jars, using the ladle and funnel, leaving ¼-inch of space at the top of the jar.
8. **Wipe the** rims of the jars with a clean, damp towel. Place the lids on the jars and secure with rings. Make sure the lids are tight, but not too tight. If you prefer frozen jam, let the jars cool on the counter for up to 8 hours. Freeze for up to two years.

To can the jam, follow these instructions for water bath canning:

9. **Process the jars,** following the instructions for your water bath canner. This jam needs 5 minutes processing at sea level, 10 minutes above 1,000 feet altitude and 15 minutes above 6,000 feet altitude.
10. **Remove jars** with lifting tongs, setting them on a clean towel. Leave them for several hours or overnight to let them seal. You will likely hear them "pop" to seal and notice that the middles are depressed; this indicates a successful seal.

Blackberry Elk Loin Chops

This recipe combines the flavors of wild berries with hearty elk loin chops for a satisfying meal!

Makes: 2 chops

Time to Make: 30 minutes

Ingredients

Sauce:
- ¾ cup blackberries
- 1½ Tbsp balsamic vinegar
- 1 Tbsp brown sugar
- 1½ Tbsp granulated sugar
- 1 dash salt
- 1 tsp butter
- 1 Tbsp cornstarch
- ¼ cup water

Elk Loin Chops:
- 2 large cuts of elk loin or rib chops (can substitute pork chops)
- 1 Tbsp olive oil
- 2 garlic cloves, chopped
- 1 purple onion, chopped

Directions
1. **For Sauce:** Combine blackberries, sugar, vinegar, salt, and butter in a small saucepan.
2. Turn to low medium heat.
3. Mix together cold water and cornstarch separately.
4. Heat berry mixture until it is bubbling.
5. Mix in cornstarch and let it simmer for another 5 minutes on low.

Elk Chops
1. **In a cast** iron skillet, heat olive oil till it sizzles, on medium low.
2. **Add** garlic cloves and let these cook for one minute.
3. **Lay** chops in the hot oil and add purple onion.
4. **Let** this first side crisp; it should cook for about 4 minutes.
5. **Flip** them, and cover with a lid.
6. **Cook** for an additional 5-7 minutes, until the internal temperature of the meat is 145°F.
7. **Plate** the chops and scoop the sauce over the top. Serve with rice and wild foraged greens.

Blackberry Pecan Salad

I first tried this recipe in a little bistro in Bend Oregon, after a long day at a powerlifting competition. I don't remember the name of the place, nor all of the flavors in that original salad, but it was so good that I decided to re-create it at home. Ever since, it has been the perfect summer dinner for when it is too hot to cook. Add ½ cup grilled chicken, wild turkey, or grouse to this salad to increase the protein content.

Makes: 4 plates of salad

Time to Make: 20 minutes

Ingredients

To Make Candied Pecans

Combine 2 cups pecans and 1/3 cup brown sugar into a saucepan. Add 1 Tbsp water. Stir until the nuts are coated with the sugar. Cook on low medium heat for about 3 minutes, until the nuts start emitting a nutty aroma and turn shiny. Cool in a single layer on a baking sheet lined with parchment paper.

Optional: Add in apples for more fruit and less fat if you don't want the cheese

- 4 cup Organic Spring Mix or wild greens
- 2 cups Dandelion greens, cut into small pieces (other options are sorrel or miners' lettuce)
- 2 cups fresh very ripe blackberries
- 4 oz goat cheese (optional)
- ½ cup candied pecans

Dressing:
- ¼ cup balsamic vinegar
- 2 Tbsp olive oil
- ¼ cup crushed blackberries (very ripe!)
- 1 tsp granulated sugar
- ¼ tsp salt

Directions

Dressing:
1. **In** a glass jar, combine the olive oil and balsamic vinegar mixture.
2. **Crush** blackberries with a fruit crusher or simply stir vigorously.
3. **Mix** into olive oil mixture. Shake well until mixed.

Salad Assembly:
1. **Toss** spring mix and dandelion greens together in a large bowl.
2. **Assemble** four plates with the greens.
3. **Top** each plate with ¼ cup blackberries, 1 oz crumbled goat cheese, and candied pecans.
4. **Drizzle** dressing over the plates of salad just before serving.

Probiotic Blackberry Lemon Balm Frozen Yogurt

Probiotics in yogurt support a healthy gut microbiome, which can improve digestion, boost immunity, and enhance nutrient absorption. Combined with the flavor of fresh blackberries, and the slight tanginess of lemon balm, this is the perfect summer treat that is secretly helping your health! See wild cherry section for a DIY yogurt recipe!

Makes: 6 ½ cup servings
Time to Make: 1 hour including freezing time

Ingredients
- ¼ cup lemon balm, fresh, chopped
- ½ cup agave syrup
- 1½ cups blackberries, fresh or frozen, thawed slightly
- 3 cups Nancys Probiotic Yogurt, whole milk (substituting half Greek nonfat yogurt is fine)
- 2 tsp vanilla extract

Directions
1. **Place** lemon balm leaves in the agave syrup.
2. **Let** sit for a couple of hours or up to overnight.
3. **Alternately,** heat until almost boiling but not quite and then let cool to infuse the lemon balm flavor this way.
4. **Strain,** reserving the liquid and discarding the leaves.
5. **In** a blender, combine blackberries, yogurt, and vanilla.
6. **Add** strained syrup to blender.
7. **Blend** until mixed well.
8. **Add** to ice cream maker and process according to directions.

Note: You can serve immediately or let it freeze more later. If you don't prefer the seeds, you can put the blackberry mixture through a strainer and use a spoon to help feed it through until the only thing in the strainer is the blackberry seeds.

Blackberry Lemonade

This is the perfect wild foraged drink!

Makes: 6 cups
Time to Make: 10 minutes

Ingredients
- 2 cups fresh blackberries, washed
- 1½ cups granulated sugar
- 4½–5 cups water
- 1 cup fresh-squeezed lemon juice (plus more, to taste)

Directions
1. **Mash** or blend blackberries to create a pulp.
2. **Strain** through a fine sieve or cheesecloth so that the seeds are removed (optional).
3. **Mix** together 2 cups water and granulated sugar until sugar is thoroughly dissolved.
4. **Add** lemon juice to water and sugar mixture.
5. **Add** in blackberry mixture or blackberry juice.
6. **If** you want to make it into concentrate to use for later, refrigerate or freeze.
7. **When** ready to serve, mix with the remaining 2 cups water. Stir thoroughly. Taste test for sweetness.
8. **Serve** with ice and lemon balm or mint leaves (optional).

Pro Tip: This lemonade makes the perfect popsicle that will leave your kids coming back for more (without the artificial dyes and flavors associated with commercially made popsicles!). To make this even more desirable for kids, omit 1 cup of water and blend with 1-2 cups of ice to make it a slushie!

Blackberry Cobbler

This recipe is a late summer favorite, passed down to me from my mother and originally my grandmother. Summer evenings at her house will always be a fond memory for me. Sitting in the cooled kitchen of her Western Washington home, after a day of playing with cousins in the hot sun, drinking watered-down grape juice poured from the silver metal pitcher she always mixed it in, and then waiting in anticipation as she dished us warm blackberry cobbler with vanilla ice cream will always be a core memory I hold dear. All of us girls would sit around the circular table, enjoying our treat, as we talked about our latest crush, quietly whispering so my little brothers couldn't hear. After the last bite had been scraped from the bowl, we would go into the adjoining living room and sit on the dark blue corduroy fabric couch to watch the original BBC version of *The Chronicles of Narnia* with my grandparents or marvel as we looked at an old book from when she was a child.

As you make this dessert and enjoy it, I invite you to think back on a memory with a loved one. Food can so often connect us to the people we hold dear.

Pro Tip: If you want to make this camping or survival style, cook it over the campfire in a cast iron skillet; just make sure it is covered with a heavy lid so ash doesn't get in. Also see salal section for a recipe where you bake a cake in boiling water over an open fire.

Makes: 8" x 8" baking pan
Time to Make: 45 minutes including baking

Ingredients

- ½ cup granulated sugar
- ¼ cup margarine
- 1 egg
- ½ cup milk
- 1 cup flour
- 2 tsp baking powder
- Dash of salt
- 1 tsp vanilla
- 2 cups blackberries (can use peaches for a different variation, or a combination of both)
- 1/3 cup honey
- 1 cup boiling water
- 1 Tbsp margarine

Directions

1. **Preheat** oven to 375°F.
2. **Cream** sugar and margarine.
3. **Add** egg.
4. **Beat** well.
5. **Stir** in milk.
6. **Sift** flour, baking powder, and salt together.
7. **Add** to sugar mixture.
8. **Beat** until smooth.
9. **Stir** in vanilla.
10. **Spread** evenly over bottom of 8" square baking pan.
11. **Mix** blackberries, honey, boiling water, and margarine.
12. **Pour** on top of batter.
13. **Bake** in 375°F oven for 45 minutes.

Note: Cake rises to the top during baking.

SPRING BOLETE

Spring boletes *(Boletus spp.)* are among the earliest wild mushrooms to emerge after winter, prized for their firm texture, rich flavor, and versatility in the kitchen. Like many wild mushrooms, they offer a modest dose of antioxidants, minerals such as potassium and selenium, and immune-supporting compounds. Their high water and fiber content make them a light, nourishing addition to seasonal meals, especially for those living off the land. They grow in many parts of the world, although the identification information provided focuses specifically on PNW harvesting.

Did You Know?

Indigenous groups, such as some Plateau and Sierra Nevada tribes, foraged and dried early boletes like *B. rex-veris* for winter use.

Identification Guide

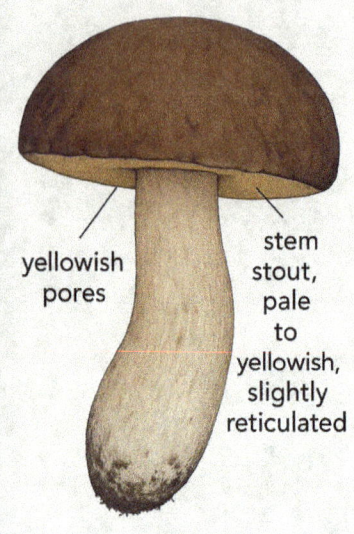

(Boletus rex-veris & relatives)

- Typically have a thick, tan to brown cap with a slightly cracked or velvety texture.
- The underside of the cap has yellowish pores instead of gills.
- Flesh is firm, pale, and should not turn blue when cut or bruised — a key ID trait

yellowish pores

stem stout, pale to yellowish, slightly reticulated

Foraging Guide

Habitat

- Found in western North America, especially the Sierra Nevada, Rocky Mountains, and Pacific Northwest
- Grows in conifer forests (especially near fir and pine) at mid to high elevations (3,000–7,000 feet)
- Look along well-drained sandy or loose dirt slopes, forest edges, and near melting snow lines in late spring
- Watch road banks as you drive along gravel roads!

Season

- April to June – Follow the snow line up; they typically appear within two weeks after snow melts

Toxic Look-Alikes and Cautions

1. **Satan's Bolete** (Boletus Satanas)
   - Large, bulbous base, red or pink pores, and flesh that stains blue
   - Poisonous
2. **Boletus sensibilis**
   - Quickly turns blue when cut
   - Can cause gastrointestinal distress
3. **Bitter Bolete** (Tylopilus felleus)
   - Edible but extremely bitter and undesirable due to taste

General Rule: Avoid boletes with red or orange pores and any that bruise blue unless confidently identified.

Cleaning

Brush gently with a pastry brush—due to their shape and lack of gills, they usually require minimal cleaning. If washing is needed, do so right before use. Spring boletes may harbor worms or insects inside; slicing them helps you check. If heavily infested with worm holes, discard. If only lightly affected, remove the worms, cut out damaged parts, and cook thoroughly. **Never eat boletes raw!**

Drying

Slice into ½-inch thick pieces. Lay flat on a dehydrator tray. Dry at 110°F for about 10 hours, until they snap when bent and feel completely dry. Store in vacuum-sealed bags in the freezer or a cold, dry place.

Flavor Profile

Spring boletes have a nutty, earthy, and slightly meaty flavor with a firm, almost silky texture.

- **Texture:** Firm, smooth, and meaty
- **Taste Notes:** Nutty, earthy, with a mild umami quality
- **Best Uses:** Sautéed in butter, added to creamy pasta sauces, grilled, or preserved by drying

Where to Buy

Farmers markets, foraging groups, and mushroom identification or bartering communities on Facebook.

Simple Fried Spring Boletes

This is a perfect addition to an off grid or camping meal! It is quick, easy, and preserves the original flavors of the bolete!

Makes: 2 fried boletes

Time to Make: 15 minutes

Ingredients
- 2 medium-large boletes, cleaned, sliced to ½ inch thickness (about 2 cups)
- 1–2 Tbsp butter or tallow
- Pinch of salt

Optional: Minced garlic or wild herbs (like yarrow or wild thyme)

Directions
1. **Heat** the butter in a cast iron skillet over medium heat until it sizzles.
2. **Add** sliced boletes in a single layer. Let them sear undisturbed for 2–3 minutes.
3. **Flip** and cook another 2–3 minutes until golden and crisp on the edges.
4. **Sprinkle** with salt and serve hot—as-is, over fry bread, or alongside wild greens.

Pro Tip: These fry beautifully over a camp stove or open fire—just don't overcrowd the pan.

Bolete & Nettle Dumplings in Bone Broth

This cozy, forager-friendly recipe turns spring boletes into an earthy stew with herbal dumplings made from wild nettles or other greens. For a bone broth recipe, see the section on cooking with elk meat.

Makes: 6 cups soup

Time to Make: 30 minutes

Ingredients

For the broth:

- 1 quart bone broth (venison, elk, or chicken)
- 1 cup chopped spring boletes
- 1 clove garlic, minced
- Salt and pepper to taste

Optional: (for added protein) 2 c chopped chicken, grouse, or elk stew meat

For the dumplings:

- 1 cup flour (use acorn flour, cattail or other foraged flour if eating completely off the grid)
- 1 tsp baking powder
- ½ tsp salt
- ½ cup cooked, finely chopped nettles (or spinach)
- ¼ cup water or broth + more as needed

Directions

1. **In** a pot, bring the broth to a simmer and add boletes, garlic, salt, and pepper. Let simmer 10–15 minutes. Add meat if using.
2. **In** a bowl, mix flour, baking powder, salt, and chopped nettles. Stir in just enough liquid to form a soft dough.
3. **Using** your hands or a greased spoon, drop small pieces of dumpling dough into the simmering broth. Cover and simmer 10 minutes or until dumplings are puffed and cooked through.
4. **Serve** hot with fresh herbs or wild greens.

Deluxe Forager's Umami Rub (Wild Herb Blend)

This makes a simple yet unique gift—and takes very little time to complete!

Makes: About ¾ cup

Time to Make: 10 minutes

Ingredients

- ½ cup mixed, dried wild mushroom (chanterelle + bolete + lobster if possible)
- 2 Tbsp smoked salt (or alder-smoked sea salt for PNW flair)
- 1 Tbsp cracked black pepper
- 1 Tbsp garlic granules
- 1 Tbsp onion granules
- 1 Tbsp dried nettle powder (adds earthy greens & minerals)
- 1 tsp dried wild thyme or oregano
- 1 tsp dried yarrow flower (for an herbal, slightly bitter backbone)
- Pinch of dried spruce tips or smoked chili flakes (optional, for a campfire edge)

Directions

1. **Grind** your dried mushrooms into a fine powder using a spice grinder or mortar and pestle. (For boletes, once fully dried, break into pieces and pulse until powdered.)
2. **Combine** mushroom powder with the remaining ingredients in a small bowl.
3. **Stir** until evenly blended.
4. **Store** in an airtight jar away from light and heat.

Serving Suggestions

- **Sprinkle** over grilled or fire-roasted meats for a smoky, wild depth of flavor.
- **Dust** onto root vegetables or squash before roasting.
- **Stir** into soups, stews, or broths to boost the earthy, savory notes.

PINEAPPLE WEED (FALSE CHAMOMILE)

False Chamomile, or **Pineapple Weed**, is one of the plants I was taught to identify as a young child. Its pineapple-like scent makes it appealing and the light flavor is delicious. Almost every year, I see a patch or two growing through the cracks in my cemented driveway! Areas like this are popular spots for it to grow. In addition to its amazing aroma, it is known for its ability to help calm nerves, promote sleep, and even relieve digestive issues! Because pineapple weed is more common as a wild plant here in the PNW, I focused on that for identification purposes. German Chamomile (or true chamomile) is more often grown in gardens.

Did you know?

Ancient Egyptians dedicated chamomile to the sun god Ra and used it to treat fevers—earning it the nickname "plant's physician."

Pineapple Weed
(*Matricaria discoidea*)
– a common wild relative of true chamomile

Cone-shaped
Flower Head

Pineapple weed looks like a small, petal-less chamomile with yellow-green, cone-shaped flower heads and finely divided, feathery leaves. It gives off a strong pineapple scent when crushed and often grows in compacted soil like sidewalks, trails, and gravel roads.

Foraging Guide

Habitat
- Found in paths, gravel roads, and compacted soil
- Resembles chamomile without petals
- Releases a strong pineapple scent when crushed

Season
- May to July

Toxic Look-Alikes and Cautions
1. **Mayweed** (*Dog Fennel*)
   - Similar in appearance
   - Smells pungent or unpleasant—not like pineapple
2. **Sneezeweed or other Asters**
   - Not toxic, but not palatable or useful
   - Sneezeweed has bright yellow daisy-like flowers with rounded dome centers and jagged-edged petals
   - Typically grows on tall, branching stems in wet meadows or along streambanks

How to Harvest
Best Time: Late morning on a dry, sunny day, after dew has evaporated
Pick: Only the flower heads, not the stems
Technique: Gently pinch or snip just below the flower
Storage: Collect in a basket or paper bag (avoid plastic—it traps moisture)

Cleaning
Wash flower heads gently under running water.

Drying
Spread them on a screen or paper towel in a warm, dry, well-ventilated place. Allow to dry for several days until crisp. Store in an airtight glass jar, out of sunlight.

Flavor Profile

Chamomile has a delicate sweetness with floral, honeyed notes and a hint of hay or earthiness. It smells like pineapple when fresh.
- **Taste Notes:** Light, floral, and slightly fruity
- **Aroma:** Pineapple-like, sweet, and calming
- **Best Uses:** Herbal teas, infused syrups, baked goods, and light desserts
- **Pairs Well With:** Citrus, vanilla, mint, honey, and oats

Where to Buy

If you can't find this in the wild, search for loose-leaf chamomile or pineapple weed online or at herbal apothecaries. See the reference guide for more.

Chamomile Tea

Makes: 1 cup   **Time to Make:** 15 minutes

Ingredients
- 1 Tbsp fresh chamomile buds or flowers
- 1 cup fresh spring water or filtered water

Directions
1. **To brew** tea of chamomile flowers, boil water.
2. **Place the flowers** or buds of chamomile into a tea strainer, pour water over top, and let steep for 10 minutes.

Chamomile French Toast

I created this recipe as a way to benefit from the calming effects of chamomile flower, without needing to drink tea. While the amount of chamomile used in this recipe does not add a huge flavor boost to the French toast, the subtle effect of the chamomile, which is to calm the nerves, can be gleaned from this delicious breakfast food. It is also easily adapted to camp cooking or off grid living!

Makes: 6 pieces
Time to Make: 25 minutes

Ingredients
- 6 pieces bread
- 2 eggs
- ½ cup milk
- 8 chamomile buds, broken up so that the little flowery parts incorporate with the milk mixture
- 1 tsp vanilla extract
- Maple syrup, for serving
- Whipped cream, for serving
- Fresh pineapple (optional) for serving
- Butter or oil, for frying

Directions
1. In a bowl, whisk together the milk, eggs, vanilla extract, and chamomile buds.
2. Heat a cast iron skillet to medium low heat and add oil or butter.
3. Immerse a piece of bread into the milk mixture; flip over so the other side becomes soaked in the milk mixture too.
4. When the oil is sizzling, remove bread from the milk mixture and place in heated pan.
5. Let cook for about 3 minutes, then flip and cook until done. Serve with fresh fruit, whipped cream, and maple syrup or wild harvested raw honey.

Mosquito Bite Anti-Itch Ointment

This ointment combines herbal infused oil with hydrocortisone cream to help reduce inflammation and itching from mosquito bites—it's perfect for camping, hiking, or your herbal first aid kit. While in Alaska this summer, I put it to the test—and it proved more valuable than gold—or sockeye salmon!

Makes: 8 one-ounce tins
Time to Make: 2–3 hours (quick method) or 4–6 weeks (slow infusion method)

Ingredients

Herbal Infused Oil
- 1 Tbsp dried chamomile
- 1 Tbsp dried calendula flowers
- 1 Tbsp dried goldenrod
- 1 Tbsp dried purple dead nettle
- 1 Tbsp dried broadleaf plantain (partially or fully dried)
- ½ cup olive oil (or mix of olive + jojoba)

Make the Infused Oil
1. **Place** dried herbs in a clean glass jar.
2. **Cover** with oil until herbs are fully submerged.
3. **Infuse** using one of the following:
   - **Slow method:** Let sit 4–6 weeks in a sunny window, shaking daily.
   - **Quick method:** Heat gently over a double boiler for 2–3 hours (do not simmer).
4. **Strain** through cheesecloth and store in a clean jar.

Ingredients

Ointment
- 1 Tbsp herbal infused oil (from above)
- 1 tsp beeswax
- ¼–½ tsp lecithin granules, hydrated in 1 tsp warm water for 15–30 minutes
- 1 tsp 1% hydrocortisone cream (store-bought)

Optional: 2–3 drops lavender or peppermint essential oil

Make the Ointment
1. **Melt** herbal oil and beeswax together in a heatproof bowl over a double boiler.
2. **Stir** in the hydrated lecithin until fully blended.
3. **Remove** from heat and let cool for 1–2 minutes.
4. **Add** hydrocortisone cream and optional essential oil. Whisk until completely smooth.
5. **Pour** into clean 1 oz tins. Let cool completely before sealing.

Use & Storage
- **Apply** a thin layer to mosquito bites 2–3 times daily.
- **Store** in a cool, dark place or in the refrigerator.
- **Use** within 2–3 months.

BONUS Recipe!

Chamomile Relaxation Bath

Add a handful of dried chamomile flowers (or 3–4 chamomile tea bags) to a cloth bag or directly to the bathwater. Let them steep in the hot water for a few minutes before getting in.

Optional: Add 1 cup of Epsom salt and a few drops of lavender essential oil for extra relaxation. Soak for 20–30 minutes to soothe your skin and calm your nerves.

CHANTERELLES

Chanterelle mushrooms (*Cantharellus* spp.) are not only prized for their rich, earthy flavor but also offer valuable health benefits. They're a good source of vitamin D, potassium, and antioxidants that support immune health and reduce inflammation. Found in temperate forests across North America, Europe, Asia, and parts of Africa, chanterelles thrive in mossy, coniferous woodlands and are a favorite among foragers worldwide. They are also a great one for beginners, due to the ease with which they can be identified! Kids love foraging for them!

Did you know?

Chanterelles were once believed to grow best under trees that had been struck by lightning.

Chanterelles

(*Cantharellus cibarius* and related sp.)

Color: Distinctive golden-yellow to orange color.

Shape: Cap is wavy or funnel-shaped, often with a smooth or slightly wrinkled surface

Gills: Underside has blunt, forked ridges (false gills) that run down the stem — not true, blade-like gills

Texture: Firm and meaty – never slimy

Scent: Has a fruity, apricot-like aroma when fresh

Spore Print: True chanterelles have a white to pale yellow spore print

Foraging Guide

Habitat

- **Forest Type:** Moist coniferous forests are ideal. Look under:
  - Douglas fir
  - Hemlock
  - Sitka spruce
  - Western hemlock (especially productive)
- **Elevation:** Found from near sea level to 3,000 feet
- **Soil:** Well-drained, mossy forest floors
- **Moisture:** Check 1–3 days after rain that lasts at least one full day
- **Temperature:** Daytime temps in the 50s–60s °F with cool nights

Season

- August to November – Depending on elevation and rainfall

Toxic Look-Alikes and Cautions

1. Jack-o'-Lantern Mushroom (*Omphalotus olivascens*)
- Has true gills, grows on wood (not soil), may glow in the dark
- **Toxic** – Causes vomiting, cramps, and diarrhea

2. False Chanterelle (*Hygrophoropsis aurantiaca*)
- Thinner, deeper orange, with true blade-like gills
- Gills are closely spaced and sharper than chanterelle ridges

Rule of Thumb: Chanterelles grow on soil, not wood, and have false gills—not blade-like true gills.

Cleaning

Inspect and Sort: Discard soggy, moldy, or bug-infested mushrooms.
Trim the Stems: Slice off dirty or woody bottoms with a small knife.
Dry Brush First: Use a soft brush or toothbrush to clean the cap and ridges; brush outward from the stem.
Washing Before Use: Rinse under cold running water and pat dry. Let air-dry for 10–15 minutes before cooking.

Storage

Store in a paper bag in the fridge for up to 5 days. Avoid plastic.

Freezing

Sauté first (about 3 minutes), then freeze in labeled bags. Do not freeze raw. Keeps up to one year.

Drying

Slice or leave whole. Dry at 110 °F for 8–10 hours until brittle. Store in jars or vacuum seal.

To Rehydrate

Run cold water over mushrooms in a bowl and soak for 15 minutes. Drain before use.

Flavor Profile

- **Taste:** Rich, buttery, with notes of apricot, earth, and mild pepper
- **Texture:** Firm and meaty—holds up well in cooking
- **Best Uses:** Cream sauces, eggs, sautés, wild game, white wine pairings
- **Pairs Well With:** Garlic, thyme, shallots, cream, white wine

Where to Buy

Farmers markets in fall or Facebook Marketplace (local foragers often post seasonal wild mushroom sales).

PNW Harvest Wild Rice and Chanterelle Stuffing

This is the perfect addition to a wild foraged Thanksgiving! The wild rice gives an earthy base to this mix of chanterelles, celery, onion, fresh sage, which you can grow at home, and dried crabapples, another wild harvested ingredient in this book! The chestnuts add a signature nutty flavor that always transports me back in time to Thanksgiving at my parents' house, where we could go out and pick the chestnuts off the tree in the front yard. You can also harvest wild chestnuts, although I haven't included those in this book.

Makes: 8"x 8" baking dish
Time to Make: 2 hours

Ingredients

- 1-½ cup wild rice
- 2-¼ cups bone broth (or vegetable broth for vegetarian)
- Salt and pepper
- 2 Tbsp olive oil
- 1 small purple onion, chopped
- 3 large chanterelles, cut into bite sized pieces, washed
- 2 ribs celery, finely chopped
- ½ tsp dried thyme
- 3 cloves garlic, minced
- 1 Tbsp chopped fresh sage
- ½ cup chestnuts (about 6-10 in shells)
- ½ cup dried crabapples (**alternate idea:** wild dried cherries, see cherry section of this book)

Directions

1. **Add** wild rice, vegetable broth, and a pinch of salt to a medium-sized saucepan.
2. **Bring** to a boil over high heat. Immediately place a lid on top then turn heat down to low heat.
3. **Simmer** for 40–45 minutes or until rice is cooked.
4. **Leave** the lid on and set pot aside to cool.
5. **Preheat** oven to 425°F.
6. **Cut** slits in the surface of chestnuts with a sharp knife so they don't explode in the oven.
7. **Lay** them on a baking sheet and bake for about 25 minutes, until shells have softened and chestnuts are tender.
8. **Set aside** to cool—skip if chestnuts are pre-cooked.
9. **Heat** a medium cast iron skillet over low-medium heat and **add** chanterelle pieces.
10. **Cook** until moisture evaporates, about 7 minutes.
11. **Remove** chanterelles from pan; **set aside**.
12. **Add** olive oil and minced garlic to the skillet, then **add** onion, celery, chopped sage, and dried thyme.
13. **Sauté** for 2 minutes, then **return** chanterelles to the pan.
14. **Cook** for an additional 5 minutes, until celery is soft but not mushy.
15. **Take off** heat and **set aside**.
16. **Cut** chestnuts in half or into large chunks.
17. **Mix** chestnuts into mushroom and vegetable mixture.
18. **Combine** with wild rice and dried apples or cranberries.
19. **Transfer** mixture to a large baking dish.
20. **Bake** at 350°F for about 30 minutes, or until heated through.

Cauliflower Chanterelle Loaded Soup

This recipe will be your best friend after a long day hunting or foraging! It is easy and can be made over an open fire or camp stove with minimal effort!

Makes: 5 cups
Time to Make: 45 minutes

Ingredients

- 8 slices bacon, cut into bite sized pieces
- 1 clove garlic, minced
- 1 small white onion, chopped
- 1 ½ cups chanterelle mushrooms, cut into chunks (about 3 large ones)
- ½ head cauliflower
- ½ cup sour cream
- 1 Tbsp flour
- 1 tsp salt, or more to taste
- 3 cups water
- 1 bunch fresh wild chives or green onions, chopped
- 1 ½ cups cheddar cheese, shredded

Directions

1. **In a stock pot**, combine minced garlic and bacon.
2. **Turn to medium heat** and cook about 5 minutes, until the bacon sizzles and begins to crisp.
3. **Add** onion and chanterelles.
4. **Cover and cook** another 3 minutes, or until onions begin to caramelize.
5. **Wash and chop** cauliflower into bite-sized chunks.
6. **Add** cauliflower to pan and **stir**.
7. **Cover again** and let steam for about 2 minutes.
8. **Add** 3 cups water and **bring to a boil** by increasing the heat.
9. **Simmer** soup for about 15 minutes on medium-low heat.
10. **Scoop** about two-thirds of the soup into a blender or food processor. *(Skip this step for a chunkier, off grid version.)*
11. **Add** sour cream, salt, and flour to the blender.
12. **Blend on low** until cauliflower is smooth but bacon pieces remain intact.
13. **Pour** the blended mixture back into the remaining soup.
14. **Stir to combine** and return to medium-high heat.
15. **Simmer** for about a minute to allow the flour to thicken the soup.
16. **Leave on low** heat for another 5 minutes.
17. **Add** half the green onions (or wild chives) and 1 cup shredded cheddar.

Serve hot, garnished with remaining cheese and chives.

Indian Butter Chicken with Chanterelles

This is likely one of the best comfort foods you will ever try with foraged foods, especially if you like Indian food! The recipe includes campfire cooking instructions. Imagine impressing your family or friends by bringing along the premade sauce, picking some chanterelles on a cold fall day, and throwing this together to fill everyone's bellies while they sit around the campfire talking about the day's hunt or foraging trip! You can even swap out the chicken for wild turkey or grouse meat!

Makes: 4 bowls
Time to Make: 2 hours including marinating time

Ingredients

Marinade

- 3 chicken breasts, cut into chunks
- ¼ cup yogurt (if living off grid, see recipe in wild cherry section for making your own yogurt)
- 2 tsp garam masala
- 1 tsp cumin
- 1 tsp chili powder

For sauce

- 2 garlic cloves, minced
- ½ white onion, chopped
- 2 tsp garam masala
- 1 cup chanterelles, cut into bite sized slices
- 2 Tbsp butter
- 1 cup tomato sauce
- 1 cup heavy cream (half 'n' half works too)
- 1 Tbsp granulated sugar
- 1¼ tsp salt

Directions

1. **Marinate** chicken in yogurt sauce for 1 hour.
2. **Lie** in a single layer on a baking sheet.
3. **Preheat** oven to 375°F.
4. **Bake** chicken for about 15 minutes, until no longer pink and the juices are running.
5. **In** a cast iron skillet, combine spices, garlic, butter, and chopped onion.
6. **Cook** until fragrant and onions are translucent, about 7 minutes, stirring often.
7. **Add** chanterelles and cook for another 5 minutes or until the juices have evaporated from the mushrooms.
8. **Now add** pasta sauce or tomato sauce (homemade or store-bought).
9. **Add** sugar and heavy cream and stir.
10. **Turn down** and let simmer for about 10 minutes so the flavors can mix.
11. **Remove** from heat. Pour about 2/3 of the mixture into a blender, leaving some mushrooms in the pan for texture.
12. **Blend** until smooth. Pour this back into the pan and mix thoroughly.
13. **Add** chicken and heat until hot if needed.
14. **Serve** with naan bread and jasmine rice.

To cook over campfire:

Prepare your sauce, minus the chanterelles (if you want to harvest them and add at the last minute). Start a fire and let it burn until there are more coals than fire and it is well established. Arrange logs to create a flat place with some direct fire below it and a lot of hot coals (or use a fire grate). Place cast iron skillet over the fire. In the cast iron pan, cook chanterelles until the moisture has evaporated. Now, add an additional 1 Tbsp of butter and fry for about 5 minutes (maybe less depending on the heat of the fire), until they begin to turn brown and have cooked through. Add the jarred sauce (with chicken). Heat thoroughly and serve with Naan bread.

Naan bread

This is an easy recipe that you can prepare ahead of time and take to the field with you or prepare at camp or in an off grid living situation. Frying it in a cast iron skillet over the fire is simple and easy!

Makes: 4 pieces of naan
Time to Make: 2 hours to overnight (slow rise)

Ingredients

- 3 cups all-purpose flour
- 1 Tbsp active dry yeast
- 2 Tbsp granulated sugar
- 1 cup milk
- 2 Tbsp olive oil + more for greasing the pan
- 1½ tsp salt

Directions

1. **Heat** milk in a saucepan just until warm but not hot to the touch (think just warmer than a baby bottle).
2. **Pour** into a large bowl.
3. **Sprinkle** yeast on top, then sprinkle sugar on top of this.
4. **Let** sit for 3 minutes or until you see a small amount of foam on the top.
5. **Add** in flour and knead to mix, sprinkling on more if needed to keep it from sticking.
6. **Cover** with a tea towel.
7. **Let** rest for 2–3 hours, or, if bringing it camping, put in the refrigerator or cooler overnight.

When Ready to Cook:

1. **Divide** dough into 4 equal pieces.
2. **Form** pieces into balls.
3. **Roll out** dough balls to desired thickness (about the size of a small tortilla).
4. **Sprinkle** additional flour on to avoid sticking in the pan. If you're out camping, stretch it by hand instead—pack gloves if water is scarce (or just leave it in the bag to do the initial stretch). Add flour (not oil) to the edges of your storage bag to prevent sticking.
5. **Heat** a dry skillet until it's hot, but not smoking. Doing this over a small fire or the coals is a good idea. You want to make sure it is getting enough heat, so play with that a little bit and you will get better at judging how much heat your fire is giving with the more you cook over open fires.
6. **Add** one piece of thin bread at a time, and cook for about 1–2 minutes, then flip and cook for an additional 1–2 minutes.
7. **Serve** hot, dipped in butter chicken or alongside your favorite foraged dish.

Garlic Sautéed Chanterelles and Leaves

This recipe is perfect for making over the fire—and only takes a couple of moments to complete. It exemplifies the flavors of the Pacific Northwest, whether grown in the garden or harvested wild!

Makes: 2 servings

Time to Make: 20 minutes

Ingredients

- 5–10 freshly picked summer chanterelles, brushed clean
- 5–10 Brussels sprout leaves or wild greens, torn
- 2 Tbsp butter
- 2 cloves garlic, chopped

Make the Dish

1. **Build** a fire until it has hot coals and a few small flames. Arrange logs to create a stable cooking surface for your pan.
2. **Place** a cast iron or metal pan directly over the logs.
3. **Add** the butter and chopped garlic to the hot pan.
4. **Toss in** the chanterelles and torn Brussels sprout leaves (or wild greens) as soon as the butter melts.
5. **Stir and cook** for about 5 minutes, depending on heat. Stir frequently to prevent sticking or burning.
6. **Remove** from heat carefully using tongs, a hot pad, or your jacket sleeve. Serve hot with crab cakes and fire-baked cheese bread.

WILD CHERRY

Wild cherries grow across much of North America, Europe, and parts of Asia, with species like chokecherry (*Prunus virginiana*) and bitter cherry (*Prunus emarginata*) common in forests, river valleys, and foothills. In the Pacific Northwest, they often thrive along sunny edges and old roadsides, offering small, astringent fruit that ripens in late summer. Thanks to birds and wildlife that feast on commercially grown cherries, they have become widespread through these animals' poop, increasing the population between true wild cherries and hybrid versions.

Though tarter and more tannic than cultivated varieties, wild cherries are rich in antioxidants, vitamin C, and anti-inflammatory compounds. They've traditionally been used in cordials, syrups, and medicine to soothe sore throats and support heart and joint health.

Did You Know?

Some Native American tribes used wild cherry bark to make cough syrup and teas for lung ailments—and modern herbalists still use it today for its natural soothing properties. The fruit may be sweet or tart, but the tree's bark holds the real medicine!

WILD CHERRY

(*Prunus spp.* — including chokecherry, bitter cherry, and black cherry)

LEAVES: Oval, finely toothed edges, pointed tips, with a noticeable midrib and two small glands where the leaf joins the stem (a key feature).

BARK Young trees have smooth, reddish-brown bark with horizontal lenticels (lines). Older bark darkens and may peel

FRUIT Small cherries (¼-½ inch), ranging from red to deep black when ripe. Grows in clusters or loose drupes.

TREE SIZE: Can range from a large shrub (like chokecherry) to a medium-sized tree (like black cherry or bitter cherry).

Foraging Guide

Habitat

• Found throughout North America, especially in woodland edges, clearings, riverbanks, old logging roads, and disturbed soils
• In the Pacific Northwest, bitter cherry (*Prunus emarginata*) thrives from sea level to mid-elevation forests, often in sunny locations

Season

• **July to September** – Depending on elevation and species

Look-Alikes and Cautions

1. **Buckthorn** (*Rhamnus cathartica*): Similar fruit, but grows on shrubs with alternate leaves and lacks cherry bark or leaf glands. **Toxic.**
2. • **Nightshade** (*Solanum spp.*): Berries are smaller and very poisonous. Leaves and growth habit look different—no woody stem or tree form.
3. • **Unripe cherries & pits:** Even real wild cherries contain cyanogenic compounds in the pits, leaves, and unripe fruit. Only eat fully ripe fruit and never consume the seeds.

Cleaning & Prep Tips

Rinse gently in cool water to remove dust and insects. Remove pits carefully before cooking or drying—never crush them. Cherries are great for boiling into juice or syrup, then straining.

Drying

Pit the cherries: Always remove the pits before drying, as they contain toxic compounds and are a choking hazard. Halve or quarter larger cherries to help them dry faster and more evenly.

Optional: Blanch in boiling water for 30 seconds, then dunk in cold water to soften skins and improve drying.

Lay cherries in a single layer on a mesh dehydrator tray or baking sheet. Dry at 135°F for 12–20 hours in a dehydrator. In the sun or oven, use the lowest setting and crack the door open for airflow. Done when leathery but not sticky—they should not squish when squeezed.

Storage: Keep in airtight jars in a cool, dark place or freeze for long-term storage.

Freezing

Rinse and remove stems and pits. Spread cherries on a baking sheet in a single layer and freeze until solid (2–4 hours). Transfer to labeled freezer bags or containers to prevent clumping. Use within 6–12 months for best flavor.

Flavor Profile

Wild cherries range from mouth-puckeringly tart (chokecherry) to slightly sweet (black cherry). Most have an astringent, bitter edge when raw, which mellows beautifully when cooked into jams, jellies, or syrups. Chokecherries can also be dried into fruit leather or used in traditional pemmican.

Where to Buy/Substitutes

Wild cherries are rarely sold fresh in grocery stores, but you can sometimes find chokecherries or black cherries at farmers markets in late summer. Foraged or frozen wild cherries may also be available through local bartering groups or online marketplaces like Etsy. If you need a substitute, try tart pie cherries (like Montmorency) or unsweetened dried cherries in recipes calling for wild varieties.

Cherry Pie Donuts—Foraged Style

These donuts are soft on the inside, golden outside, and made for sharing—especially fresh from the pan over an open fire.

Makes: 8 donuts
Time to Make: 1½ hours including rising time

Ingredients
- 1¼ tsp active dry yeast
- ¾ cup warm milk (about 110°F)
- 3 Tbsp granulated sugar
- 2 Tbsp butter, melted
- 1 egg
- ½ tsp salt
- 2½ cups all-purpose flour (plus more for kneading)
- Oil for frying (vegetable, canola, or lard)

Directions
1. **Activate Yeast:**
   In a bowl, stir yeast into the warm milk with sugar. Let sit for 5–10 minutes until foamy.
2. **Make the Dough:**
   In a large bowl, mix the sugar, melted butter, egg, salt, and foamy yeast mixture. Stir in the flour gradually until a soft dough forms.
3. **Knead:**
   Turn the dough out onto a floured surface and knead for about 5–7 minutes until smooth and elastic.
4. **Let Rise:**
   Place dough in a greased bowl, cover, and let rise in a warm spot until doubled—about 1 hour.
5. **Pro Tip (When Camping):** You can let this rest overnight in a greased Ziploc bag stored in a cold cooler to slow the rise.
6. **Shape Donuts:**
   Divide into equal balls of dough. Poke a hole all the way through and shape it until the hole is about the size of a nickel.
7. **Fry:**
   Heat oil to 350°F. If cooking over a fire, test it by dropping in a small scrap of dough—it should sizzle. Fry donuts in batches, 1–2 minutes per side, until golden brown. Drain on paper towels.
8. **Finish:**
   Drop donuts into a bowl or bag of powdered sugar and shake to coat. Serve with cherry sauce or pie filling for dipping.

Cherry Pie Sauce

In a small pan or cast-iron skillet, over a fire or medium heat burner, add 2 cups pitted, sweet wild cherries. Sprinkle the remaining powdered sugar from the donut bag on top of the cherries. If they are tart cherries, add up to an additional ½ cup sugar or to taste. Let these cook for about 6 minutes, mashing the cherries to help them release their juices. Stir often to avoid burning. It will thicken quickly. Remove from heat; spoon into the middle of the donuts or simply dip each one into the sauce before eating!

Pemmican

Pemmican is a traditional Native American food made from three simple ingredients—dried meat, dried berries, and tallow! This easy recipe teaches you how to make it—as authentic as our ancestors who made it—using modern equipment that helps ensure food safety and a shelf stable final product, which is the perfect survival food for someone on the trail—or off the grid! **Note:** See elk section for information about tallow: what it is, and how to make it.

Makes: 8-12 individual pieces or squares
Time to Make: Two Days (including dehydrating and process)

Ingredients
- 1 lb lean wild game (elk, venison, or lean beef), sliced thin
- ½–1 cup dried wild cherries (or substitute dried cranberries or blueberries)
- ½ cup rendered tallow (or beef suet, bear fat, etc.)

Optional: pinch of salt, smoked salt, or wild herbs (spruce tips, thyme, juniper)

Directions

1. Dehydrate the Meat:
- Slice meat into thin strips (¼-inch or thinner), trimming off all fat.
- Dehydrate at 145–160°F until completely dry and brittle—usually 6–10 hours depending on thickness.
- Once dry, let cool, then grind or crush into a powder using a food processor or mortar and pestle.

2. Prepare the Berries:
- If not already dried, dry your pitted wild cherries (or chokecherries) until leathery—but not sticky.
- Pulse in a food processor or chop by hand until in small bits or paste-like.

3. Render the Fat (if not done already):
- Melt raw fat over low heat until fully liquid, then strain through cheesecloth or a coffee filter to remove solids.
- Let cool slightly—you want it warm, not hot.

4. Mix It All Together:
- In a bowl, combine powdered meat and dried berry bits.
- Slowly add melted fat until mixture holds together (like thick granola bar mix). You may not need all the fat—just enough to bind.

5. Form and Store:
- Press mixture into molds, silicone trays, or shape into patties or bars by hand.
- Let cool completely and store in airtight containers or vacuum-seal.
- Store in a cool, dark place for up to 1 month, or freeze for up to a year.

Traditional Notes:
- Ratio can vary—generally equal parts meat and fat, with berries optional (but ¼–½ part works well).
- Used by many Indigenous nations, including the Métis and Plains tribes, as trail food and winter sustenance.

Simple Yogurt with Wild Cherry Compote

Why Yogurt Matters—Especially if You're Off grid

I've been making yogurt from scratch since I was 13, driven by a curiosity to learn how to do it with as few tools as possible. All you really need is milk, a little time, and about two Tbsp of plain yogurt with live cultures to use as a starter—similar to how sourdough needs a bit of the old batch to begin the next. When you're living off the land, gut health becomes a core part of your survival strategy. Probiotics—those beneficial microbes found in yogurt—support digestion, improve nutrient absorption, and help strengthen your immune system. In a world without pharmacies, a strong gut is your frontline defense, and a little homemade yogurt can offer a daily dose of resilience.

Makes: 4 cups yogurt

Time to Make: 1 day (time for yogurt to set)

Ingredients
- 4 cups milk (cow, goat, or shelf-stable boxed milk works)
- 2 Tbsp plain yogurt with live cultures (store-bought or leftover from a previous batch)

Directions
1. **Heat milk** in a pot until it reaches 180°F (just before boiling). Stir occasionally so it doesn't scorch.
2. **Cool it down** to 110°F (warm but not hot to the touch).
3. **Stir in yogurt**, whisking well so it distributes evenly.
4. **Cover the pot** and place somewhere warm (a cooler, near a campfire, or wrapped in a towel). Let sit undisturbed for 8–12 hours.
5. **Check texture**: it should be thick and tangy. Chill before serving.

Tips:
If you're off grid, place the covered pot in a warm sleeping bag or next to a warm fire overnight.

Wild Cherry Yogurt (Add-On)

How to Add Wild Cherries to Homemade Yogurt:
1. **Make a simple cherry compote:**
   - Combine 1 cup pitted wild cherries, 1–2 Tbsp honey, and a splash of water in a small pot.
   - Simmer over low heat for 10–15 minutes until the cherries break down and thicken slightly.
2. **Cool completely**, then layer or swirl into chilled yogurt.
   - For rustic texture, leave the fruit chunky.
   - For a smoother blend, mash or puree before stirring in.
3. **Optional:** Add a pinch of cinnamon, vanilla, or lemon zest for extra depth.

Perfect as a breakfast with granola, or packed into a jar for a trailside snack.

Pro(tein) Tip: To make this into Greek yogurt, simply strain the plain yogurt through a cheesecloth, reserving the thick part and letting the juice go. Do this a couple of times to get thicker, higher protein content yogurt. You can mix the cherry compote in after the straining process is complete.

CHICKEN OF THE WOODS MUSHROOM

Chicken of the Woods (*Laetiporus spp.*) grow in temperate forests across North America, Europe, and parts of Asia, often found on decaying hardwood trees, in late spring through fall. They're a good source of plant-based protein, with 10% of their mass by weight being made up of protein macros—making them a hearty, nourishing wild food for foragers around the world.

Did You Know?

Chicken of the Woods doesn't just taste like chicken—it was actually used as a meat substitute by early settlers and Indigenous peoples long before plant-based meat was trendy! Its dense texture and savory flavor make it perfect for frying, grilling, or shredding like pulled chicken.

CHICKEN OF THE WOODS

(*Laetiporus*)

sulfur-yellow undersides

Bright yellow to orange-caps with sulfur-yellow undersides (no gills, just pores)

Grows in overlapping, fan-shaped shelves, sometimes as large as dinner plates

Foraging Guide

Habitat

- Grows on wood, not on the ground
- Common on dead or dying hardwoods like oak, cherry, and beech
- In the Pacific Northwest, may grow on oak, willow, and occasionally coniferous trees like Douglas fir (though some species on conifers may cause GI upset)
- Grows in shelves or rosettes, often brightly colored and very visible

Season

- August to October

How to Harvest

Only harvest young, tender growth. Older mushrooms become tough and woody. The best part is often the outer edges of the shelves. Use a sharp knife to slice off clean sections. Don't collect from polluted or sprayed areas (roadsides, treated wood, or industrial zones).

Look-Alikes and Cautions

Toxic Look-Alikes

1. **Jack-O'-Lantern Mushroom** (*Omphalotus olivascens / O. illudens*)
   - Has true gills, unlike Chicken of the Woods
   - Grows from the ground near wood—not directly on wood
   - Bioluminescent (glows faintly in the dark)
   - Toxic – causes severe cramps, vomiting, and diarrhea
2. **Old Chicken of the Woods**
   - Not a different species, but over-mature specimens can cause GI distress due to spoilage
   - If it smells sour, fishy, or looks dry/cracked—skip it

Additional Cautions

- Always cook thoroughly—never eat raw
- Start with a small portion the first time; some people are allergic
- Avoid mushrooms growing on conifers, eucalyptus, or locust trees—they may cause gastrointestinal upset
- Do not eat if the mushroom is crumbly, dry, or bitter-tasting

Cleaning

Brush off debris with a soft brush or cloth. Rinse lightly under cool water if needed, but don't soak them. Check for bugs or larvae, especially in older specimens. Pat dry with a towel or let air-dry before storing.

Storage

Refrigerate in paper bags for up to 5–7 days.

Freezing

Sauté in butter for 3 minutes. Cool on a cookie sheet. Freeze in vacuum-sealed bags. Ensure mushrooms are cooked thoroughly when thawed before consuming.

Drying

Slice into 2-inch strips. Lay in a single layer on a dehydrator tray. Dehydrate at 110°F for around 8 hours, until it snaps when bent.

Flavor Profile

Taste: Mild, earthy, and subtly lemony with a distinct savory richness. When sautéed, it develops a meaty, umami-forward flavor reminiscent of roasted chicken or crab.
Texture: Firm, juicy, and fibrous—similar to chicken breast or tofu. The edges can be delicately tender, while thicker sections are hearty and satisfying.
Best Uses: Grilled, pan-fried, or simmered in stews. Excellent in tacos, stir-fries, or as a meat substitute in sandwiches and casseroles.

Where to Buy

Check farmers markets in the fall. If you can't locate them locally or via Facebook Marketplace, try online sources.

Chicken of the Woods Over Homemade Alfredo and Pasta

This is a perfect recipe for people who prefer not to consume meat—the high protein content, coupled with the meaty texture, makes it a perfect way to get vegetarian nutrition—at home, or in your off the grid home in the wild!

Makes: 4 servings
Time to Make: 30 minutes

Ingredients
- 1 cup young chicken of the woods mushroom (the small, still bright orange ones)
- 2 Tbsp butter
- 2 Tbsp white wine
- 2 cups spiral pasta

Alfredo Sauce:
- 3 garlic cloves (I buy mine frozen and pre-peeled)
- 2 Tbsp butter
- 1½ cup half 'n' half or heavy cream
- 1 cup Parmesan cheese
- Salt, to taste, around ¼ tsp
- Garlic and herb spice (optional)

Directions
1. **Cook the Mushrooms:**
   In a skillet, heat butter.
   Add cleaned and thinly sliced chicken of the woods mushroom. **Fry** in butter for about 6 minutes, stirring often to ensure even cooking.
   Add white wine and **simmer** for an additional 3 minutes. Meanwhile, **cook** pasta until al dente.
2. **Make the Alfredo Sauce:**
   Chop your garlic cloves while the butter is warming in a saucepan over medium heat.
   Drop them in, **let sizzle** for about a minute, and **turn** the pan down to low.
   Add half and half. **Stir** and **let simmer** for about two minutes.
   Turn off the heat, **add** Parmesan cheese, and **stir well**.
   Season with salt and garlic spice, if desired.

Chicken of the Woods Sweet Curry

This recipe was a favorite from one of my grandmothers. It is easy to make, and swapping out the chicken for its namesake mushroom was a simple way to include more wild mushrooms into our diet!

Makes: 6 servings

Ingredients

- 1 cup diced crabapples
- ¼ cup chopped onion
- 1 tsp curry powder
- 2 Tbsp butter
- 2 Tbsp sugar
- 1 cup chicken of the woods, cleaned and chopped into small bites
- 1 (12 oz) can cream of mushroom soup (or cream of chicken)
- ½ **cup** water

Time to Make: 30 minutes

Directions

1. **Put** apples, curry powder, onion, butter, and chicken of the woods in a saucepan.
2. **Fry** until onion is tender, about 5 minutes.
3. **Stir in** cream of mushroom (or chicken) soup and water.
4. **Simmer** for about 20 minutes until everything is soft and the flavors are blended.
5. **Serve** hot over jasmine rice.

Pulled Chicken of the Woods Sandwiches (Wild BBQ Style)

Simmered in a tangy, smoky sauce, chicken of the woods pulls apart just like shredded chicken. This wild BBQ recipe turns a forest harvest into a hearty sandwich that feels right at home around the campfire.

Makes: 4 servings
Time to Make: 40 minutes

Ingredients

- 1 lb. young chicken of the woods, cut into thick strips
- 2 Tbsp oil or rendered fat
- 1 small wild onion (or ½ cup diced garden onion)
- 2 cloves garlic, minced
- ½ cup huckleberries or crabapples (for tangy base)
- ¼ cups vinegar (apple cider or spruce tip–infused if available)
- 2 Tbsp honey or sugar
- 1 tsp smoked paprika (or alder-smoked chili flakes)
- ½ tsp salt
- ¼ tsp cracked black pepper
- 4 bannock rounds, flatbreads, or sandwich buns

Directions

1. **Prepare the mushrooms:** Clean and slice chicken of the woods into thick strips.
2. **Sear:** Heat oil or fat in a cast iron pan. Add mushrooms, onion, and garlic. Cook until mushrooms begin to soften and edges turn golden.
3. **Make the wild BBQ sauce:** In a small pot or the same pan, mash the huckleberries or crabapples with vinegar, honey, paprika, salt, and pepper. Simmer until thickened.
4. **Simmer together:** Stir sauce into the pan with mushrooms. Cover and simmer 10–15 minutes, adding a splash of water if needed, until mushrooms are tender and soak up the sauce.
5. **Shred:** Using two forks, pull apart the mushroom strips into "shredded chicken" texture.
6. **Serve:** Spoon onto bannock, flatbread, or buns.

Pro Tip:

- **Add crunch** with wild greens (lamb's quarters, dandelion, or miner's lettuce).
- **Top with pickled vegetables** for extra zing.
- **Wrap in foil** and warm at the edge of the campfire for trail meals.

CAULIFLOWER MUSHROOM

Cauliflower mushrooms grow in temperate forests across North America, Europe, and Asia, often found at the base of conifer trees in late summer to fall. Known for their unique texture and mild, nutty flavor, they're also rich in fiber, antioxidants, and beta-glucans that support immune health and digestion—a valuable wild find both nutritionally and culinarily. The primary species of cauliflower mushroom found in the Pacific Northwest is Sparassis radicata (sometimes still referred to as *Sparassis crispa*, though this name typically refers to European species).

Did You Know?

Cauliflower mushrooms (*Sparassis radicata*) often grow back in the exact same spot year after year—making them one of the few wild mushrooms you can "visit" like an old friend each season! Keep track of your patch and you may get a harvest every fall.

Cauliflower mushrooms
(*Sparassis radicata*)

Appearance: Resembles a pale, brain-like or ruffled mass — often compared to a head of cauliflower or egg noodles.

Color: Creamy white to pale yellow or tan when fresh; darkens with age

Size: Typically 6-10 inches across, but can grow over 20 inches and weigh several pounds.

Texture: Firm, rubbery, and somewhat brittle with thin, deeply contorted folds or fronds

Smell: Mild, nutty, or slightly earthy — not pungent

Spore Print: White

Foraging Guide

Habitat

- Moist, coniferous forests, especially with older trees
- Strongly associated with Douglas-fir (*Pseudotsuga menziesii*) in the PNW
- Grows from buried roots or decaying stumps, sometimes partially underground
- Found from sea level up into mid-elevation forests

Season

- Late August through November, depending on rainfall and elevation

Look-Alikes and Cautions

1. **False Coral Mushrooms** (*Ramaria spp.*): May appear similar at a glance but have tree-like branching rather than ruffled folds. Many species can cause stomach upset if eaten
2. **Meripilus sumstinei** (*Black-Staining Polypore*): Features overlapping, fan-shaped caps—not deeply folded or lobed like cauliflower mushrooms
3. **Sparassis spathulata**: Found in eastern North America. It's less ruffled and differs in habitat and shape compared to *Sparassis radicata*

Key Distinguishing Features

The true cauliflower mushroom (*Sparassis radicata*) has a distinct ruffled, noodle-like structure that's hard to confuse once you know it. It grows near conifers, often from underground wood, and can become large, dense, and heavy.

Cleaning

Wait to clean until you're ready to cook—don't wash ahead of time. Trim the base of the mushroom with a knife. Cut like a cabbage: slice into sections, letting the "leaves" or ruffles fall apart naturally. Keep pieces large so they still resemble their pasta-like shape.

Washing Instructions

Place a single layer of mushroom pieces in a colander or strainer. Run cold water over them while gently stirring with your hand to clean all sides. Repeat the process with remaining pieces until all are clean.

Storage

Store in a paper bag in the fridge for up to one week.

Freezing

Bring a large pot of water to a boil. Place cleaned mushroom pieces in a colander or strainer. Submerge the colander/strainer into the boiling water. Blanch for no more than 3 minutes. Remove from water and drain thoroughly. Spread mushrooms on a towel-lined cookie sheet to cool completely. Once cooled, place in vacuum-sealed bags. Vacuum out the air, but stop if liquid starts to be pulled out. Switch your machine to "seal only" mode to finish sealing. Store in the freezer for up to 1 year.

Drying

Break into smaller, uniform pieces so they dry evenly.
Dehydrator: Dry at 110–125°F for 6–10 hours until crisp.
Air-dry: In a dry, well-ventilated area on a screen or rack (can take several days).
Storage: Once fully dry and brittle, store in an airtight jar in a cool, dark place.

Rehydrating

Soak in hot water for 15–20 minutes. They'll rehydrate with a tender, noodle-like texture perfect for soups, stir-fries, or stews.

Flavor Profile

Cauliflower mushrooms have a mild, nutty flavor with hints of almond and a slightly earthy, buttery undertone. Their unique, chewy texture absorbs flavors well, making them ideal for stir-fries, soups, and creamy sauces. Pairs beautifully with garlic, soy, herbs, and rich broths.

Where to Buy

Check farmers markets in the fall. If you can't locate them through farmers markets or Facebook Marketplace, your next best option is buying them.

Cauliflower mushroom chicken noodle soup

This hearty soup is perfect for making ahead and freezing or taking with you for a winter time off grid campout! Try dehydrating the vegetables and making it into ramen like packets—just add broth and meat later on—for a completely shelf-stable meal!

Makes: 8 servings
Time to Make: 1 hour

Ingredients

- 2 cloves garlic, chopped
- 2 Tbsp olive oil
- 1 tsp oregano
- 1 tsp basil
- 3 stalks celery, chopped
- ½ white onion, chopped
- 2 carrots, chopped
- 2 chicken breasts, frozen or fresh
- ½ cauliflower mushroom (around 3 cups)
- 1 tsp salt
- 6 cups water
- Liquid Aminos, to taste
- Parmesan cheese, for serving

Directions

1. **In a stock pot, combine** olive oil, minced garlic, carrots, onions, and celery. Heat until sizzling and garlic becomes fragrant. Stir in oregano and basil. Cover with a lid.
2. **Cook** on medium heat for about 5 minutes. Add chicken breasts and pour in 6 cups of water. Bring to a rolling boil, then reduce to medium-low to maintain a gentle boil.
3. **Simmer** for 30 minutes (40 if chicken is frozen). Meanwhile, clean your cauliflower mushroom thoroughly.
4. **Remove** chicken from the pot and cut into bite-sized chunks. Return chicken to the pot. If the broth has reduced too much, add 1–2 cups water.
5. **Add** cauliflower mushroom. Simmer for another 5–10 minutes until mushrooms are tender. Stir in salt and taste to adjust seasoning.
6. **Serve** hot with a splash of Bragg Liquid Aminos and a sprinkle of Parmesan cheese, if desired.

Sautéed Cauliflower Mushroom with Garlic and Herbs

This recipe highlights the texture and flavor of cauliflower mushroom—without adding so many flavors that it becomes overbearing.

Makes: 3--5 servings

Time to Make: 25 minutes (including cleaning and prep time)

Ingredients

- 1 small cauliflower mushroom (cleaned and cut into large "noodle" pieces)
- 2–3 Tbsp butter or oil (olive oil or tallow works well)

- 2 garlic cloves, minced
- Salt and pepper to taste

Optional: Chopped wild chives or fresh parsley

Directions

1. **Clean and prep the mushroom**
   Tear or cut into large pieces, rinse well under cold water to remove dirt and bugs. Pat dry with a towel or let air dry briefly.
2. **Heat the pan**
   In a cast iron skillet or camp pan, melt the butter or heat your oil over medium heat.
3. **Sauté the garlic**
   Add garlic and cook for 30 seconds to 1 minute, until fragrant but not browned.
4. **Add the mushroom**
   Toss in the cauliflower mushroom pieces and sauté for 6–8 minutes. Stir occasionally. The mushroom will release moisture—let it cook off so it can brown slightly.
5. **Season and serve**
   Add salt, pepper, and herbs. Serve hot as a side dish or over rice, wild grains, or alongside game meat.

CHIVES

Wild chives (*Allium schoenoprasum*) can be found in abundance in the Pacific Northwest, starting in late March. They also grow in temperate regions throughout the world, including Europe, Asia, and many parts of North America. They are often found on sunny slopes or waterfront areas under cottonwoods. They make a great addition to many home cooked meals, including egg dishes, soups, and marinades! Similar to garlic, wild chives are rich in vitamins A and C, and contain natural antibacterial and anti-inflammatory compounds that support immune health and digestion.

Did You Know?

Wild chives are one of the few wild plants that can double as both food and pest control—their strong onion-like scent naturally repels insects and even some animals from your campsite or garden!

WILD CHIVES
Allium schoenoprasum

Leaves:
Hollow, slender, round, grass-like stalks growing in clumps. Bright green and onion-scented when crushed.

Smell: Strong onion or garlic smell when bruised—this is critical for ID

Height: 8–20 inches tall.

Flowers:
Ball-like clusters of star-shaped, purple-pink flowers atop leafless stalks (late spring–summer)

Small, white to pale purple, and onion-like underground.

Foraging Guide

Habitat

Moist, sunny meadows, streambanks, forest edges, and disturbed ground. Often near gardens or older homesteads. Check city parks along rivers. Be sure to avoid harvesting in areas where the park may have been sprayed or where other pollution has occurred.

Season

- Spring through early summer (March–May)

Toxic Look-Alikes and Cautions

1. **Death Camas** (*Zigadenus spp.*)
   – Leaves: Similar in shape but not hollow and lack any onion smell
   – Flowers: White or cream-colored, not purple, and star-like

   – Smell: No onion or garlic odor—a strong warning sign
   – Toxicity: Extremely poisonous. Even a small amount can be fatal
2. **Star of Bethlehem** (*Ornithogalum umbellatum*)
   – Leaves: Narrow and grass-like with a central white stripe, not hollow
   – Flowers: White with a green stripe underneath
   – Smell: No onion smell. Toxic to humans and pets

Golden Rule: If it doesn't smell like onion or garlic—**do not eat it.**

Cleaning & Processing Wild Chives

Harvest Carefully

Use clean scissors or a knife to cut 2–3 inches above the bulb to allow regrowth. Avoid harvesting near roads or polluted water sources.

Clean Thoroughly

Rinse under cool running water to remove dirt, insects, and debris.
Soak briefly in a bowl of water with a splash of vinegar to remove hidden pests.
Pat dry with a towel or spin in a salad spinner.

Storage

Store fresh in a paper bag in the fridge for up to a week.

Freezing

Chop and freeze in ice cube trays with a little oil for longer-term use.

Drying

Chop into small bits (about ½-inch or shorter stalks). Wash using a strainer. Spread onto a dehydrator tray. Dry at 110°F for about 8 hours.

Flavor Profile

Taste: Mild, fresh onion flavor with subtle grassy and garlicky notes
Aroma: Clean and pungent, similar to scallions or green onions, with a hint of wildness
Texture: Crisp when raw; softens and mellows when cooked
Best Compared To: A blend between green onions and garlic greens, but gentler
Pairs Well With: Creamy, egg-based, or starchy dishes—but their delicate flavor can be overpowered if overcooked

Where to Buy/Substitutes

If you can't find these in the wild, the best option would be to grow your own chives. However, since this does take time, you can easily substitute commercially grown chives or green onions, available readily at grocery stores, in the following recipes.

Chive and Lemon Balm Quinoa Salad

Makes: 4 servings

Time to Make: 5 minutes (quinoa is cooked in advance)

Ingredients

- 2 cups cooked, cooled quinoa
- ½ cup chopped parsley
- ½ cup chopped wild chives
- 2 Tbsp chopped mint
- 1 Tbsp chopped lemon balm
- 1 Tbsp chopped basil

- 1 garlic clove, minced
- ¼ to ½ cup lemon juice (taste test after ¼ and keep adding to desired tanginess)
- ¼ cup extra virgin olive oil
- ¼ tsp salt
- 1/8 tsp fresh ground pepper

Directions

1. **Toss** all ingredients and chill for one hour.

2. **Garnish** with fresh lemon balm and mint to serve.

Ranch Dressing

The secret to gaining the perfect thickness for ranch dressing is xanthan gum. It is a plant-derived thickening agent that helps bind ingredients without the need for thickening. The amount I use in this recipe is only ¼ tsp. This recipe also calls for parsley and dill weed as options. Personally, I like a basic recipe with only garlic and chives, but everyone likes different flavors. Play around with the spices till you figure out what you prefer.

Makes: about 2 cups
Time to Make: 5 minutes

Ingredients
- 1 cup milk
- ½ cup mayonnaise
- ½ cup sour cream
- 1 small bunch wild chives, finely chopped
- 2 tsp parsley (optional)
- 1 tsp dill weed (optional)
- 1¼ tsp salt (start with 1 tsp and adjust to taste)
- 1½ tsp garlic powder
- 1/8 tsp xanthan gum
- Pepper, to taste (optional)
- **Optional:** 2 fresh garlic cloves (for stronger garlic flavor)

Directions
1. **Combine** all ingredients in a blender.
2. **Blend** until smooth. Taste and adjust salt as needed.
3. **Pour** into a mason jar or salad dressing bottle.
4. **Chill** in the refrigerator. Dressing will thicken as it cools.

Meatballs with Feta and Chives

This is similar to the feta meatloaf later in the book, but even simpler. It's a perfect springtime meal served with truffle butter rice, and roasted asparagus or a salad.

Makes: 4 servings
Time to Make: 1 hour, including baking time

Ingredients
- 1 lb. grass-fed ground beef (can use Elk or a combination of venison and ground beef)
- 4 oz Feta cheese, crumbled
- 1 tsp salt
- 2 Tbsp chopped freshly harvested wild chives

Directions
1. **Knead** ingredients together.
2. **Shape** into balls and place in 8"x8" baking dish.
3. **Bake** at 400 for 35 minutes.

Chive Smashed Potatoes

Makes: 4 servings
Time to Make: 35 minutes

Ingredients
- 8–12 small red or yellow potatoes, halved, peeled if desired
- 1/3 cup sour cream
- 1 bunch chopped chives
- 2 Tbsp butter
- Salt, to taste

Directions
1. **Start** by boiling the potatoes in water for about 25 minutes, until they are soft when pierced with a fork.
2. **Drain.**
3. **Add** sour cream, chives, butter, and salt to taste.
4. **Mix** just until sour cream is combined but potatoes are still somewhat lumpy.
5. **Serve** with lemon balm balsamic spring chinook (see salmon section).

BONUS Recipe!

Wild Chive Rodent-Repellent Sachets

A natural solution for keeping mice and rats away from your shelter, pantry, or gear.

Makes: 4 sachets
Time to Make: 15 minutes

Ingredients
- 1 cup dried wild chive greens (or substitute dried garden chives)
- ½ cup dried mint (peppermint or lemon balm work best)
- ½ cup cedar shavings or fir tips, crushed
- 10 drops peppermint or eucalyptus essential oil (optional but highly effective)
- Small cloth sachets or pieces of muslin/cotton tied with string

Directions
1. **Mix** the dried chives, mint, and cedar/fir tips in a bowl.
2. **Add** a few drops of essential oil if using. Mix again.
3. **Spoon** into sachets or wrap in cloth and tie shut.
4. **Place** the sachets in corners, near food storage, under bedding, or anywhere you've seen signs of rodent activity.

Pro Tip: Replace sachets every 4–6 weeks or if they lose scent. You can also sprinkle the loose mix directly in rodent entry points or burn some on a fire-safe dish near an open vent.

Why it Works:
- **Wild chives** and **mint** emit strong sulfurous and menthol compounds that irritate rodent senses.
- **Cedar and fir** naturally deter pests due to their aromatic oils.
- Essential oils boost potency, especially in enclosed spaces.

CRABAPPLE & WILD APPLE

Crabapples (*Malus spp.)* are one of the most accessible wild fruits—often hiding in plain sight. I debated on adding this section, toying with the question—are they wild or just off-shoots of cultivated apples? Though some may be the descendants of cultivated trees brought by settlers, these tart little apples thrive along roadsides, forest edges, and forgotten homesteads across the Pacific Northwest and beyond, making them wild enough in my books! While they may be smaller and sourer than their grocery store cousins, they're packed with nutrients and ideal for canning, drying, or making jellies and chutneys.

Photo by Jon Sailer

Did You Know?

Crabapples contain high levels of pectin, which makes them perfect for natural jelly-making—no added pectin needed! Their tart skins are also packed with vitamin C and antioxidants, supporting immune health and digestion.

CRABAPPLES
(*Malus spp.*)

- **Size:** ½ to 2 inches in diameter

- **Shape:** Round or slightly oval, usually with a small dimple at the blossom end

- **Color:** Varies — red, green, yellow, or a mix; sometimes striped or speckled

- **Leaves:** Oval with finely toothed edges and pointed tips

- **Bark:** Smooth and gray on young trees; rougher as the tree matures

- **Fruit Clusters:** Grow singly or in small bunches; fruit is firm and apple-like

- **Tree Size:** Usually 10–25 feet tall; found near parks, abandoned orchards, old roads, and field edges

Foraging Guide

Habitat

- Found along rural roadsides, old homesteads, orchard edges, and disturbed areas
- Common near fields, pasture perimeters, and forest edges, especially in areas with a history of settlement
- Often grows wild in the Willamette Valley, coastal ranges, and lower elevations throughout the Pacific Northwest
- Widely distributed across North America, Europe, and Asia—not limited to the PNW

Season

- Late summer to early fall (August–October)

Look-Alikes and Cautions
1. **Hawthorn Berries** (*Crataegus spp.*)
   - Similar size, but contain a single large seed, not a multi-seeded core
   - Edible when ripe, but seeds contain cyanide compounds—don't eat in quantity

Key Tip: Has a core with multiple small seeds like domestic apples. Firm texture and thin, edible skin. Grows on trees with alternate, serrated leaves and woody stems.

Cleaning

Rinse thoroughly in cold water to remove dirt, bugs, and debris. Discard any fruit with worm holes or soft spots. Pat dry or air-dry before storage or processing.

Freezing

Wash, core, and chop into small chunks. Store in airtight freezer bags—no peeling required unless preferred.
Optional: sprinkle with cinnamon and brown sugar before freezing (especially if using for pies or applesauce eventually).

Drying

Core and slice thinly (about ¼-inch thick). **Optional:** soak in lemon water to prevent browning.
Dehydrate at 125–135°F for 8–12 hours until leathery. Store in airtight containers in a cool, dark place.

Flavor Profile

Taste: Tart, tangy, mildly bitter, sometimes lightly sweet when ripe
Texture: Firm when raw; softens when cooked
Best Uses: Jellies, syrups, vinegars, pickles, chutneys, baked goods
Pairs Well With: Cinnamon, cloves, ginger, apple cider, sugar, pork, and root vegetables

Where to Buy/Substitutes

Substitute farm-grown apples

Wild Crabapple Vinegar

Crabapple vinegar is rich in acetic acid, which supports digestion and gut health. Historically, it was used in old-world medicine for everything from wound cleaning to cold remedies. Today, it's used for everything from fermentation to gut balancing. Personally, I drink some of this every morning in a glass of water for a gut balancing start to the day!

Makes: about 2 quarts depending on size of apples and amount of water   **Time to Make:** 1 month (fermentation time included)

Ingredients
- 6–8 cups washed, chopped crabapples (no need to peel or core)
- ½–1 cup granulated sugar or honey (adjust to taste)
- Filtered water (enough to cover the fruit)

Optional: 1 Tbsp raw, unpasteurized apple cider vinegar (as a starter culture)

Directions
1. **Fill** your jar about ¾ full with chopped crabapples. Bruised or overripe fruit is great for vinegar-making.
2. **Dissolve** sugar or honey in filtered water and pour over the fruit until fully submerged.
3. **Optional:** Add a Tbsp of raw apple cider vinegar to help kickstart fermentation.
4. **Cover** the jar with cheesecloth or a clean towel and secure with a rubber band. This allows airflow but keeps bugs out.
5. **Stir** daily with a clean utensil to prevent mold. Bubbles and foam are normal!
6. **After** 1–2 weeks, strain out the solids. Return the liquid to a clean jar and cover again with the cloth.
7. **Let** it ferment another 3–4 weeks, tasting weekly. Once it has a tangy, vinegar-like smell and taste, it's ready!
8. **Transfer** to a sealed bottle or jar for storage. No refrigeration needed. Flavor improves with age.

Secret Ingredient Crabapple Crisp

This recipe was a favorite among my family growing up. My parents often made it when guests came over and then asked the guests to guess the secret ingredient (peanut butter). Serve warm with a big scoop of vanilla ice cream. It will blow your tastebuds!

Makes: 9x9" pan
Time to Make: 1 hour including prep time

Ingredients

For Filling:
- 8 cups sliced or chopped crabapples
- 2 Tbsp flour
- ½ cup granulated sugar
- 2 tsp cinnamon
- ¼ tsp salt
- 2 Tbsp water

For Topping:
- ½ cup oats
- ½ tsp salt
- ¼ cup butter
- ¼ cup creamy peanut butter
- 2/3 cup brown sugar

Directions
1. **Preheat** oven to 350°F.
2. **Combine** crabapples, flour, sugar, cinnamon, salt, and water.
3. **Grease** a 9x9" casserole dish with butter or oil.
4. **Place** apple mixture into the greased dish.
5. **Cut** topping ingredients together with a pastry blender until crumbly.
6. **Sprinkle** topping evenly over the apple mixture.
7. **Bake** in preheated oven for 35 minutes, until the top is golden brown and the apples are cooked through.

Slow Cooker Crabapple Butter

This recipe offers the perfect way to preserve apples for winter. This apple butter can be spread on toast, or even served with meat like pork chops. I never peel my apples, as this recipe will be blended before packaging. However, for a smoother finish, you can peel apples before preparing this.

Makes: 6-8 pints

Time to Make: Overnight

Ingredients
- 6 cups chopped apples
- 3½ cup granulated sugar
- 2 tsp cinnamon
- ½ tsp ginger
- 1 tsp apple pie spice
- ½ tsp allspice
- 4 tsp salt
- 1 cup water

Directions
1. **Combine** all ingredients in a slow cooker.
2. **Mix** until spices are fully incorporated.
3. **Turn** to the low setting and cook for 8–10 hours (overnight or during the day).
4. **Enjoy** the incredible aroma as it cooks!
5. **Blend** in a blender if you prefer a smoother texture.
6. **Preserve** by pouring into glass jars and freezing.
7. **Can** if desired: use the boiling water bath method (see blackberry section). Process **pint jars** for 10 minutes per 1000 feet elevation; **quart jars** for 15 minutes.

Overnight Crabapple Oatmeal

If you like oatmeal, this is a delicious breakfast. You can also make this with dried apples and give as gifts in jars, as long as your apples are completely dried and you include instructions for cooking, including adding the wet ingredients.

Makes: 6 servings
Time to Make: Overnight

Ingredients
- 3 cups oatmeal
- 1 ½ cups crabapples, chopped (use dried apples if making this part in advance)
- 1 Tbsp cinnamon (adjust if you don't like it as strong)
- 1 tsp apple pie spice
- ¼ cup brown sugar
- 1 tsp salt

Directions
1. **Shake** all dry ingredients together in a jar to store for later.
2. **When ready to make**, add **6 cups water** and shake again to mix.
3. **Place** in a slow cooker.
4. **Turn** to the low (8–10 hour) setting the night before serving.
5. **Wake up** to a house filled with warm, spicy aroma—perfect for cold mornings or holiday gatherings.

Crabapple and Chanterelle Chutney

Use early season summer chanterelles—often found near the coastline—and crabapples, to make this foragers chutney. Serve with crackers, a little cheese, or even smoked salmon!

Makes: ~2 cups

Time to Make: About 1 hour

Ingredients
- 2 cups crabapples (halved or quartered, cores removed if desired)
- 1 cup fresh chanterelle mushrooms, cleaned and chopped
- ½ cup yellow onion, finely chopped
- 1 clove garlic, minced
- ½ cup apple cider vinegar
- ⅓ cup brown sugar (or honey for a more natural option)
- 1 Tbsp fresh grated ginger (or 1 tsp ground)
- ¼ tsp cinnamon
- ⅛ tsp cloves
- ⅛ tsp red pepper flakes (optional, for mild heat)
- ½ tsp salt
- ¼ cup water (as needed)

Directions
1. **Sauté the Mushrooms:**
   Heat a splash of oil in a pan over medium heat.
   Add chopped chanterelles and **sauté** for about 5–7 minutes, until softened and most moisture has evaporated.
   Remove from pan and set aside.
2. **Cook the Base:**
   In the same pan, **add** a little more oil and **sauté** the onion over medium heat until translucent, about 5 minutes.
   Stir in garlic and cook 1 more minute.
3. **Add Fruit and Flavorings:**
   Add crabapples, sautéed mushrooms, vinegar, brown sugar (or honey), ginger, cinnamon, cloves, red pepper flakes, and salt.
   Pour in water and **bring** to a simmer.
4. **Simmer and Soften:**
   Cook uncovered for 30–40 minutes, stirring occasionally, until the crabapples have softened and broken down.
   Add more water if needed to prevent sticking.
5. **Mash and Adjust:**
   Gently mash larger chunks with a spoon or potato masher if desired, but leave some texture.
   Taste and adjust seasoning—more vinegar for tang, sugar for sweetness, or salt for balance.
6. **Cool and Store:**
   Let cool completely before transferring to a jar.
   Store in the fridge for up to 2 weeks, or process in a water bath for longer shelf life.

Dungeness Crab

- White-tipped claws
- Smooth carapace
- Ten carapace spines

Red Rock Crab

- Black-tipped claws
- Rough carapace
- Fewer carapace spines

CRAB

Crabs are fairly easy to find in the Pacific Northwest and throughout the world. Crab is a lean source of protein rich in omega-3 fatty acids, vitamin B12, and minerals like zinc and selenium, which support heart health, brain function, and immune defense. Here in the PNW, throwing crab pots baited with chicken legs, fish carcasses, herring, or other small bait fish is the move. Taking leftover meat or native-to-an-area bait fish is often suitable crab bait. Crabs like a lot of different baits, and anything smelly is right up their alley! The big challenge with finding crabs, especially when you are harvesting from a dock, as opposed to from a boat, where you can get further out in the ocean or bay, is finding crabs that are legal. In most places, you can keep only males, and there are often size limits as well. Ensure you have read regulations thoroughly before going and make sure you have the correct license. We have found more success when going in late fall, but before December, when the commercial harvest is at its peak. As always, I will include links to more comprehensive resources in the recommended reading section of this book.

Did You Know?

The shells of crabs can be crushed and boiled to make a mineral-rich broth or ground into calcium powder for long-term use. Nothing goes to waste!

Common Crabs to Harvest in the PNW & Identification

MALE CRAB
(Jimmy)

FEMALE CRAB
(Sook)

Narrow, pointed apron (resembles a lighthouse or Washington Monument)
• Typically larger claws
• Often more meat per crab, especially in species like Dungeness

• Wide, rounded apron (like a dome or beehive – used to carry eggs)

Important Notes for Foragers

- In many regions, especially in the Pacific Northwest, it is illegal to harvest female crabs
- Always check local fishing regulations before keeping any crab
- Return egg-bearing females to the water immediately to support healthy crab populations

Foraging Guide

Locations

- Estuaries, bays, jetties, and nearshore ocean

Gear

- Crab pots/traps: Best for docks or boats
- Ring nets: Simple and good for short-term soaking

Bait

- Raw chicken, fish carcasses, squid, or razor clam scraps work well
- The key here is to use zip ties or a crab pot with an enclosed bait compartment—otherwise the crabs **will** take all your bait (without a thank-you for the meal) and take off!

Best Time

- Slack tide is ideal. When the tide is strong, crabs may bury themselves in the sand
- Crabbing is best from late summer to early winter

Cleaning

Boil whole crabs (see below). Rinse with cold water to cool. Flip crab over, remove the apron (the belly flap), and lift off the top shell. Pull out and discard the gills and guts. Rinse again, then break crab into halves or quarters.

How to Cook Crabs

1. **Bring a large pot of salted** water to a rolling boil (many people cook them in the water they inhabited).
   - Add ~¼ cup salt per gallon (unnecessary if you are using ocean water)
   - Optional: Include lemon, bay leaves, garlic, or crab boil spices

2. **Drop in the cleaned or live crabs**
   - Whole crabs: Boil 15–18 minutes
   - Halved/cleaned crabs: Boil 10–12 minutes
   - Crabs are done when bright orange-red
3. Cool in an ice bath or under cold water to stop cooking.

Flavor Profile

- **Dungeness Crab**
  – Flavor: Sweet, briny, and delicately nutty
  – Texture: Tender but firm—ideal for salads, pastas, crab cakes, or just dipped in butter

- **Red Rock Crab**
  – Flavor: Sweet and slightly stronger; more robust than Dungeness
  – Texture: Firmer meat with smaller claws—great for soups, sauces, or cracking and snacking

Where to Buy

If you can't harvest your own crabs, the next best option would be to buy fresh, live seafood. In many cases, Asian markets are a wonderful way to get the next best thing, with high quality products. Look for live crabs. Also check markets in coastal regions, if that is feasible for you, where fresh seafood is easily acquired. If all else fails, you can purchase acceptable crab meat from grocery stores like Safeway.

Crab Fondue

My bestie shared this recipe—all the way from Alaska, where she often harvested crabs and fish as a child.

Makes: 6 cups fondue
Time to Make: 25 minutes

Ingredients
- 2 cups medium white sauce (see recipe at the end of this recipe)
- 8 oz cream cheese
- 4 oz sour cream
- 5 oz Monterey jack cheese
- 4 oz mild cheddar cheese
- 6 oz Swiss cheese
- 1/8 tsp lemon juice
- ½ tsp garlic salt
- ¼ tsp cayenne pepper
- ½ cup white wine
- 4 wild chives or green onions
- 1 ½ lb crab

Directions
1. **Make** white sauce.
2. **Add sour** cream, cheeses, seasonings, and crab.
3. **Serve** warm with rice or French bread cubes.

Easy White Sauce Recipe

Makes: 2 cups
Time to Make: 10 minutes

Ingredients
- 2 Tbsp butter (or tallow)
- 2 Tbsp all-purpose flour (could even use acorn or other foraged flour)
- 1½ cups milk (whole milk preferred, or substitute with broth for a lighter version)
- Salt and pepper to taste

Optional: Pinch of garlic powder

Directions
1. **Melt the butter** in a saucepan over medium heat.
2. **Whisk in the flour** and cook for 1–2 minutes, stirring constantly to form a smooth roux (don't let it brown).
3. **Slowly add the milk**, whisking continuously to prevent lumps.
4. **Simmer gently** until the sauce thickens (about 5–7 minutes).
5. **Season to taste** with salt, pepper, and any optional flavorings.

Fire Cooked Crab Cakes

Makes: 6-8 crab cakes
Time to Make: 30 minutes

Ingredients
- 1 lb lump crab meat (picked over for shells)
- 1 large egg
- ¼ cup mayonnaise
- 1½ tsp Dijon mustard
- 1 tsp Worcestershire sauce
- 1 tsp Old Bay seasoning (or homemade spice blend)
- ½ tsp sea salt
- ¼ tsp black pepper
- 2 tsp lemon juice
- 2 Tbsp chopped fresh parsley
- ½ cup finely crushed saltine crackers (or panko)
- 2–3 Tbsp butter or oil for pan-frying

Directions
1. **Mix the binder:**
   In a medium bowl, whisk together the egg, mayonnaise, mustard, Worcestershire, Old Bay, lemon juice, salt, and pepper.
2. **Combine:**
   Gently fold in crab meat, parsley, and crushed crackers. Be careful not to break up the crab too much—you want chunks!
3. **Chill:**
   Cover and refrigerate the mixture for 30–60 minutes. This helps the cakes hold together.
4. **Form cakes:**
   Shape into 6–8 patties, about ¾ inch thick.
5. **Cook:**
   Heat butter or oil in a skillet over medium heat. Fry cakes for 3–4 minutes per side or until golden brown and crisp. Handle gently when flipping!
6. **Serve:**
   Great hot or room temp. Try with a lemon wedge, spicy aioli, or homemade tartar sauce.

Simple Crab Dipping Sauce

Many people enjoy crab legs or whole crabs straight from the pot after cooking. To make a simple dipping sauce, all you need is melted butter, garlic cloves, and Parmesan cheese (optional). Combine 1 minced garlic clove per ¼ cup melted butter and 1 Tbsp Parmesan if using. Dip freshly cooked crab legs in this sauce and enjoy! Serve alongside a meal of sautéed lobster mushrooms, early chanterelles, and clams fried in oil and vinegar (see clam section). Finish off the meal with wild cherry donuts (see cherry section) or a Bannock cooked over the campfire, drizzled with wild raw honey!

Campfire Crab Boil (PNW Style)

Down South, seafood boils are a lively tradition—pots brimming with crawfish or crab, corn, potatoes, and spices, all dumped out on a table for friends and family to gather around. This is the Pacific Northwest version, made with Dungeness crab and foraged herbs, cooked right at the water's edge. Instead of Cajun seasoning, we let seawater, wild greens, and coastal aromatics shine.

Makes: 4 servings
Time to Make: 45 minutes

Ingredients
- 2 whole live crabs (Dungeness preferred, or local catch)
- 8 small potatoes, halved
- 2 ears corn, cut into chunks (optional but classic)
- 2 handfuls nettle tops or wild greens (lamb's quarters, dandelion)
- 1 wild onion (or ½ cup garden onion), quartered
- 2 cloves garlic, smashed
- A few sprigs wild herbs (yarrow, fennel fronds, or spruce tips)
- Seawater (or 8 cups fresh water with ⅓ cup sea salt)
- 2 Tbsp butter or oil (optional, for finishing)

Directions
1. **Prepare the fire:** Build a strong fire and bring a large pot of seawater (or salted fresh water) to a rolling boil.
2. **Add the vegetables and crab:** Drop in potatoes, onions, garlic, and crab and cook 12-15 minutes until crab shells turn bright orange.
3. **Add greens:** In the last 2–3 minutes, toss in nettles or other wild greens.
4. **Drain and serve:** Pour out the pot onto a flat stone, rustic table, or spread of leaves. Drizzle with butter or oil if available.
5. **Dig in:** Crack crab and eat with potatoes, greens, and broth-soaked vegetables.

CLAM

Digging clams can be a fun activity in the Pacific Northwest and beyond! Clams are a nutrient-dense shellfish packed with lean protein, iron, vitamin B12, and omega-3s, supporting energy levels, brain health, and a strong immune system. Kids can easily get the hang of clam digging and it takes very little experience to find your limits. With this being said, always read local regulations thoroughly. Check for which species are legal, what license or tag you may need, and always pay attention to size specifications and daily and yearly bag limits. When it comes to digging, I find that a shovel works much better for smaller clams, as opposed to a clam gun. Having both and being flexible can help a lot. Find an area, wait for low tide, look for holes in the sand, and start digging! The amount below the surface of the sand varies for each clam. There are many excellent resources on clam digging available. See recommended reading section to learn more.

Did You Know?

Clams can burrow up to a foot deep in the sand and filter gallons of seawater each day, making them natural ocean cleaners! In a survival situation, they provide not only protein and minerals, but their shells can also be used to scrape, scoop, or even sharpen into tools.

Common Clams in the PNW

Butter Clams
(Saxidomus gigantea)

Shell: Thick, oval, white to yellowish; concentric growth rings

Gaper Clams
(Tresus capax / T, nuttallii)

Shell: Large, oblong, chalky white with fragile edges. Siphon often sticks out and can't retract

Razor Clams
(Siliqua patula)

Shell: Long, narrow, smooth and shiny—like a straight razor

Cockles
(Clinocardium nuttallii)

Shell: Round, deeply ribbed, usually white or gray with brown patches

Foraging Guide

- **Location:** Bays, estuaries, and intertidal zones
- **Tools:** Bucket, shovel or clam gun, and shellfish license
- **Tide Timing:** Go at low tide (preferably -1.0 ft or lower); dig near "clam shows"—small holes, dimples, or squirts in the sand
- **Tip:** Look for areas where everyone else is digging!

Regulations & Tips

- License required—check local regulations
- Limits: Vary by species—check local regulations
- Keep Only Legal Clams: Measure carefully and don't cull—if it's below size, leave it in the ground
- Respect Closures: Red tide (domoic acid) and pollution can make clams toxic. Always check current advisories

Cleaning

1. **Purge Sand**
   - Place live clams in a cooler with ice for up to 12 hours
   - Optional: Add 1–2 Tbsp of cornmeal to help purge grit
   - Rinse thoroughly afterward
2. **Scrub Shells**
   - Use a stiff brush under cold running water to scrub off mud, barnacles, or algae
3. **Open the Clam (Without Prying)**
   If you're not steaming the clam open and want to clean it raw:

   - **Step 1:** Place the clam flat-side up on a cutting board
   - **Step 2:** Using a sharp paring or boning knife, insert the tip gently between the shells at the hinge end or near the side where the two shells slightly gap
   - **Step 3:** Slice carefully around the inside edge of the shell, keeping the blade flush with the inside of the top shell. This will sever the adductor muscles holding the shell closed
   - **Step 4:** Repeat the same motion along the other side of the clam, cutting around the inside of the bottom shell
   - **Step 5:** Open the shell carefully and remove the meat with your fingers or the knife, trimming away any dark or tough parts if desired

Tip: For gapers or large butter clams, slit and rinse the siphon to remove grit—it can be chewy but tasty

Flavor Profile

- **Butter Clams:** Buttery, full-flavored, with a rich finish—ideal for chowders
- **Razor Clams:** Delicate and slightly sweet, excellent fried or in ceviche
- **Gaper Clams:** Mild and chewy—best chopped or in soups
- **Cockles:** Firm and salty, perfect for steaming, pasta, or paella

Where to Buy

Much like crabs, buying from a local vendor at the coast is the absolute best option. However, when this is not feasible, search for local Asian markets. Look for clams kept on ice, but not submerged completely in water. Make sure that there is no strong odor and that the clams are still closed. Some Asian markets will be able to cut and clean them for you. If all else fails, canned clams will be fine for clam chowder or pasta dishes.

Oil and Vinegar Whole Clams

This simple recipe keeps the oceanic flavor of clams—adding a simple highlight of vinegar to bring out the flavors even more! Cook at home or over the campfire! Perfect for off grid meals as they require very little preparation ahead of time!

Makes: 6 clams

Time to Make: 10 minutes

Ingredients
- ¼ cup olive oil
- 3 garlic cloves, sliced
- 2 Tbsp white wine
- 6 clams, sliced down the middle, rinsed

Directions
1. **Heat** a cast iron skillet to medium-low heat.
2. **Add** 2 Tbsp of the vinegar and oil mixture to the pan.
3. **When** it is simmering, **add** your clam, face down.
4. **Cook** for 3 minutes.
5. **Remove** and **serve** immediately.

Clam and Crab Chowder

This simple recipe combines clams and crabs for a filling soup—straight from the ocean!

Makes: 6 servings   **Time to Make:** 35 minutes

Ingredients

- 1 purple onion, chopped
- 2 garlic cloves, minced
- 4 slices bacon, cut into ½-inch pieces
- 2 slices celery
- 5 red potatoes, peeled if desired (I never peel my potatoes)
- 4-oz fresh clams, cleaned, juice reserved
- ½ cup crab leg or claw meat (canned is fine)
- 1 tsp oregano
- 1 tsp basil
- 1 tsp parsley
- 1 tsp salt
- ½ tsp pepper
- 1 Tbsp flour
- 2 cups water
- 1 cup whole milk
- ½ cup heavy cream
- Butter, for serving

Directions

1. **In a large stock pot or saucepan**, combine onion, garlic, celery, and bacon.
2. **Turn** to medium-low heat and cook for about 5 minutes, until the onion is tender and the bacon starts to curl.
3. **Add** spices and stir.
4. **Drain** clam juice into the pot.
5. **Add** water to cover potatoes.
6. **Bring** to a boil and then turn the heat down so it begins to simmer.
7. **Cover** with a lid and let cook about 15 minutes, until potatoes are soft when pierced with a fork.
8. **Remove** 2 cups of the potato and water soup base into a food processor or blender.
9. **Add** 1 cup milk and 1 Tbsp flour.
10. **Blend** just until mixed and potatoes are mashed.
11. **Return** to pot and stir in.
12. **Pour** in clams and crab meat.
13. **Add** cream.
14. **Leave** on low heat for about 5 minutes, letting it simmer but not come to a full boil. It should thicken significantly.
15. **Remove** from heat.
16. **Ladle** into bowls and serve with a spoonful of butter and some saltine crackers.
17. **Easy Clams in Cream Sauce**

Note: Prepare this over the campfire for a creamy treat—serve with pasta, or steamed cauliflower mushroom—for a healthier, lower carb pasta option!

Easy Clams in Cream Sauce

Prepare this over the campfire for a creamy treat—serve with pasta, or steamed cauliflower mushroom—for a healthier, lower carb pasta option!

Makes: 4 servings

Time to Make: 20 minutes

Ingredients

- 1 lb fresh clams, cleaned and de-shelled, chopped into small bites
- 2 Tbsp butter
- 2 garlic cloves, minced

- ½ cup dry white wine or broth
- ½ cup heavy cream
- Salt and black pepper to taste

Optional: Fresh parsley, lemon zest, or red pepper flakes

Directions

1. **In a large pan**, melt the butter over medium heat. Add garlic and sauté until fragrant (1–2 minutes).
2. **Pour in** the wine or broth and bring to a simmer.
3. **Add** the clams, cover the pan, and sauté for 3–5 minutes, or until the clams are cooked.
4. **Stir** the cream into the pan and simmer for 2–3 minutes until slightly thickened.
5. **Season** with salt and pepper.
6. **Garnish** with parsley or lemon zest and serve hot—great with crusty bread, over pasta, or served with steamed wild greens.

DANDELION

Dandelions (*Taraxacum officinale*) grow abundantly across North America, Europe, Asia, and beyond—thriving in meadows, lawns, roadsides, and disturbed soils from early spring through fall. Often dismissed as a weed, every part of the dandelion is edible and medicinal: the leaves are rich in vitamins A, C, and K, the roots support liver and digestive health, and the flowers contain antioxidants that help reduce inflammation. This resilient plant has been used for centuries as a nourishing food and powerful herbal remedy.

Did You Know?

Dandelion has been used for centuries as a natural detoxifier. In tough times, pioneers and Indigenous communities roasted the roots for coffee, used the leaves for greens, and turned the flowers into wine or syrup!

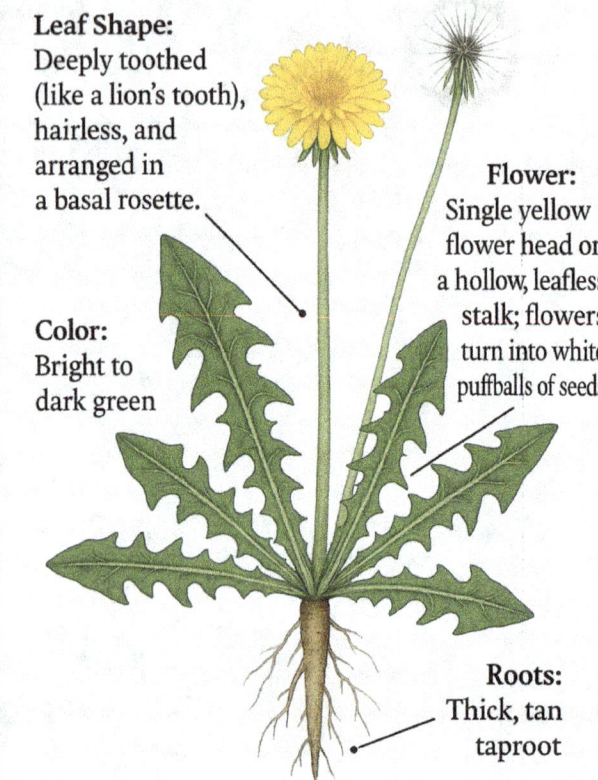

Dandelion
(*Taraxacum officinale*)

Leaf Shape:
Deeply toothed (like a lion's tooth), hairless, and arranged in a basal rosette.

Color:
Bright to dark green

Flower:
Single yellow flower head on a hollow, leafless stalk; flowers turn into white puffballs of seeds

Roots:
Thick, tan taproot

Foraging Guide

Habitat

- Lawns, meadows, roadsides, vacant lots, gardens—almost anywhere with disturbed soil
- Range: Widespread across North America and Europe
- Growth Habit: Low to the ground; leaves radiate outward from a central point

Season

- Early spring to mid-summer, especially before flowering for tender, less bitter leaves.
- Can be harvested again in fall.

Look-Alikes and Cautions

1. **Cat's Ear** (*Hypochaeris radicata*)
   - Similar yellow flower
   - Leaves are fuzzy and less deeply toothed
   - Usually has branched flower stems (unlike dandelion's single flower stalk)
2. **Wild Lettuce** (*Lactuca spp.*)
   - Taller and more upright
   - Leaves less lobed, may be spiny underneath
3. **Sow Thistle** (*Sonchus spp.*)
   - Leaves have prickly edges and milky sap
   - Flowers are similar but plant grows taller with a hollow stem

Key Difference: True dandelions have smooth, hairless leaves and a single unbranched flower stalk that exudes milky sap when broken.

Harvesting Tips

- Use scissors or a knife to cut young leaves close to the base of the rosette
- Harvest in early morning when leaves are perky
- Choose leaves before flowering for best taste and tenderness
- Avoid areas treated with herbicides, pesticides, or frequented by pets

Cleaning

Rinse leaves in cold water to remove dirt and bugs. Soak in a bowl of cold water with a splash of vinegar for 10 minutes. Rinse thoroughly and pat dry with a towel or use a salad spinner. Discard any wilted, spotted, or tough leaves.

Drying

Air Drying: Lay cleaned leaves in a single layer on a mesh rack or screen in a warm, dry place out of direct sun. Allow 5–7 days to fully dry.
Dehydrator: Use at 95–115°F for 4–8 hours, or until brittle.
Store in an airtight jar in a cool, dark place.

Flavor Profile

- Raw: Earthy, slightly bitter, with a peppery edge—similar to arugula
- Cooked: Bitterness mellows; becomes more nutty and spinach-like
- Best Uses: Salads (young leaves), sautéed greens, soups, smoothies, and as a tea when dried

Where to Buy

See references at the end of this book

Dandelion Green Salad with Strawberries and Goat Cheese

This is an early summer favorite for me. If I want more protein, I will serve with half a salmon filet, cooked on the grill to avoid heating the house (or over the fire in a foil packet). The bitterness in the dandelion greens complements the sweetness of fresh, wild strawberries, and the balsamic dressing brings out the sweetness even more. The goat cheese adds a creamy touch that perfectly blends it all together.

Makes: 6 plates

Time to Make: 15 minutes

Ingredients

- 6 cups organic spring mix
- 1 cup dandelion greens, cut into small pieces
- 2 cups fresh very ripe strawberries, preferably wild harvested or from a local PNW farm

- 4 oz goat cheese
- ½ cup sliced almonds (optional)
- 1 cup mung bean sprouts (optional, adds a nice crunch and extra protein)

For Dressing

- ¼ cup balsamic vinegar
- 2 Tbsp olive oil

- 1 dash salt

Directions

1. **Toss** spring mix and dandelion greens together in a large bowl.
2. **Assemble** four plates with the greens.
3. **Top** each plate with ¼ cup strawberries, 1 oz crumbled goat cheese, sliced almonds, and mung bean sprouts if desired.
4. **In a glass jar,** combine the olive oil and balsamic vinegar.
5. **Drizzle** dressing over the plates of salad just before serving.

Dandelion Limeade

This is the perfect health drink—only you can't tell that based on the taste, because it is so sweet that even kids love it!

Makes: 2 cups

Time to Make: 30 minutes

Ingredients

- 2 cups water, divided
- 1 cup dandelion flowers (remove green parts and keep only the petals)
- ¼ cup raw honey
- ¼ cup freshly squeezed lime juice
- Ice

Directions

1. **Cover** 1 cup dandelion petals with 1 cup water in a saucepan.
2. **Bring** to a boil. Take off heat and **let sit** for 10 minutes.
3. **Strain,** reserving the liquid and a few petals if desired. (Save remaining petals for dandelion pasta recipe if desired; see recipe later in this section.)
4. **Add** honey to the warm infusion and **stir** until it dissolves.
5. **Mix in** lime juice and the remaining 1 cup water (adjust to taste).
6. **Add** ice cubes to chill the mixture.
7. **Serve** over additional ice.

Dandelion Honey Ice cream

This is a delicious summer treat that is easy to make,
beautiful to look at, and even better tasting!

Makes: 3 ½ cup ice cream

Time to Make: 3 hours-overnight

Ingredients

- ½ cup raw honey (or use half honey, half sugar)
- 1½ cup heavy cream
- 1 cup half & half
- 1 cup dandelion petals
- 3 egg yolks
- 1 tsp vanilla (optional)
- 1 dash salt

Directions

1. **Add** half & half and dandelion petals to a saucepan. **Bring** to a low simmer, then **remove** from heat.
2. **Let sit** for 45 minutes to infuse.
3. **Strain,** reserving the half & half and ¼ cup of the petals. Discard the rest.
4. **Pour** the infused half & half into a clean saucepan. **Add** honey and heavy cream.
5. **Warm** gently over low heat. **Beat in** the egg yolks slowly as it warms.
6. **Heat** until it's hot to the touch but not boiling (test with your pinky—warm but not scorching).
7. **Remove** from heat. **Add** a dash of salt and vanilla, if using.
8. **Cool** completely for at least 2 hours or overnight in the fridge.
9. **Add** to your ice cream maker. **Surround** the canister with alternating layers of ice and rock salt.
10. **Churn** until thickened and ice cream forms.

Dandelion Pasta with Goat Cheese and Chicken

This is an easy spring meal; swap the chicken for wild game bird if desired.

Makes: 4 servings
Time to Make: 35 minutes

Ingredients
- 1 chicken breast, cooked
- 1 cup rotini pasta, cooked
- 1 cup dandelion petals, boiled for 5 minutes in water, drained
- ½ cup alfredo sauce
- 1.5 oz goat cheese
- 1 slice bacon, cooked and crumbled
- 1 cup chopped broccoli (optional)

Directions
1. **Assemble** chicken, pasta, and dandelion petals in a baking dish.
2. **Pour** alfredo sauce over top.
3. **Crumble** bacon and goat cheese on top.
4. **Bake** for 25 minutes at 350°F, until cheese is softened and casserole is bubbly.

French Press Dandelion Coffee

Grind your dried dandelion root. Add equal parts ground coffee and dried dandelion root to a French press. I do 2 Tbsp of ground coffee per 1 cup of water; adjust based on the strength of your coffee, but do at least this much dandelion root. Pour boiling water over top. Steep for 10-15 minutes; press and prepare how you take your coffee!

Roasted Dandelion Root Tea

This easy tea can be made as a way to enjoy the health benefits of dandelion roots—you can also add berry leaves (just make sure they're the edible ones), grated orange peel, or chamomile to glean an array of flavors if you don't like the taste of plain dandelion root.

Makes: 1 cup

Time to Make: 5 minutes (not including roasting time)

Ingredients
- 1 Tbsp roasted dandelion root (coarsely chopped or ground)
- 1½ cups water

Optional: splash of milk, honey, cinnamon, or vanilla

Directions
1. **In a small pot**, combine the roasted dandelion root and water.
2. **Bring to a boil, then** reduce to a simmer for 10–15 minutes.
3. **Strain into** a mug and enjoy as-is or with your favorite add-ins.

Tip: You can roast your own root by chopping fresh, cleaned dandelion roots and baking at 300°F for 30–40 minutes, turning occasionally, until dark brown and aromatic.

ELDERBERRIES

Elderberries (*Sambucus* spp.) grow widely across North America, especially in moist areas like forest edges, stream banks, and meadows, thriving in both temperate and mountainous regions. These dark blue berries, known for their high levels of vitamin C, also have many lesser-known health benefits. Personally, elderberries are a go-to for my whole family. For those of us who don't have the luxury of living off grid or distancing ourselves from everyone, elderberry can be a wonderful healing tonic, combating everyday illness such as the kind that kids pick up incessantly during the winter months. When my two children attended public school, it seemed like every other week one of them was home with a cough, runny nose, sore throat, or stomach virus. Knowing I couldn't afford to catch every illness they shared, I began taking a daily dose of my homemade elderberry syrup—and I didn't come down with a single sore throat all year. Most recently, I had great success using it to fend off a stomach bug my ten-year-old caught three times last winter.

Did you know?

Elderberry dye was traditionally used for textiles and face painting in ceremonial practices, and the elder tree was believed to house protective spirits.

Elderberry

Sambucus Nigra and Sambucus Cerulea

Type: Deciduous shrub or small tree

Flowers:

• Small, white, five-petaled Flat clusters bloom late spring–early summer

Leaves:

• Compound with 5–9 serrated, pointed leaflets (2–6")
• Opposite; slightly unpleasant scent when crushed

Berries:

• Small, dark purple-black in drooping clusters

Blue elderberries (*Sambucus cerulea*) look powdery light blue when ripe due to a natural waxy coating, while black elderberries (*Sambucus* nigra) ripen to a shiny, deep black with no coating.

Foraging Guide

Habitat

- Mountain slopes and foothills
- Streambanks and riparian zones
- Woodland edges and clearings
- Sunny forest openings
- Low to mid elevations in the Pacific Northwest

Blue elderberries grow as large, bushy shrubs or small trees, often reaching 10–30 feet tall. Look for them in sunny, moist environments, especially near creeks and ditches. They have compound leaves with serrated edges and grow in large, umbrella-shaped clusters.

Season

- Late August to early October (varies by elevation)

Toxic Look-Alikes and Cautions

1. **Red Elderberries** (*Sambucus racemosa*)
   - Ripen earlier in summer
   - Grow in tighter cone-shaped clusters
   - **Toxic when raw:** even cooked, using in cooking is debatable
2. **Pokeweed** (*Phytolacca americana*)
   - Berries grow on reddish-purple stems and are shiny, deep purple-black when ripe
   - Leaves and berries are highly toxic to humans
   - Can cause nausea, vomiting, and respiratory failure if ingested
3. **Devil's Walking Stick** (*Aralia spinosa*)
   - Berries grow in large umbrella-like clusters
   - Berries resemble elderberries but grow on a spiny woody stalk
   - Toxic to humans and pets if consumed
4. **Virginia Creeper** (*Parthenocissus quinquefolia*)
   - Berries are small, dark blue, and grow in loose clusters
   - Vines have five leaflets (not compound leaves like elderberry)
   - Contains oxalate crystals that can cause irritation and are toxic if eaten

All elderberries must be cooked before eating – Raw berries contain cyanogenic glycosides, which can cause nausea or worse in large amounts. Always cook thoroughly before consuming.
Avoid the leaves, bark, and stems – These parts are toxic.

Cleaning

Use a fork to gently strip ripe berries from the stems, working over a bowl. Rinse them in cool water and remove any green, underripe berries or stray stems.

Storage

Fresh elderberries spoil quickly and should be used or processed within a day or two. Store them unwashed in the refrigerator in a breathable container.

Freezing

After cleaning, spread the berries on a baking sheet and freeze until solid. Transfer to freezer-safe bags and label. Frozen elderberries are excellent for wintertime syrup-making or baking.

Flavor Profile

Tart and tannic when raw, cooked elderberries develop a rich, wine-like flavor with hints of blueberry, plum, and dark grape. Their deep purple juice is excellent in syrups, jellies, pie fillings, or mead, and they pair well with warming spices like cinnamon, ginger, and cloves.

Where to Buy

Blue elderberries are rarely available fresh in stores, but you can often find them frozen, dried, or as syrup in natural food stores or online. Farmers' markets and wild harvesters sometimes offer them in season. Look for *Sambucus nigra* ssp. *cerulea* to ensure you're getting the safe, edible variety.

Elderberry Pancake Syrup

Makes: 2 cups

Time to Make: 1 hour

Ingredients

- 2 cups elderberries, washed
- 1 cup granulated sugar
- 4 Tbsp cornstarch
- ⅓ cup water
- 1 tsp vanilla extract (optional)
- 1 dash salt

Directions

1. **Place** elderberries in a saucepan and add water just until covered.
2. **Bring** to a boil, then reduce to a low simmer. Cover, cracking the lid if needed for steam to escape.
3. **Simmer** for about 45 minutes, ensuring the heat stays low so water doesn't evaporate too fast.
4. **Remove** from heat and strain the elderberries through cheesecloth, reserving all the juice.
5. **Pour** the juice back into a clean pan. Add sugar and stir over low-medium heat until fully dissolved.
6. **Taste test** and add more sugar if desired—elderberries are naturally tart!
7. **Whisk** cornstarch with ⅓ cup water in a separate bowl until smooth.
8. **Slowly add** the cornstarch mixture to the elderberry syrup, stirring constantly.
9. **Add** a dash of salt and vanilla extract if using. Stir until the syrup thickens.
10. **Remove** from heat and serve warm over pancakes, waffles, or biscuits.

Elderberry Medicine Syrup

Note: If you don't have fresh berries, you can substitute twice the amount in dried berries compared with fresh. You may need to cook longer this way.

This medicine is pure gold when it comes to the common cold and even sore throats brought on by allergies! One thing I learned a couple of years ago, is that raw, local honey—when added without completely cooking—boosts its own health benefit, especially for those with allergies! Because a lot of allergies are related to flowers and plants, and the bees are harvesting their pollen from these same plants, using local, raw honey helps to boost the system's natural immunity to these allergens—in a small dosage type of way—through the honey!

Makes: about 2 quarts or 4 pints
Time to Make: 2 hours

Ingredients
- 6 cups fresh blue elderberries
- 6 cups water
- 2 cups raw honey (or to taste)
- Cheesecloth
- Large pot (stainless-steel preferred)

Directions
1. **Wash** the berries thoroughly and remove any insects or stems.
2. **Place** elderberries in a large pot and add water (equal parts berries to water).
3. **Bring** to a boil, then reduce to a simmer. Keep the lid cracked and simmer for 45 minutes, until the liquid turns deep purple and lightly coats a spoon.
4. **Strain** through cheesecloth into a bowl. Gather and hang the cloth to allow full draining of juice.
5. **Discard** the pulp and let the juice cool to lukewarm.
6. **Stir in** raw honey once cooled (not hot!) to preserve its medicinal benefits. Start with 1 cup and add more to taste—children often prefer it sweeter.
7. **Pour** the syrup into clean jars, leaving 1 inch of headspace.
8. **Store** by freezing (best for preserving medicinal value for up to a year), or process in a boiling water canner for shelf stability:
   ○ 10 minutes at sea level
   ○ Add 5 minutes for every 2,000 feet of elevation

Dried Elderberry & Echinacea Tea Blend

Make this in the late summer and store it for the long flu season in the winter or gift this at Christmas to your fellow forager friends!

Elderberry
antiviral, supports respiratory health

Echinacea
immune stimulant, may shorten duration of colds

Yarrow
supports fevers and circulation

Mint
soothes digestion and clears sinuses

Ginger (if used)
warming and anti-inflammatory

Chamomille (if used):
Calming, good for sleep

Ingredients
- ½ cup dried elderberries
- ¼ cup dried echinacea root or flower
- 2 Tbsp dried yarrow leaves or flowers
- 2 Tbsp dried peppermint or wild mint
- 2 tsp dried ginger root pieces (optional)
- 2 tsp dried chamomile flower (optional)

Directions
1. **Mix** together and label with cute labels if using as gifts.
2. **Store** in a cool dry place. Attach following usage instructions to jars you give away.

To Use:
- Steep **1 heaping Tbsp** of the blend in **2 cups hot water**.
- Simmer covered for **15 minutes** (especially if using roots and berries).
- Let steep another **5–10 minutes**, strain, and sweeten if desired.

Storage:
Keep the dry blend in an airtight jar in a cool, dark place for up to **1 year**. Label with ingredients and date for easy tracking.

Elderberry & Wild Plum BBQ Sauce

Wild plums soften the sharp tang of elderberries, creating a deep, fruity BBQ sauce that's both sweet and savory. Brush it on venison, duck, or even grilled mushrooms for a rich, smoky glaze that feels straight from the forest.

Makes: About 2 ½ cups
Time to Make: 40 minutes

Ingredients

- 1 cup fresh elderberries
- 2 cups wild plums, pitted and chopped
- 1 small wild onion (or ½ cup garden onion), diced
- 2 cloves garlic, minced
- 2 Tbsp oil or rendered fat
- ¼ cup vinegar (apple cider or spruce tip–infused)
- ¾ cup brown sugar
- 2 Tbsp tomato paste (optional, for extra body)
- 1 tsp smoked paprika (or alder-smoked chili flakes)
- ½ tsp salt
- ¼ tsp cracked black pepper

Directions

1. **Wash** elderberries. Cover with water and bring to a boil in a saucepan.
2. **Cook** for 25 minutes.
3. **Strain** through a fine sieve or strainer. Reserve juice.
4. **Heat** oil in a saucepan or cast-iron pan. Add onion and garlic; cook until soft and fragrant.
5. **Stir** in plums and elderberry juice. Cook 5–7 minutes until plums begin to break down.
6. **Add** vinegar, brown sugar, paprika, salt, and pepper.
7. **Cook** 20–25 minutes, stirring often, until fruit is fully softened and sauce thickens. Add a splash of water if needed.
8. **Mash** with the back of a spoon or blend smooth, depending on preference.
9. **Cool and store:** Keeps 1 week in the fridge, or freeze for longer storage.

Pro Tip

- **Brush** over venison or duck in the last minutes of roasting for a glossy finish.
- **Stir** into pulled chicken of the woods or smoked fish for a wild BBQ sandwich.
- **Bottle** small jars and bring along for campfire feasts—it reheats well.

BONUS Recipe!

Elderberry Dye for Yarn (Using Leftover Pomace)

I decided to research how to dye yarn (you can also do this with fabric) using the leftovers from the elderberry syrup! I believe in using the entire plant and re-using it to ensure there is never any waste!

What You Need:
- Undyed natural yarn (preferably wool or alpaca)
- Elderberry pomace (leftover skins/seeds)
- Salt (for mordanting)
- Water
- Large pot (non-reactive like stainless steel)
- Wooden spoon or stick (don't use for food after)

How-To:

1. Pre-soak the yarn (mordant step):
- Mix **4 cups water + ¼ cup salt** in a pot.
- Add the yarn and simmer gently for **30–60 minutes**.
- Let it cool in the liquid, then rinse gently.

2. Prepare the dye bath:
- Place elderberry pomace in a clean pot.
- Add enough water to generously cover.
- Simmer gently for **30–45 minutes**. Avoid boiling to preserve color.

Optional: Strain for a smooth dye bath or leave bits in for texture.

3. Dye the yarn:
- Add the pre-mordanted, damp yarn.
- Simmer on low for **45–60 minutes**, gently stirring.
- Let the yarn **cool in the dye bath overnight** for richer color.

4. Rinse and dry:
- Carefully remove yarn and rinse in **cool water** until it runs clear.
- Hang to dry in the shade.

Tips:
- Try different mordants (like vinegar, iron, or alum) to shift the tones.
- Elderberry dyes tend to fade slightly over time; store dyed yarn out of direct sunlight.
- Use gloves—elderberries can stain your hands purple!

ELK

In addition to being a breathtaking sight, elk symbolize strength, stamina, and nobility, often representing perseverance through life's challenges. In many Native American traditions, elk are seen as spirit messengers of masculinity, and deep spiritual connection to the natural world. Harvesting one is an incredibly spiritual and sacred experience that should be revered. Elk is also one of the healthiest meats you can harvest. Elk meat is lean and protein-rich, offering around 22–25 grams of protein per 3-ounce serving, with less fat than beef or pork. When simmered into bone broth, elk bones also release natural collagen, which supports joint health, skin elasticity, and gut repair.

Flavor Profile
Elk has a rich, slightly sweet, and subtly gamey flavor with a clean, lean finish. It's milder than venison but more flavorful than beef, with a fine grain and tender texture when cooked properly. Because it's naturally low in fat, elk benefits from gentle cooking or added moisture to prevent drying.

Texture: Lean, tender, and slightly firm
Taste Notes: Earthy, clean, slightly sweet, less "wild" than other game
Pairs Well With: Juniper, rosemary, red wine, garlic, mushrooms, berries (especially huckleberry or cranberry)
Best Cooking Methods: Grilled, seared, roasted, stewed, or ground for burgers and sausages

Where to Buy/Substitutes
Grass-fed ground beef, bison, venison

Did you know?

Indigenous hunters used elk tallow not only for food but to waterproof hides and condition wooden tools.

Photo by Stockcake

Elk Burger with Chanterelles and Bacon

This recipe is an absolute classic; derived from wild meat and wild mushrooms, you can prepare this at elk camp or bring along some of last year's ground elk to cook into juicy burgers over the camp grill, throwing in chanterelles to top it off!

Makes: 4 burgers

Time to Make: 35 minutes

Ingredients

2 cups fresh chanterelle mushrooms
5 slices bacon
½ white onion (optional)
1 lb. ground elk (can substitute venison or grass-fed beef)

Salt and pepper, to taste
4 hamburger buns
4 slices Swiss cheese

Directions

Cook the Chanterelles and Bacon:

1. **Slice** cleaned chanterelles lengthwise, then into bite-sized pieces if desired.
2. **Place** in a dry cast iron skillet over low-medium heat. Cook, stirring often, until they release their juices and most liquid is absorbed (10–15 minutes).
3. **Chop** onion while mushrooms cook. When mushrooms start to sizzle, **snip** bacon into bite-sized pieces directly into the pan.
4. **Add** onion and stir to coat in bacon grease.
5. **Cover** and cook for 3 minutes for softer onions, then uncover and cook 1 more minute until bacon is crispy.

Cook the Burgers:

6. **Season** ground elk with salt and pepper (add an egg if desired). Divide into four portions and roll into balls.
7. **Flatten** each into patties slightly larger than your buns.
8. **Preheat** grill to high (400–450°F) or position over open fire.
9. **Grill** burgers 2–3 minutes per side for medium-rare, flipping only once. Adjust time for desired doneness (160°F for well done).
10. **Add** Swiss cheese slices during final minute of cooking. Toast buns if desired.
11. **Assemble** burgers with chanterelle-bacon topping. Add BBQ sauce or enjoy as-is—a wild, fire-cooked feast!

Smoky Pine Needle Elk Jerky Over the Fire

This recipe will teach you how to make jerky over the fire—no fancy equipment needed!

Note: Only use safe, edible pine like Eastern White Pine or Douglas Fir. Avoid Yew, Ponderosa, and Lodgepole Pine—they can be toxic. Always ID before using.

Makes: 1 lb jerky
Time to Make: 1 day

Ingredients
1 lb elk meat, sliced thin (¼-inch or thinner, across the grain)
¼ cup soy sauce or liquid aminos
1/8 tsp curing salt
2 Tbsp Worcestershire sauce
1 Tbsp honey or maple syrup
1 tsp garlic powder
1 tsp onion powder
½ tsp black pepper
½ tsp smoked paprika (optional)
A few sprigs of fresh pine needles (from a non-toxic variety like Ponderosa, lodgepole, or white pine)

Directions

Marinate the meat:
Combine all ingredients except the meat and pine needles. Add elk slices and marinate in a cool place for 4–12 hours. A cooler is great if you are camping or an ice house if you are off grid.

Build your fire:
Start a campfire and let it burn down to a bed of hot coals. Set up a grate or a greenwood rack 12–18 inches above the coals.

Add pine needles for smoke:
Just before you add the meat, toss a small handful of clean, fresh pine needles onto the coals. The needles will smoke quickly—don't overdo it, just a few at a time every 30 minutes or so.

Dry the meat:
Lay elk slices over the grate or hang them on sticks. Let them slowly dry and smoke for 2–4 hours, turning occasionally. Keep heat low and smoke steady.

Check for doneness:
Jerky is ready when it's darkened, dry to the touch, and bends without snapping.

Cool and store:
Let the jerky cool completely before eating or storing in a breathable pouch or container.

Easy Elk Bone Broth

If you've heard of the many benefits of collagen, or have, at any time, jumped on the bone broth bandwagon, you may know the essential health benefits associated with it. This recipe will show you, drawing from the concept of no waste, how to make the most of your bones from big game, while reaping the ultimate health benefits. You can exchange the type of animal bone for venison or even bear. At the end of this recipe, you will find pressure canning instructions, although you can also freeze the broth in glass jars (just leave a couple of inches headspace so the jars don't break when the liquid expands in the freezer). Additionally, I want to talk about tallow. Tallow is the whiteish layer of fat that floats to the top of the broth as it cools down. If you want to harvest it, cool your broth down in the pot after making it (you can reheat it to can, or individually harvest the tallow off each jar as you open it later on). As it gets cold, the tallow will harden on the top. You can then use it to make a survival-style fire starter (recipe below).

Best Bones to Use:
Marrow bones (femur, shank) for richness and collagen
Knuckle joints for high gelatin content
Neck, ribs, or spine for flavor and connective tissue

Makes: a large stockpot, depending on how many bones you have
Time to Make: 1 day

Ingredients

3–4 lbs elk bones (cut if needed to expose marrow)
1 onion, quartered
2–3 garlic cloves, smashed

2 Tbsp apple cider vinegar (helps extract minerals)
Optional: Carrot, celery, bay leaf, peppercorns, or wild herbs
Water to cover

Directions

Optional roasting: Roast bones at 400°F for 30–40 minutes for a deeper flavor.
Simmer: Add bones, vinegar, and aromatics to a large pot or slow cooker. Cover with water and bring to a boil.
Skim & reduce: Skim off foam, then reduce to a low simmer. Cover and cook for 12–24 hours, adding water as needed.
Strain: Remove bones and strain the broth through a fine mesh sieve.
Cool & store: Let cool, skim off fat if desired, and store in the fridge for up to a week or freeze for later use.
For a firepit version: Use a stockpot or large cast iron pot over a low, steady campfire and simmer all day, moving it to a cooler spot if the boil gets too strong.

How to Pressure Can Elk Bone Broth

Canning your elk bone broth makes it shelf-stable for up to a year, perfect for off grid storage, long-term use, or field cooking without relying on refrigeration. Because broth is a low-acid food, you must use a pressure canner (not a water bath) to safely kill harmful bacteria like *Clostridium botulinum*.

What You'll Need:

A tested pressure canner (not just a pressure cooker)
Clean pint or quart-sized mason jars
New lids and clean screw bands

A jar lifter, funnel, and towel
Your strained, hot elk bone broth

Directions

Sterilize and Prep Jars:
Wash your jars in hot soapy water or run them through the dishwasher. Keep them hot until use (either in hot water or your canner filled with a few inches of simmering water).

Heat the Lids:
Place your new canning lids in a small pot of simmering water (not boiling) to soften the seals. Keep them warm until ready to use.

Ladle in the Broth:
Use a funnel to pour hot, strained bone broth into the jars, leaving 1 inch of headspace at the top. This gap is important to allow for expansion during processing.

Remove Air Bubbles:
Use a plastic knife or canning tool to gently stir around the inside edges of the jar to release any trapped air.

Wipe & Seal:
Wipe jar rims with a clean damp cloth. Place lids on and screw bands on finger-tight (not too tight—just snug).

Load the Canner:
Add 2–3 inches of water to your pressure canner (check your model's directions). Place jars in the rack inside the canner, making sure they're upright and not touching.

Seal the Canner & Vent Steam:
Lock the canner lid into place. Turn the heat to high and allow the canner to vent a steady stream of steam for 10 full minutes before placing the weight or closing the valve (this is crucial for safe processing).

Pressurize & Process:
After venting, bring the canner up to pressure:

Jar Size	Dial Gauge (Sea Level)	Weighted Gauge	Time
Pints	11 PSI	10 PSI	20 min
Quarts	11 PSI	10 PSI	25 min

Increase pressure based on your elevation (e.g., 12 PSI for 1,000–2,000 ft).

Cool Down Safely:
Once the time is up, turn off the heat and let the canner depressurize naturally. Don't force the lid open or remove the weight until the pressure gauge reads zero.

Remove & Rest:
Carefully lift jars out using a jar lifter and set on a towel. Let them cool undisturbed for 12–24 hours.

Check Seals & Store:
After cooling, press the center of each lid. If it doesn't pop, the seal is good. Label and store in a cool, dark place.

Rendering Elk Tallow

What Is Tallow?

Tallow is the hard fat from big game animals like elk, deer, or bear. It renders down into a dense, long-burning fat that can be stored, cooked with, or turned into essential tools— like soap, balm, or in this case, fire starters that work even in damp conditions.

PART 1: Rendering Tallow (The Clean Way)

What You'll Need:

Elk fat or hardened tallow skimmed from broth

A small pot or skillet

Fine mesh strainer or cheesecloth

A clean jar or tin for storage

Directions

Chop or break up large chunks of tallow for quicker melting.

Place in a pot over very low heat. Do not fry it—just slowly melt. Stir occasionally.

As it melts, foam and bits will rise—that's connective tissue and impurities.

Once fully liquid and golden, strain through cheesecloth or a fine mesh sieve into a clean jar.

Let cool and solidify. It should be pale and firm at room temp. Store with a lid in a cool, dry place.

Rendered tallow will last months without refrigeration and doesn't go rancid easily, especially if you were very thorough with removing impurities from it during the rendering process. Store in a fridge or freezer to extend shelf life even longer, especially if using for cooking.

DIY Tallow Fire Starters Using Tallow (Camp-Ready)

These fire starters are compact, scent-free, and packable in your hunting or foraging kit. In addition to this, making them yourself means there is nothing toxic in your campfire smoke!

What You'll Need:

Rendered tallow (softened)

Dryer lint, wood shavings, sawdust, or pine needles

Pine Resin

Muffin tin, paper egg carton, or paper cupcake liners

String or cotton wick (optional for hand-lighting)

Directions

Pack your base material (lint, shavings, etc.) into each cup or liner. Don't overpack—leave room for fat to coat.

Mix melted tallow and pine resin. Pour melted tallow mixture over each filled cup until fully saturated.

Optional: Insert a 1–2" cotton wick or string in the center before the tallow hardens for easy lighting.

Let cool and harden fully.

Store wrapped in wax paper or in a sealed tin. They're waterproof once solid.

Survival Tip:

One starter will burn 4–8 minutes, even on damp ground—enough time to light kindling.

FIREWEED

Fireweed (*Chamerion angustifolium*) is a striking wildflower that brings vivid color to open meadows, roadsides, and forest edges throughout summer. Its tall stems and bright pink blooms are more than just beautiful—they're incredibly versatile. Nearly every part of the plant is edible or medicinal. Indigenous peoples have long used fireweed for tea, salves, and food. From tender spring shoots to late-season blossoms perfect for jelly, fireweed offers a bounty of wild benefits in one elegant plant.

Did You Know?

Fireweed is often the first plant to grow back after a wildfire, earning it the nickname "the phoenix flower." Its vibrant pink blossoms not only signal ecological recovery but are also rich in nectar—making them a favorite among bees and foragers alike.

Fireweed
(*Chamerion angustifolilium*)

Leaves
Long, narrow, and lance-shaped with smooth edges, 4–8 inches long.

Flowers
Bright pink to magenta with four deeply notched petals. Grow in tall vertical clusters at the top of the stalk.

Stems
Unbranched, reddish or green, and can reach 3–6 ft tall. Smooth or lightly hairy

Key Feature
Often grows in dense colonies after wildfires or logging. Tall stalk with vivid pink flowers and narrow, spiraled leaves

Seedpods
Long, slender pods split open to release fluffy, wind–dispersed seeds

Foraging Guide

Habitat
- Found in open meadows, forest edges, roadsides, and disturbed ground
- Thrives in full sun and moist, well-drained soils
- Common at mid to high elevations in the Pacific Northwest and across northern regions of North America

Season
- **Shoots:** Early-spring (April–May)
- **Leaves:** Late-spring through mid-summer
- **Flowers:** Mid to late summer (July–August)

Notes
- Young shoots resemble asparagus and can be eaten raw or lightly cooked
- Leaves can be harvested for tea before flowering
- Flowers are used in jellies, syrups, and garnishes
- Harvest early in the morning for best flavor and potency
- Always leave some stems and flowers for pollinators and reseeding

Toxic Look-Alikes and Cautions

1. **Dogbane** (*Apocynum spp.*)
   - Similar height and leaf shape in young growth
   - Milky white sap when broken (fireweed has clear sap)
   - Highly toxic—avoid if unsure
2. **Purple Loosestrife** (*Lythrum salicaria*)
   - Also grows in similar habitats
   - Square stems vs. fireweed's round stems
   - More clustered, spiked flowers—not as loose or wand-like as fireweed's
   - Considered invasive and not safe for consumption

Caution:
- Always positively ID before harvesting, especially in spring when fireweed shoots can resemble other upright herbs
- Avoid harvesting near roadsides or contaminated soil—fireweed readily grows in disturbed areas, which may have pollutants

Cleaning

Harvest Carefully: Choose vibrant, young fireweed leaves, shoots, or blossoms that are free of bug damage or discoloration

Rinse Gently: Place your harvest in a bowl of cold water. Swish gently to loosen dirt or insects. Avoid aggressive rubbing, especially with flowers, as they bruise easily

Inspect: Remove any wilted, brown, or questionable parts. Check for small insects inside flower clusters

Dry Surface Moisture: Lay cleaned fireweed parts on a clean towel or paper towel and gently pat dry before proceeding to air dry or dehydrate

Drying Fireweed

For Leaves or Shoots (Tea, Infusions, Medicinal Use):
- **Air Drying:** Bundle stems and hang upside down in a dry, shaded, well-ventilated area for 7–10 days
- **Dehydrator:** Place leaves in a single layer on dehydrator trays. Dry at 95–110°F for 4–6 hours, or until leaves are crisp

For Flowers (Tea or Jelly Use):
- Air Drying: Spread flowers loosely on a mesh screen or clean towel in a shaded space. Stir daily to prevent clumping. Dry for 3–5 days
- Dehydrator: Use a fine mesh or parchment paper to prevent flowers from falling through. Dry at the lowest setting (90–95°F) for 2–4 hours

Storage Tip: Once fully dry, store in airtight jars away from heat and light. Label with the date. Properly dried fireweed can last up to 1 year.

Flavor Profile

Fireweed has a fresh, slightly peppery taste. Flowers and leaves add a floral, mildly sweet accent to teas, jellies, and salads.

Where to Buy

Fireweed tea, honey, and jelly are sometimes available at farmers' markets, local herbal shops, or specialty wildcrafting stores.

Fireweed Jelly with Crabapple Pectin

When making wild jelly, many recipes call for store-bought pectin—but if you're living off grid or just want to keep things fully foraged, crabapples are your secret weapon. These tart, wild fruits are naturally high in both pectin and acid, making them perfect for thickening jams and jellies without any additives. By simmering the whole fruit—skins, seeds, and all—you can extract a powerful, natural pectin that helps your jelly set beautifully. In this recipe, we pair vibrant fireweed blossoms with homemade crabapple pectin to create a truly wild, stunningly purple-pink jelly that's as practical as it is delicious.

Makes: 4-5 pints
Time to Make: 35 minutes

Ingredients
- 4 cups fresh fireweed flowers (no stems)
- 5 cups water
- 2 cups crabapples (cut in half, skins & seeds intact)
- 1 Tbsp lemon juice
- 3½ cups granulated sugar

Optional: Switch out half of the fireweed for wild rose petals

Directions

1. **Make the Fireweed Tea:**
   Rinse fireweed flowers. Add them and 3½ cups of water to a pot. Bring to a boil, then remove from heat. Cover and steep for 10–15 minutes. Strain through cheesecloth or a fine mesh strainer to remove solids.

2. **Extract Crabapple Pectin:**
   In a separate saucepan, add crabapples and the remaining 2 cups of water. Simmer for 1 hour or until fruit is soft and broken down. If there is still a lot of liquid, cook it down further to concentrate the pectin. Strain the liquid through cheesecloth, pressing gently. You want about ½ cup of crabapple juice—this will act as your pectin.

3. **Combine & Cook Jelly:**
   Pour the strained fireweed tea and crabapple pectin into a clean pot (about 3½ cups total liquid). Add lemon juice. Bring to a boil, then add the sugar. Stir constantly and boil hard for 20-25 minutes. Test for gelling by spooning a little on a cold plate and checking if it wrinkles when pushed.

4. **Jar It:**
   Skim off foam if needed. Pour into sterilized jars, leaving ¼-inch headspace. Wipe rims, add lids and rings.

5. **Process:**
   Process in a boiling water bath for 10 minutes. Let cool and check seals before storing.

Yield: 4–5 half-pint jars

Fireweed Tincture

Fireweed has long been valued for calming inflammation and soothing the digestive system. A tincture captures its benefits in concentrated form, easy to carry on the trail or store in a survival kit.

Makes: About 1 cup
Time to Make: 10 minutes active, plus 4–6 weeks steeping

Ingredients
- 1 cup fresh fireweed flowers (or ½ cup dried)
- 1 ½ cup 80–100 proof vodka, brandy, or other clear alcohol

Directions
1. **Prepare:** Chop fresh fireweed or lightly crush dried to expose more surface area.
2. **Fill jar:** Place plant material in a clean glass jar, filling about halfway.
3. **Cover:** Pour alcohol over the fireweed until fully submerged, leaving 1 inch of space at the top.
4. **Steep:** Seal and store in a cool, dark place for 4–6 weeks. Shake occasionally.
5. **Strain:** Filter through cheesecloth into a clean jar or dropper bottles.

Pro Tip: Standard dosage is ½–1 teaspoon (or 10–30 drops) diluted in water or tea, up to 3 times daily. Label clearly with plant name and date.

Fireweed Tea

A simple herbal tea made from fireweed leaves and blossoms. Traditionally used to ease stomach upset, sore throats, and general inflammation.

Makes: 2 cups
Time to Make: 10 minutes

Ingredients
- 2 tsp dried fireweed leaves and/or flowers (or 1 Tbsp fresh)
- 2 cups boiling water

Directions
1. **Prepare:** Place fireweed in a teapot, mug, or heatproof jar.
2. **Steep:** Pour boiling water over the herbs. Cover and let sit 5–10 minutes.
3. **Strain and serve:** Drink warm, or cool and sip as a refreshing tonic.

Pro Tip
- Add honey for sore throats or combine with mint or chamomile for extra digestive relief.
- Fireweed tea is gentle enough for regular use and makes a soothing evening drink.

BONUS! Recipe

Fireweed & Calendula Skin Soothing Salve

Fireweed is known for its anti-inflammatory and skin-soothing properties. Traditionally used to relieve rashes, burns, and dryness, it's a great base for a wilderness-first-aid salve. Calendula is renowned for its gentle antimicrobial and skin-repairing properties, which is why it's the perfect companion to fireweed in a healing salve that soothes, restores, and protects irritated skin.

Makes: 1¼ cups

Time to Make: 1 day-4 weeks

Ingredients

- 1 cup dried fireweed leaves and flowers
- ½ cup dried calendula flowers
- 1 cup olive oil (or substitute jojoba, sweet almond, or sunflower oil)
- 2 Tbsp beeswax pellets

Optional: 5–10 drops lavender or tea tree essential oil (for added calming or antimicrobial benefits)

Directions

1. **Infuse the Oil:**
   - Place the dried fireweed and calendula in a clean glass jar and cover with oil.
   - Let it sit for 4–6 weeks in a sunny window, shaking gently every few days.
   - *Quick method:* Heat gently in a double boiler or slow cooker on low (never boiling) for 2–3 hours.
2. **Strain:**
   - Use cheesecloth or a fine mesh strainer to remove plant material. Press well to extract all the oil.
3. **Make the Salve:**
   - In a clean double boiler, combine the infused oil with beeswax.
   - Heat gently, stirring, until the beeswax melts completely.
1. **Add Essential Oils (optional):**
   - Stir in essential oil once removed from heat.
2. **Pour & Cool:**
   - Pour into clean tins or glass jars. Let cool and solidify at room temperature.
3. **Label & Store:**
   - Store in a cool, dark place. Use within 6–12 months.

FIR TIP

Young fir tips—the tender, bright-green new growth at the ends of fir tree branches—have been used for centuries by Indigenous peoples and foragers alike. These spring tips are rich in vitamin C, antioxidants, and natural resins that can help soothe sore throats and coughs. Fir tip tea or syrup is a traditional remedy for colds, offering a mild expectorant effect and a boost to the immune system during the long, damp months. Fir trees (like Douglas fir, Grand fir, and Balsam fir) are abundant across North America, especially the Pacific Northwest, Northern Rockies, and parts of the Northeast. Look for healthy, mature fir trees in forests, along logging roads, and in clearings where new growth is easy to reach.

Did You Know?

Fir (*genus Abies*) tips aren't just for decoration—they're packed with vitamin C and were traditionally brewed by Indigenous peoples into teas to ward off scurvy, colds, and fatigue. Their bright, citrusy flavor also makes a refreshing addition to syrups, salts, and wild-crafted sodas.

Fir (genus Abies)

- Look for the bright, soft new growth in spring to early summer — these tips are a vibrant light green and feel tender compared to the darker, older needles.

- **Needles:** Fir needles are flat, soft, and attached singly to the branch. When you roll them between your fingers, they won't feel sharp like spruce

- **Bark & cones:** Fir trees have smooth to slightly furrowed bark (depending on species) and upright cones that disintegrate

- **Scent:** Crushing a fir tip releases a fresh, citrusy evergreen aroma — not sharp like pine but gentler

Foraging Guide

Habitat

- Grows throughout North America in mountainous or forested regions
- Commonly found in mixed conifer forests at mid to high elevations
- In the Pacific Northwest, look for Douglas fir, grand fir, noble fir, and subalpine fir

Season

- Early to mid-spring (typically April–June, depending on elevation and climate)

Toxic Look-Alikes and Cautions

1. **Yew** (*Taxus spp.*)
   – Grows in similar forest environments
   – Needles are flat and dark green with no citrus scent
   – Contains **taxine alkaloids**—extremely toxic if ingested
2. **Pine or Spruce Tips** (*Pinus spp., Picea spp.*)
   – Not all are toxic, but some can cause digestive upset if consumed in large amounts
   – More resinous, and flavor is often harsh compared to true fir

Key ID Tip: True firs (Abies spp.) have soft, flat needles that are fragrant and citrusy when crushed. If the plant lacks this smell or produces milky sap—**do not harvest.**

Foraging Tips

- Snip just a few tips from each branch to avoid damaging the tree
- Only take the tender, current-year growth—these are sweetest and least resinous
- Harvest in early to mid-spring when tips are still soft and light green
- To dry them, simply hang your branch from the rafters for a couple of days—until the needles feel dry and snap instead of bend when broken

Flavor Profile

Fresh fir tips taste bright, citrusy, and slightly resinous, like a lemony evergreen. They work beautifully in syrups, teas, candies, or even wild jellies. Their gentle pine flavor pairs well with honey, citrus, and wild mint.

Where to Buy

Fir needles can be bought online on Amazon or Etsy as well as other retailers.

Fir Tip Syrup

Bright, citrusy, and pine-scented—this syrup is excellent in cocktails, teas, ice cream, or drizzled on pancakes.

Makes: 2 cups
Time to Make: 45 minutes

Ingredients
- 2 cups young fir tips (clean, bright green, spring growth)
- 2 cups water
- 2 cups granulated sugar (or 1½ cups honey for a richer version)

Directions
1. **Rinse** fir tips and place in a saucepan with water.
2. **Bring** to a boil, then reduce heat and simmer for 30 minutes.
3. **Strain** out fir tips. **Add** sugar to the infused water.
4. **Return** to heat and stir until sugar is dissolved. **Simmer** gently for 10 more minutes.
5. **Pour** into a sterilized jar.
6. **Store** in the fridge for up to 2 months.

Fir Tip Soda (Naturally Fermented)

This recipe is chock full of health benefits and highlights the scents of the forest—in a simple to make, homemade soda! Because it uses honey, you are truly getting a benefit from not only the fir tips, but also honey!

Makes: 5 cups
Time to Make: 3 days

Ingredients
- 1 cup fresh fir tips (young, bright green tips from Douglas fir are best)
- ½ cup sugar or raw honey (adjust to taste)
- 1 lemon, sliced (optional for brightness)
- 5 cups non-chlorinated water (filtered is best)
- 1 quart-size mason jar with a lid, or flip-top bottle for fermenting

Directions
1. **Harvest & Clean:**
   - Rinse your fir tips in cool water to remove any dirt or bugs.
   - Avoid tips that are too old, woody, or brown.
2. **Infuse:**
   - Add fir tips, lemon slices (if using), and sugar or honey to your jar.
   - Pour in the water and stir well until the sugar dissolves.
3. **Cover & Ferment:**
   - Cover loosely with a cloth or a lid that's not airtight.
   - Leave the jar at room temperature (65–75°F) for 2–3 days.
   - Stir once or twice a day and check for bubbles.
4. **Strain & Bottle:**
   - Once bubbles appear and the flavor is slightly tangy and fizzy, strain out the solids.
   - Pour the liquid into a clean flip-top bottle or tightly sealed mason jar.
5. **Build Carbonation (Optional):**
   - Leave the sealed bottle at room temperature for another 1–2 days to naturally carbonate.
   - *Important:* "Burp" the bottle once a day to release pressure and avoid explosions.
6. **Chill & Serve:**
   - Refrigerate once fizzy.
   - Serve cold, over ice, with a slice of lemon or sprig of fir for garnish.

Shelf Life:
Best enjoyed within 1 week. Always keep refrigerated once bottled.

Fir Pitch Medicine

Fir trees produce sticky resin (pitch) when injured, and this resin is naturally antiseptic. For survival, it can be collected and used to seal minor cuts, scrapes, or blisters, keeping dirt out and helping to protect against infection.

Makes: Variable (depends on how much resin is collected)
Time to Make: 15 minutes active, plus collection time

Ingredients
- Fresh fir pitch (resin), carefully collected from the tree
- Small tin or glass jar for storage

Directions
1. **Collect:** Look for hardened or semi-hardened pitch on fir trees. Scrape only small amounts with a clean knife, choosing resin that has already oozed naturally.
2. **Soften (optional):** Warm gently near a fire if you want a more pliable texture.
3. **Apply:** Spread directly over minor wounds to seal and disinfect.

Pro Tip: Harvest sparingly and never cut into live wood—only take resin that the tree has already produced, so the tree can continue healing itself.

Pitch is sticky—carry a dedicated knife or stick for collecting and applying.

Note: Fir Needle Steam Inhalation

Fir needles are rich in aromatic oils that help clear congestion. To use, pour **2–3 cups boiling water** over a handful of fresh needles in a bowl. Lean over, cover your head with a towel, and breathe the steam for **5–10 minutes**. A simple survival remedy for coughs, colds, or chest tightness.

BONUS Recipe!

Pine, Fir Tip & Lemon Balm Tallow Candle

Bring the forest indoors with this old-fashioned, wild-foraged candle that blends the earthy resin scent of pine and fir tips with the bright, citrusy note of wild lemon balm. Using rendered tallow—a true pioneer staple—you create a rustic candle that's deeply practical, naturally fragrant, and a beautiful reminder that survival can be comforting, too.

Whether you're lighting your off-grid cabin or just want the scent of fresh evergreens at home, this candle is a simple way to use wild ingredients you can harvest by hand.

Makes: 1 candle
Time to Make: 3 hours

Ingredients
- 1 cup rendered tallow (or 50% tallow + 50% beeswax for a firmer candle)
- ¼–½ cup fresh or dried pine needles (Ponderosa, lodgepole, or other safe pine)
- ¼–½ cup fresh fir tips (or spruce tips)
- ¼ cup dried lemon balm leaves
- Cotton or wood wicks
- Jars, tins, or molds

Optional: a few drops of pine or lemon essential oil for stronger scent

Directions
1. **Clean & Dry Herbs:**
   Rinse fir tips, pine needles, and lemon balm. Pat dry thoroughly or let air dry overnight to avoid moisture in your candles.
2. **Melt Tallow (and Beeswax):**
   In a double boiler, gently melt the tallow. If using beeswax too, add it and stir until fully melted and combined.
3. **Infuse the Scent:**
   Add pine needles, fir tips, and lemon balm to the melted tallow. Keep the heat low and **infuse for 1–2 hours**, stirring occasionally so the plant oils release into the fat.
4. **Strain:**
   Strain the mixture through cheesecloth or a fine mesh sieve to remove plant material. Discard the herbs or compost them.
5. **Boost the Aroma (Optional):**
   If you'd like a stronger scent, add a few drops of pine, fir, or lemon essential oil once the melted mix cools slightly (under 140°F).
6. **Pour & Wick:**
   Place your wick in the center of each jar or mold. Pour the scented tallow blend into containers, securing the wick with a clothespin or chopsticks so it stays centered.
7. **Set & Trim:**
   Let candles cool and harden fully at room temperature. Trim wicks to ¼-inch before burning.

Scent Notes
- **Fir tips & pine needles:** Warm evergreen forest smell—grounding, fresh, and resinous.
- **Lemon balm:** Bright, lemony-mint layer that lifts the scent, making it feel clean and refreshing.

Tallow Candle Tips

Tallow burns beautifully but softer than wax—combining it with beeswax gives a harder candle.
Store away from heat; tallow can soften in warm weather.
Keep wicks trimmed to reduce smoke.

GROUSE

I often find and shoot grouse while I am deer hunting or mushroom foraging. While this is not a hunting guide, I have included a section on cleaning grouse, both whole, and if you just want the breast. Nutritionally, they compare to chicken... minus the growth hormones, high levels of gluten from grain fed-birds, and throw in benefits from a wild, plant-based diet!

Did You Know?

The male *ruffed grouse* drums his wings so rapidly on a log that it creates a deep, echoing sound— without ever touching anything. This "drumming" is a territorial display that can be heard from over a quarter mile away and is often mistaken for a distant motor starting.

Grouse Cleaning Guide (Field & Kitchen)

What You'll Need

- Sharp knife or game shears (optional)
- Clean water (or damp cloth)
- Ziplock bags or game bags
- Gloves (optional)

Field Cleaning (Pluck-Free "Breast Out" Method)

This is the quickest and most popular method for cleaning grouse on the spot.

Step-by-Step:

1. **Lay the** bird on its back, breast side up.
2. **Step on the wings:** Place a foot firmly on each wing where they meet the body.
3. **Grab the legs:** Hold both legs tightly.
4. **Pull up steadily:** With a firm, smooth motion, pull the legs up and away from the wings.
    - → The breast and entrails will separate from the wings and lower body
5. **Trim it up:**
    - Remove entrails (if any remain)
    - Use a knife to separate the breast meat from the backbone if needed
    - You can also take the thighs if they came off cleanly
6. **Wipe clean or rinse with water,** then place the meat in a clean bag.

Full-Plucking & Gutting (If You Want the Whole Bird)

This is ideal if you're roasting the grouse whole or want legs, thighs, and skin-on meat.

Step-by-Step:

1. **Pluck while warm:** It's easiest before the bird cools down.
    - Start from the breast and pull feathers against their growth
2. **Remove feathers down** to the skin across the whole body.
3. **Make a small cut** below the breastbone, near the vent.
4. **Reach inside** and pull out all the entrails.
    - Be careful not to puncture the intestines or crop
5. **Cut off head, feet,** and oil gland (at base of the tail).
6. **Rinse inside** and out with cool water.

After Cleaning

Pat the meat dry with a paper towel. Cool quickly (ice packs or fridge). Store in a clean container or bag. Use within 3 days or freeze.

Safety Tips

- Clean birds as soon as possible
- Keep meat cold and dry
- Wash hands, knives, and surfaces after handling
- If you see green bile (from the gallbladder), rinse meat immediately—it can make it bitter

Flavor Profile

Grouse has a rich, earthy flavor with a mild gamey edge. The meat is lean, dark, and slightly more intense than chicken or pheasant, especially in older birds. Wild herbs, pine, and berries from their diet often subtly infuse the flesh, giving it a foresty, savory depth. Best suited for roasting, pan-searing, or braising with robust herbs like thyme or juniper.

Texture: Firm, slightly chewy, especially in the legs

Pairs Well With: Juniper, rosemary, mushrooms, red wine, berries, root vegetables

Where to Buy/Substitutes

Farm-raised chicken, wild or farm-grown turkey (bigger, but comparative flavor-wise), other wild game birds

Grouse or Pheasant Enchiladas

Makes: 6 servings

Time to Make: 45 minutes

Ingredients

- 3 ½ cups grouse meat, cooked, chopped (can use grouse breasts and bake at 350 for 1 hour, covered with tin foil to keep them moist)
- 1 (2 cups) container sour cream (option to substitute 1 cup of sour cream for green enchilada sauce)
- 1 (10 ¾ oz) can cream of chicken soup
- ½ (4oz) can chopped green chilies (or 1 whole can, if you prefer more spice)

- ¼ white onion, finely chopped
- 1 ¼ tsp cumin
- 1 tsp salt (or more to taste)
- 1/8 c salsa
- 2 cups shredded mozzarella or cheddar cheese
- 8 corn tortillas (or more, depending on the size and how many it takes to use filling)

Directions

1. **Mix** together sour cream, cream of chicken soup, chopped green chilies, cumin, salt, and salsa in a large bowl. **Reserve** 1 cup of the mixture.
2. **Add** chopped grouse to the bowl of sour cream mixture and stir to combine.
3. **Preheat** oven to 350°F.
4. **Fill** each tortilla with enough enchilada mixture so it can still roll up or fold over.
5. **Arrange** tortillas tightly in a greased 8x8" or 9x13" baking dish.
6. **Spread** reserved sour cream sauce over the top.
7. **Sprinkle** chopped onions and shredded cheese evenly over everything.
8. **Cover** with greased parchment paper, then foil, to prevent cheese from sticking.
9. **Bake** for 30 minutes or until bubbly and the cheese is melted.

Roast Grouse (Stovetop or Over a Fire)

I created this recipe so that, even if an oven is not available, you can easily cook what you have harvested—in the field, or at home! This can be done with a camp stove while at the hunting camp, or over an open fire if you have a heavy cast iron pot deep enough to fit the whole grouse—and a tight-fitting lid. The only non-readily available item that is essential, is a thermometer, to ensure the meat has thoroughly cooked.

Easy Stovetop Roast Grouse

You can exchange the grouse for any game bird and adjust the cooking time based on the size of the bird. When doing something as large as a wild turkey, it may take several hours for the inside to get completely done, so make sure you have a quality thermometer (and a lot of patience!).

Serves: 2   **Time to Make:** 35 minutes

Ingredients
- 1 whole grouse, cleaned and patted dry
- 2 Tbsp butter or oil (or a mix)
- 2 garlic cloves, smashed
- 2-3 sprigs fresh thyme or rosemary (optional)
- Salt and freshly ground black pepper, to taste
- ½ cup chicken broth or water
- 1 small onion, sliced (optional)

Directions
1. **Season the grouse:** Generously season the grouse inside and out with salt and pepper.
2. **Heat the pan:** Heat butter and/or oil in a heavy skillet (cast iron works great) over medium-high heat. If doing this over the fire, make sure it has heat below it, but it doesn't need to be in the middle of the fire. Adjust if it is taking too long to sizzle and get hot.
3. **Sear the grouse:** Place the grouse breast-side down and sear for about 5-7 minutes until golden brown. Turn and sear the other sides, about 3-5 minutes per side, so the skin is nicely browned all around.
4. **Add aromatics:** Add smashed garlic, herbs, and sliced onion around the bird in the pan.
5. **Simmer and cook through:** Pour in the chicken broth or water to create steam and cover the skillet with a tight-fitting lid. Reduce heat to medium-low and cook for 12-15 minutes, turning the grouse once halfway through, until the internal temperature reaches 160°F and juices run clear.
6. **Rest:** Remove the grouse from the pan and let it rest for 5 minutes before carving.

Serve with sautéed chanterelle, lobster mushroom, or any other freshly foraged ingredient like wild greens! Throw in a recipe of my truffle oil fry bread to round out the meal—almost completely from the wild!

Simple Pan Sauce for Grouse

Ingredients
- Broth/drippings from the cooked grouse
- ¼ cup dry white wine or chicken broth (unnecessary if you have a lot of broth from the grouse)
- 1 tsp Dijon mustard (optional)
- 1 Tbsp butter
- Salt and pepper to taste

Directions
1. **Remove grouse:** After cooking, transfer the grouse to a plate and keep warm.
2. **Deglaze the pan:** Place the skillet back on medium heat. Pour in the white wine or chicken broth and scrape up any browned bits from the bottom with a wooden spoon.
3. **Add mustard:** Stir in the Dijon mustard, if using, to add depth.
4. **Reduce:** Let the liquid simmer and reduce by about half, about 3-5 minutes.
5. **Finish with butter:** Whisk in the butter to give the sauce a nice glossy finish and rich flavor.
6. **Season:** Taste and adjust salt and pepper as needed.

Drizzle this sauce over your carved grouse for a delicious finishing touch!

Grouse Pot Pie

This is a classic with a wild twist—easy to prepare, filling, comfort food!

Makes: 1 pie plate or 8"x8" pan
Time to Make: 1½ hours

Ingredients
- 2 grouse breasts, chopped
- 3 garlic cloves
- 4 cups filtered water
- 2 carrots, chopped
- 4 stalks celery, chopped
- 1 cup green peas
- 1/3 cup butter, divided
- ¼ cup flour
- 1 tsp garlic powder
- 1½ tsp thyme
- 1½ tsp salt
- 1 cup half & half or milk
- 1 pie crust mix (makes two crusts)

Directions
1. **Place** grouse breasts in a saucepan and cover with 4 cups water. Bring to a boil, then reduce to a low boil. Cover and cook for about 25 minutes.
2. **Prepare** vegetables while the grouse cooks.
3. **Drain** the grouse, reserving the broth.
4. **Melt** 2 Tbsp of butter in a new pan.
5. **Add** onion, carrots, celery, and thyme. Cover and cook for 3 minutes until vegetables are tender.
6. **Add** peas and cook for 1 more minute. Remove from heat and combine with cooked grouse.
7. **Return** the pan to the heat and melt remaining butter.
8. **Sprinkle** in flour and whisk to combine. Slowly add 1 cup of reserved broth and 1 cup of half & half, whisking constantly.
9. **Add** garlic powder, salt, and pepper. Cook until thickened to a gravy-like texture. Add a bit more flour if needed.
10. **Stir** in the grouse and vegetable mixture. Taste and adjust seasoning as desired.
11. **Roll** out your pie crusts. Line the pie dish with the bottom crust.
12. **Pour** filling into crust, cover with top crust, pinch edges, and cut slits to vent.
13. **Bake** at 400°F for 30–45 minutes until crust is golden brown and filling is bubbly.

HEDGEHOG MUSHROOMS

About six years back, my favorite hedgehog spot was logged. It had been a beloved sanctuary of this forest we hunted since the day I discovered it. Thickly planted fir trees provided a cover that blocked 75% of the sunlight, making this the perfect spot for fungi to grow. By mid-November, towards the end of fall, chanterelles and hedgehogs would be popping thickly in this woodland haven. The ground was covered with basketball sized rocks coated in thick green moss, Oregon grape bushes, and the occasional downed log that had long since rotted. If you bent down to forest level, often you would see the beautiful pinkish brown of a tiny hedgehog mushroom with its face pointed towards the sunlight far above. If you then glanced around from that plant perspective vantage point, you would likely see many more of these tiny mushrooms. Often, they might be mistaken for a small chanterelle, or a honey cap mushroom, but as soon as you picked it and turned it over, you would see the spikes pointing downwards (or upwards once it is turned over) that identified it clearly as a hedgehog mushroom.

Hedgehog mushrooms (*Hydnum repandum* and *Hydnum umbilicatum*) are a nutritious wild edible, offering a good source of protein, fiber, and antioxidants that support immune health and reduce inflammation. They also contain B vitamins and trace minerals like copper and potassium, which aid energy metabolism and nervous system function.

In the U.S., hedgehogs grow primarily in the Pacific Northwest, northern California, the Rocky Mountains, and parts of the Northeast—often found in coniferous or mixed hardwood forests from late summer through fall.

Did You Know?

Hedgehog mushrooms are one of the few wild mushrooms that *don't* have gills—they have soft, tooth-like spines under their caps instead! This makes them incredibly easy to identify and one of the safest mushrooms for beginner foragers. Bonus: they store well, resist bugs, and have a sweet, nutty flavor prized in French cuisine.

Hedgehog Mushrooms

Hydnum repandum and *Hydnum umbilicatum*

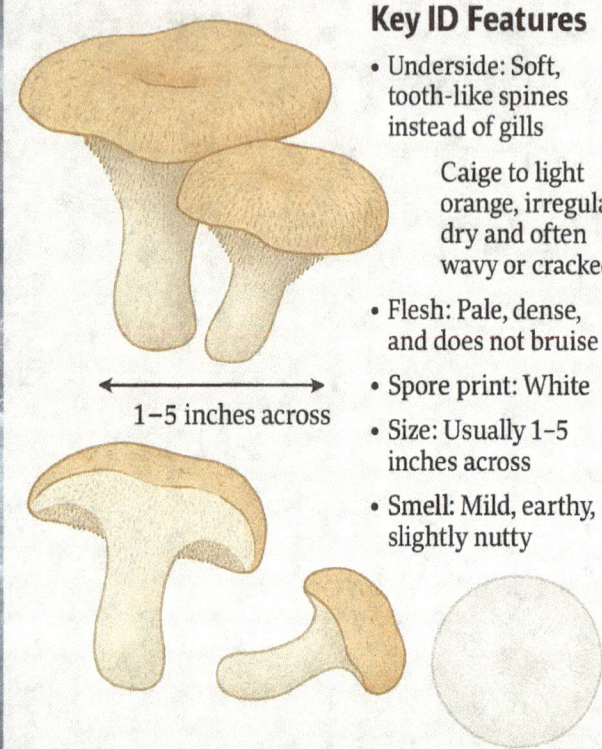

Key ID Features

- **Underside:** Soft, tooth-like spines instead of gills

  Caige to light orange, irregular, dry and often wavy or cracked

- **Flesh:** Pale, dense, and does not bruise

- **Spore print:** White

- **Size:** Usually 1–5 inches across

- **Smell:** Mild, earthy, slightly nutty

1–5 inches across

Foraging Guide

Habitat

- Mossy forest floors
- Beneath conifer and hardwood trees
- Edges of old logging roads
- Along trails in damp, shaded woods
- Mixed forests throughout the Pacific Northwest

Hedgehog mushrooms grow directly on the ground and are typically found in the same habitats as chanterelles. Look under Douglas fir, hemlock, spruce, and alder. They often blend into the forest floor due to their pale color and wavy caps.

Season

- Late summer through fall
- Best after the first heavy rains

Toxic Look-Alikes and Cautions

Hedgehogs are generally easy to distinguish from other mushrooms due to their unique spikes. However, always consult multiple resources if this is your first time harvesting.

1. **Spiny Puffball** (*Lycoperdon echinatum*)
   - Covered in spines or warts when young
   - Lacks gills or teeth; interior becomes spore-filled as it matures
   - Can resemble a toothy cap from above, but cutting it open reveals it's solid
   - Not deadly but **inedible and may cause stomach upset**
2. **Bitter Tooth** (*Sarcodon scabrosus*) *(Rare)*
   - Has teeth like hedgehog mushrooms but with a darker, scaly cap
   - Very bitter taste makes it inedible
   - Not toxic but **not palatable**, and sometimes confused when young

Foraging Note:

- Always check for bugs or soft spots—they're especially attractive to beetles
- As with all wild mushrooms, never consume raw

Cleaning

Use a soft brush or damp towel to gently wipe away dirt and fir needles. You can slice off the dirty base of the stem. Do not soak, as they absorb water easily.

Storage

Store unwashed in a paper bag in the fridge for up to a week. Avoid plastic bags, which cause sweating and spoilage.

Freezing

Lightly sauté first, then freeze in portions.

Drying

Slice and dehydrate at 110–120°F until crisp. Rehydrate in warm water for soups and sauces.

Flavor Profile

Mild, nutty, and slightly sweet, with a meaty texture that holds up in cooking. When sautéed, they release a delicate, earthy aroma. Excellent in pasta dishes, soups, omelets, or simply fried in butter. Their firm texture also makes them ideal for fire-cooked or cast-iron recipes.

Where to Buy

Hedgehogs are sometimes sold at high-end markets, co-ops, or by local mushroom foragers. Look for fresh ones in season (usually fall). They are also available dried online, but are less common than morels or porcini.

Sautéed Hedgehogs

This is the most basic way to prepare hedgehogs, and one of my absolute favorite ways. Because they are so good by themselves, you can sauté them and serve as a side dish, on top of burgers, pasta, meatloaf, or with any other meal you desire. It only takes about 10 minutes!

Makes: 2 servings

Time to Make: 15 minutes

Ingredients

- 15–20 freshly harvested hedgehog mushrooms, cleaned and brushed
- 1 Tbsp butter
- Coarse ground sea salt, to taste

Directions

1. **Slice** the hedgehogs lengthwise, removing any fir needles or dirt between the stems.
2. **Cut** again in half or into thinner slices if desired.
3. **Place** mushrooms in a dry cast iron skillet over low-medium heat.
4. **Cook** for about 5 minutes, stirring often, until moisture has dissipated.
5. **Add** the butter and stir to coat.
6. **Fry** until mushrooms are slightly crispy or reach your preferred doneness.
7. **Sprinkle** with sea salt, if desired, and **serve** warm.

Hedgehog Mushroom Pizza

I love a good homemade pizza! Hedgehogs are light and airy, making them the perfect mushroom for pizza! This recipe is easy to do over the fire in a skillet and I have included a stone cooked variation at the end as well!

Makes: 1 8" round pizza
Time to Make: 1 hour

Ingredients

Pizza Dough
- 1 packet (2¼ tsp) yeast
- 1¼ cups warm water (just warmer than baby bottle temp)
- 4 cups all-purpose flour
- 2 tsp salt
- 2 Tbsp olive oil
- 1 Tbsp granulated sugar

Toppings
- Grated cheese
- Alfredo sauce
- Pepperoni or other meat (optional)
- Hedgehog mushrooms (cleaned and sliced)

Directions

Make the Dough
1. **Sprinkle** yeast over warm water in a mixing bowl, then **add** sugar.
2. **Stir** lightly and let sit for 10 minutes, until frothy.
3. **Mix** flour and salt in a separate bowl.
4. **Add** olive oil to the yeast mixture, then slowly add flour mixture.
5. **Mix** until a coarse ball forms, about 4 minutes.
6. **Knead** for about 6 folds, then **let rest** while preparing toppings.

Cook the Mushrooms
1. **Wash** mushrooms thoroughly, checking the undersides for fir needles or dirt.
2. **Cut** lengthwise along the stem and slice tops into bite-sized pieces.
3. **Heat** a cast iron skillet over medium-low heat.
4. **Add** mushrooms and cook for 1 minute until they begin to release moisture.
5. **Stir** and **add** 2 Tbsp butter.
6. **Sauté** for another 5 minutes until soft and sizzling.

Assemble the Pizza
1. **Roll out** dough to desired thickness and shape.
2. **Spread** Alfredo sauce evenly over the dough.
3. **Add** grated cheese, mushrooms, and any other toppings.
4. **Bake** at 425°F for 15 minutes, or until golden and bubbly.

To Bake Over the Fire
1. **Prep** a large flat rock by heating it in the fire for 25 minutes.
2. **Flour** the bottom of the pizza and sprinkle flour on the hot rock.
3. **Slide** the pizza onto the rock using a peel or spatula.
4. **Cover** loosely with a metal bowl or lid, if possible.
5. **Cook** for 10–15 minutes, rotating as needed with tongs or a peel.
6. **Watch** for bubbling cheese and golden-brown crust.

Cool and Serve
1. **Remove** pizza carefully with a spatula.
2. **Let rest** for 1 minute, then **slice** and enjoy!

Philly Cheese Steak and Hedgehog Sandwiches

Makes: 5 sandwiches

Time to Make: 15 minutes

Ingredients

- 2 Tbsp butter
- ½ onion, chopped
- ¼ green pepper, sliced
- 2 garlic cloves, minced
- ½ tsp salt

- 5 hedgehog mushrooms, sliced and washed
- 8 oz ribeye steak, thinly sliced
- 5 slices provolone cheese
- 5 hoagie rolls

Directions

1. **Dry fry** the hedgehog mushrooms in a skillet over medium heat for about 2 minutes. **Remove** and set aside.
2. **Add** butter, garlic, onion, green pepper, and sliced steak to the skillet.
3. **Cook** for about 5 minutes, or until the steak is browned and the vegetables are tender.
4. **Return** mushrooms to the pan and **stir** in salt to taste.
5. **Toast** hoagie rolls in the air fryer or oven at 350°F for 2 minutes.
6. **Scoop** the meat and mushroom mixture into each toasted roll.
7. **Top** with a slice of provolone cheese and **toast** for 1 more minute, just until the cheese melts.
8. **Serve** hot.

Campfire Tip:

This recipe works great over a campfire or camp stove. **Cook** the filling in a cast iron skillet over open flames. **Toast** the hoagie rolls using a marshmallow roaster or place them on a rack near the fire.

Hedgehog Mushrooms and Honey Chicken Kabobs

This recipe is so good and so easy to assemble! These kabobs can be grilled, baked, or roasted over an open fire!

Makes: 12 skewers
Time to Make: 3 hours (including marination time)

Ingredients

- ½ cup olive oil
- ⅔ cup honey
- ⅔ cup soy sauce
- ½ tsp pepper
- 8 oz skinless, boneless chicken breasts, cut into 1" cubes
- 2 garlic cloves, minced
- 1 large onion, cut into 2" pieces
- 2 red or yellow peppers, sliced into 2" pieces
- 1 can pineapple chunks (large size)
- 5–10 hedgehog mushrooms (or other firm mushrooms, cut into chunks)

Directions

1. **Mix** honey, soy sauce, pepper, and minced garlic in a jar. Shake until fully combined.
2. **Place** chicken, onions, and peppers in a gallon-sized Ziploc bag.
3. **Pour** the marinade over the mixture, reserving ½ cup of it for basting. Seal and refrigerate for at least 2 hours or up to overnight.
4. **Thread** chicken, vegetables, pineapple, and mushrooms onto skewers, alternating ingredients. For mushrooms, thread through the stem to help keep them intact.
5. **Grill** over medium heat for about 3 minutes per side, or until the chicken is cooked through and vegetables are tender.
6. **Baste** with reserved marinade while grilling and flip once.
7. **Serve** hot, with additional marinade as a dipping sauce if desired.

HORSETAIL

Horsetail (*Equisetum arvense* among other species) is a plant that I have known about for a long time, but recently began using for its many health benefits. Among the most notable is the silica found in horsetail, which helps with collagen production. It is therefore a miracle worker for hair, skin, nails, and bone density because silica helps aid the absorption of calcium.

Did You Know?

Horsetail was once used by Indigenous peoples and early settlers as a natural scouring tool—thanks to its high silica content, the stems work like fine sandpaper and were used to clean pots, tools, and even sharpen arrows.

Horsetail

(Equisetum arvense among other species)

IDENTIFICATION GUIDE

Key Features:

- Hollow, jointed, and ridged; easily pulled apart at the segments
- Structure: Resembles a miniature bamboo or pine sapling
- Color: Bright to dark green; cone-like spore heads appear on some species
- Leaves: Reduced to small, dark toothed scales forming a ring at each joint

Growth Habit:

Grows in dense patches; stems ean reach 6–24 inches tall

Early fertile stems

(spring only)

Pale, tan, unbranched with a spore cone on top

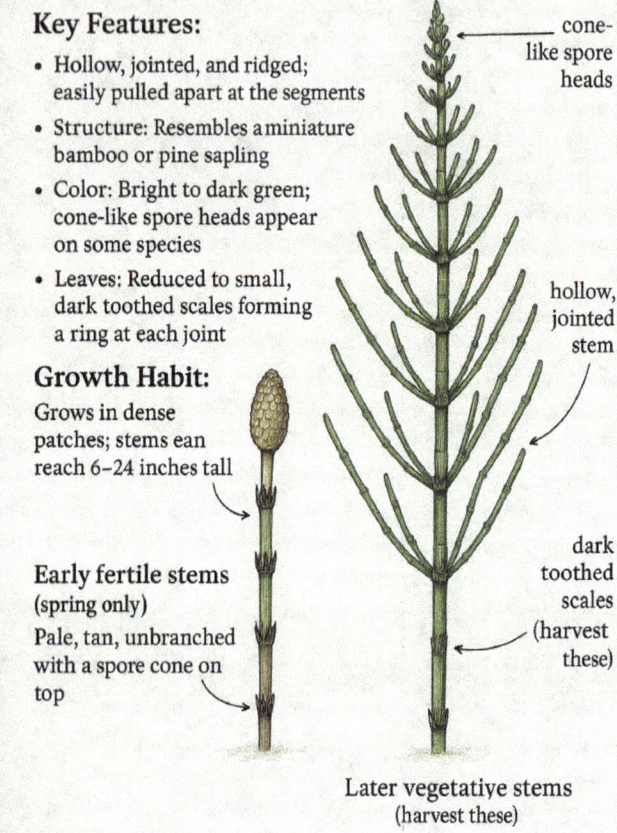

cone-like spore heads

hollow, jointed stem

dark toothed scales (harvest these)

Later vegetatiye stems (harvest these)

Foraging Guide

Habitat

Horsetail thrives in:

- Moist, sandy, or clay-heavy soils
- Streambanks, ditches, forest edges, and wet meadows
- Lowland to subalpine zones
- Often found in large colonies, especially in disturbed or wet ground

Season

Spring to early summer for young shoots; green stems available throughout summer

Toxic Look-Alikes and Cautions

1. **Scouring Rush** *(Equisetum hyemale)*
   - Closely related, technically edible but much coarser, tough, and contains more silica
   - Tall, unbranched, dark green stalks with black rings
   - Best avoided for consumption due to high abrasiveness
2. **Young Ferns** *(Bracken)*
   - When very young, bracken fern fiddleheads might look similar to fertile horsetail stems
   - Bracken fern is toxic if eaten raw or in large quantities

Key Difference: Ferns have coiled tops (fiddleheads) and frond-like leaves.
Safe ID Tip: Horsetail stems pull apart cleanly at joints and feel rough. No leaves or fronds form—only the bottlebrush-like branches.

Safety Note

- Do not consume large amounts. Horsetail contains thiaminase, which can deplete vitamin B1 (especially raw or in tea)
- Avoid if pregnant or if you have kidney issues
- Best used in moderation and often externally in traditional medicine

Cleaning

Rinse well under cold water to remove grit and bugs (they often grow in muddy areas). Snap off and discard any brown, withered, or tough lower segments. Use fresh or dry completely for later herbal use (see below).

Drying

Lay in a single layer on a screen or hang in bundles in a dry, dark, ventilated area until crisp

Flavor Profile

Not typically consumed for flavor. Horsetail has a grassy, mineral-rich, and slightly bitter taste. It is mainly used for herbal tea or external applications rather than culinary use.

Where to Buy

Dried horsetail is commonly available at herbal apothecaries, natural food stores, or online through bulk herb suppliers such as Mountain Rose Herbs or Starwest Botanicals.

Horsetail Hair Growth Wash

Makes: Varies
Time to Make: 1 day

Ingredients

- Horsetail Plant, fresh (best to harvest in the springtime, but you can do so at any time)
- Nettles (fresh is ideal, dried or in tea bags works well!)
- Green Tea (I used Organic tea bags bought from Amazon)
- Water

Directions

Cut as many stalks of horsetail as you can. If it is early spring, try to harvest the actual stalk, or the main part of the plant. The first time I did this, I harvested in December, so I used the little needle-like parts that protruded from the main stalk, as well. I stuffed these into a pot, maybe filling the pot halfway. I then put in about 10 tea bags of Green Tea, and 7 of nettles. If using fresh nettles, use about ¾ the amount nettles as how much horsetail. Add mint if desired. Simply bring this to a boil, turn it off, and let it sit for 12 hours. At the end of this time, the product is ready to use! Store in a glass jar in the fridge and to scalp before washing. Add a small amount of a preservative if desired, to make it last longer.

Horsetail and Herb Spray for Hair Thickness

This hair growth spray works much like commercial ones do! If you are health conscious and don't want harsh chemicals or additives on your skin, this is the way to go! And of course, you can make this completely from scratch if you want to do this off grid...all the ingredients can be grown in your garden or harvested.

Makes: 3 cups

Time to Make: 2 hours

Ingredients

- 1 bunch parsley
- 1 bunch basil
- 1 bunch mint
- 1 bunch horsetail

- 2 cups water
- 20 drops peppermint essential oil
- 20 drops onion oil

Directions

1. **Boil** all herbs with water in a pot.
2. **Remove** from heat and let sit for 2 hours to infuse.
3. **Strain** the liquid, discarding herbs.
4. **Add** essential oils to the cooled herbal infusion.
5. **Pour** into a clean spray bottle.
6. **Spray** directly onto stress points of the scalp or areas with thinning hair.
7. **Apply** twice daily for 4 weeks to observe results.

Horsetail Nail & Skin Salve

Horsetail is packed with silica, making it a traditional ally for strengthening nails, soothing rough skin, and promoting healing. This salve captures those minerals in an easy-to-use form for everyday use or survival care.

Makes: About 1 cup
Time to Make: 20 minutes active, plus 2 weeks infusion

Ingredients
- 1 cup dried horsetail, chopped
- 1 cup carrier oil (olive, sunflower, or rendered fat)
- 2 Tbsp beeswax

Directions
1. **Infuse oil:** Place horsetail in a clean jar and cover completely with oil. Let sit in a warm spot for 2 weeks, shaking occasionally. (For quicker results, gently heat in a double boiler for 2–3 hours.)
2. **Strain:** Pour infused oil through cheesecloth into a saucepan.
3. **Add beeswax:** Stir in beeswax and warm gently until melted.
4. **Pour & cool:** Pour into tins or jars. Let solidify before use.
5. **Apply:** Rub into nails, cuticles, or dry patches of skin as needed.

Pro Tip: Add a few drops of spruce or fir essential oil (or a wild mint leaf during infusion) for extra antiseptic power and a fresh scent. This salve keeps for several months if stored in a cool, dark place.

Note: Horsetail Seasonal Harvest

The **green, fertile shoots** that appear in **late spring through summer** hold the highest concentration of silica and are best for skin and nail remedies. Young spring shoots are more tender and suited for teas, while mature summer stems, though coarser, are richest in minerals for salves and infusions. Always harvest carefully, taking just a few stems from a patch to let it regenerate.

BONUS Recipe!

Fish Fertilizer

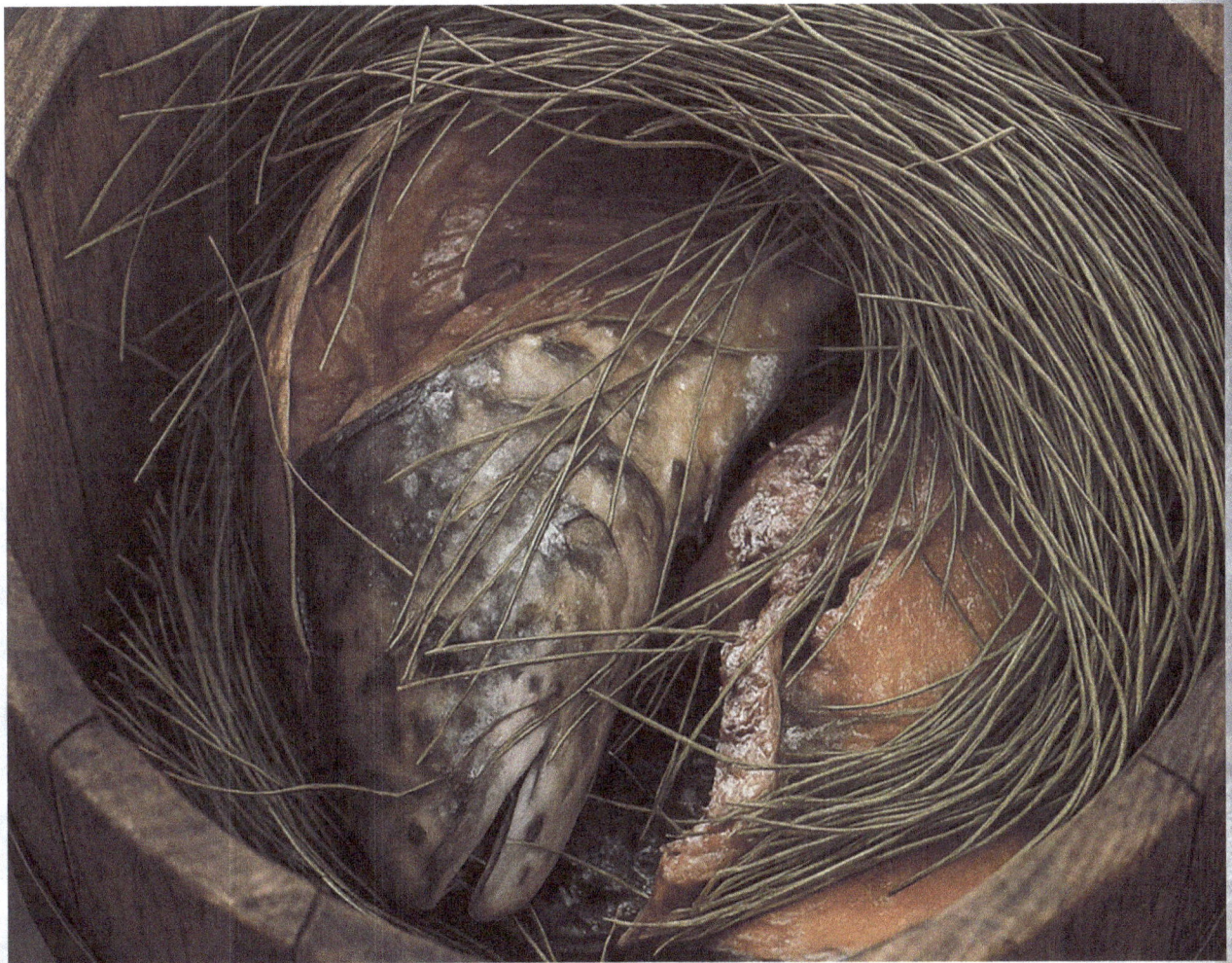

Makes: 2 gallons

Time to Make: 3 weeks to 5 months

Ingredients:
- 1 whole fish carcass (steelhead or salmon)
- Horsetail plant
- 1/4 cup molasses
- Water

Directions
1. **Start** with a clean five-gallon bucket.
2. **Add** one whole fish carcass (steelhead or salmon preferred, or multiple smaller fish such as bass).
3. **Toss in** a large handful of dried or fresh horsetail plant.
4. **Pour in** ¼ cup molasses.
5. **Cover** the contents with water, leaving a little space at the top.
6. **Seal** with a lid and let ferment. This may take 3–4 weeks in warm weather or all winter if started in colder months. It will last for several months, so if you want to keep letting it ferment until you are ready to use, this works.
7. **Check** for a fully fermented, strong-smelling liquid with no visible raw fish left.
8. **Dilute** before using: mix 1 part fertilizer to 2 parts water.
9. **Pour** around the base of your plants as needed during the growing season.
10. **When** finished using it, add to a compost pile at the end of the summer with all the plants you pull out of the garden.

HUCKLEBERRIES

Huckleberries (*Vaccinium sp.*) are small, sweet-tart berries native to the Pacific Northwest, Northern Rockies, and parts of Canada, thriving in mountain forests and alpine areas. Rich in antioxidants, vitamins, and fiber, they support heart health and immune function while adding vibrant flavor to many dishes.

Did you know?

Some tribes considered huckleberry patches sacred and would sing songs of thanks during harvest.

Huckleberries

(*Vaccinium spp.*)

Commen edible species include *V. membranaceem*, *V. ovalifolium*, and *V. deliciosum*.

While several types exist, they share key traits:

- Shrubs 1–6 feet tall
- Leaves: Oval, smooth or finely toothed, often shiny; turn red in fall
- Berries: ¼–½ inch, round, grow singly (not in clusters), in shades from deep purple to blue-black, red, or pink (blue are sweetest)
- Stems: Woody, often reddish or green
- Seeds: Tiny, edible, barely noticeable
- Flavor: Rich, sweet-tart, and fruity

Pro Tip: Ripe huckleberries roll off the stem easily when gently pinched.

Foraging Guide
Habitat

Wild huckleberries thrive in:

- Mountainous forests, often in higher elevations
- Open meadows, clearcuts, and coniferous forests
- Moist, acidic soil—often near firs, pines, or hemlocks
- Sunny or partially shaded areas with good drainage

Look for them along hiking trails, in subalpine forests, or on hillsides and ridgelines.

Season

- Mid to-late summer (July–September)

Toxic Look-Alikes and Cautions

1. **Red Baneberry** (*Actaea rubra*)
   - Habitat overlap: Moist forest areas
   - Berries: Shiny red (or white), growing in tight clusters, not singly
   - Leaves: Deeply lobed, more fern-like
   - Toxicity: Poisonous—causes nausea, dizziness, vomiting

Key Difference: Baneberry has clustered berries and lacy, compound leaves—huckleberries do not.

2. **Nightshade Berries** (*Solanum spp.*)
   - Berries: Glossy black or dark purple, growing in small clusters
   - Leaves: Wavy or lobed, sometimes with a pungent smell
   - Toxicity: Highly toxic—even a few berries can cause symptoms

Key Difference: Nightshade berries have a smooth, tomato-like skin and clustered growth, unlike huckleberries.

Safe ID Tip: True huckleberries always grow individually, have a slightly matte skin, and grow on woody shrubs with oval leaves.

Cleaning Instructions

Rinse gently in a colander under cool water. Sort out leaves, stems, and debris by hand. Drain thoroughly and lay berries on a towel to air-dry before refrigerating or freezing. Use or chill within 2–3 days—or freeze immediately for long-term storage.

Freezing

Lay in a single layer on a cookie sheet. Freeze for several hours or until completely frozen. Transfer to Ziploc bag or vacuum seal bag.

Drying

Lay in a single layer on a dehydrator tray. Dry at 135°F for 12 to 24 hours. You know they are dry when they are hard and rattle when shaken. Store in a glass jar or vacuum seal bag.

Flavor Profile

Wild huckleberries are prized for their intensely fruity, sweet-tart flavor, often described as a deeper, more complex cousin to blueberries. Depending on the species and ripeness, they can range from candy-sweet to bright and tangy.

Texture: Juicy, with soft skin and a burst of flavor

Taste Notes: Sweet-tart, fruity, wine-like, with notes of blackberry and blueberry

Pairs Well With: Lemon, sugar, vanilla, wild game (especially duck and venison), chocolate, cream, and spices like cinnamon or clove

Best Uses: Eaten fresh, in jams, syrups, pies, pancakes, muffins, sauces, or dried for trail snacks

Where to Buy

In the summer months, many huckleberry stands are available near the mountains—with vendors offering their freshly harvested berries for purchase! You can also buy these dried—or, if all else fails, substitute wild or farm-raised blueberries.

Huckleberry No Bake Cheesecake

This has been a favorite summer treat since I was about 12 when I created this recipe. Originally made with blueberries, I adapted it to use foraged huckleberries—with no regrets!

Makes: 8" x 8" pan

Time to Make: 1 hour

Ingredients
- 1.5 packages graham cracker (8 per package)
- 1 stick (½ cup) butter, soft
- ½ cup granulated sugar

Crust Directions

Crush graham crackers. Stir together with butter and sugar. Press into 8'x 8' baking dish.

Filling
- 1-8 oz package cream cheese, softened (leave out for a few hours or put in a pan of hot water before using)
- 1 cup powdered sugar
- 2 cups heavy whipping cream
- 2 tsp vanilla Extract

Filling Directions

Beat whipping cream until soft peaks form. You can also do this in a blender if you don't have a mixer. Add cream cheese, powdered sugar, and vanilla. Beat until everything is folded in, without over beating the whipping cream.

Berry Sauce
- 2 cups huckleberries
- ¼ cup sugar (optional)
- 2 Tbsp Cornstarch
- 1 Tbsp Water
- Dash salt

Berry Sauce Directions

Combine berries, cornstarch, sugar, and water over medium low heat. Add dash of salt. Stir together and cook about 8 minutes. It will get thick and stay light colored, but cook until the cornstarch in the mixture changes to take on the color of the berries.

See my website for gluten free graham cracker recipe.

Huckleberry Breakfast Scones

As a young child, I combed the newspapers for recipes, always looking for ways to create food my parents and siblings would enjoy. As I got older, I began tweaking the recipes to use foraged ingredients that were readily available in my parents' backyard (a tree farm in the PNW). This recipe was one that my mother was kind enough to save for me in a cookbook that I put together with a glue stick, construction paper, and scissors when I was a young child.

Makes: 10 scones
Time to Make: 45 minutes

Ingredients

- 1½ cups all-purpose flour
- 1 cup oats, quick or old fashioned, uncooked
- ¼ cup granulated sugar (plus 1 Tbsp for topping)
- 1 ½ tsp baking powder
- ½ tsp baking soda
- 1 tsp grated lemon zest
- 1 tsp ground ginger
- ¼ tsp salt
- 4 Tbsp butter, chilled
- ¾ cup dried huckleberries
- ¼ cup dried blueberries (can substitute fresh but reduce milk to ½ cup)
- 2/3 cup buttermilk (add 1 Tbsp vinegar to regular milk, let sit for 2 minutes and stir, to make buttermilk)
- 1 egg, lightly beaten

Directions

1. **Preheat** your oven to 400°F.
2. **Prepare** a cookie sheet by lightly spraying it with cooking spray or greasing it with butter.
3. **In a large bowl**, combine the following dry ingredients:
   - 1 cup flour
   - 1 cup oats
   - ¼ cup sugar
   - 1 Tbsp baking powder
   - 1 tsp grated lemon peel
   - ½ tsp ground ginger
   - ¼ tsp baking soda
   - ¼ tsp salt

   Mix well.
4. **Cut in the butter** using two knives or a pastry cutter until the mixture resembles coarse crumbs.
5. **Stir in** dried berries.
6. **In a small bowl**, whisk together buttermilk and egg.
7. **Add the wet mixture** to the dry ingredients. Mix with a fork just until the dry ingredients are moistened—do not overmix.
8. **Transfer the dough** to the prepared cookie sheet.
9. **Pat the dough** into an 8-inch circle about ¾ inch thick.
10. **Sprinkle** the top with the remaining 1 Tbsp of sugar.
11. **Cut into wedges** using a sharp knife and separate the wedges slightly.
12. **Bake** for 12 to 14 minutes, or until the tops are lightly golden brown.
13. **Remove from the oven** and gently separate the wedges if needed.
14. **Transfer** the scones to a cooling rack.
15. **Serve warm** and enjoy!

Foraged Huckleberry Trail Mix

This mix balances sweet, tart, nutty, and herbal flavors inspired by the wild landscapes where huckleberries grow.

Makes: 1 1/3 c trail mix

Time to Make: Not including drying berries (5 minutes)

Ingredients
- ½ cup dried huckleberries
- ½ cup roasted hazelnuts, acorns, or walnuts (if using acorns, be sure to buy from a reputable source or ensure proper safety precautions to remove tannins when cooking)
- 1/3 cup pumpkin seeds (pepitas)
- ¼ cup dried wild cherries (for tartness)
- ¼ cup dried fir or pine nuts (if you can source them safely)

Directions
1. **Combine** all ingredients in a bowl and mix gently.
2. **Store** in a glass jar or small reusable bag for easy snacking on the trail.

Wild Berry Chia Granola

This recipe is simple. It combines local and wild harvested ingredients with staples like rolled oats to offer a filling breakfast that is perfect for packing on camping or hunting trips. Make a big batch and it should last a while on the counter top in a jar (if you don't eat it for snacks because of how good it is!)

Makes: 6 half c servings
Time to Make: 35 minutes

Ingredients
- 1/3 cup butter
- 1/3 cup Maple syrup or honey
- 3 Tbsp brown sugar
- 1½ tsp vanilla
- 2 dashes salt
- 3 cups rolled oats
- 2 Tbsp chia seeds
- 1 cup dried—huckleberries, wild blueberries, wild strawberries, salmonberries, or any other wild berry you choose

Directions
1. **Preheat** oven to 325°F.
2. **Combine** honey, butter, salt, and brown sugar in a saucepan.
3. **Heat** the mixture over medium heat until it begins to bubble.
4. **Let it bubble** for 1 minute.
5. **Remove from heat** and stir in vanilla.
6. **Add** rolled oats and chia seeds. Mix until evenly coated.
7. **Spread** the mixture onto a baking sheet.
8. **Bake** for 15–20 minutes, until lightly golden but not too dry.
9. **Remove** from oven and immediately transfer to a bowl.
10. **Stir in** huckleberries or other dried berries of choice.
11. **Cool** completely before storing or serving.

Easy Camping Pancake Mix

This is a base recipe to add to your survival bag—or camp cooking stash! Add in huckleberries—or whatever wild berries you want when preparing!

Ingredients

Dry Mix (prepare at home):
- 1 cup all-purpose flour
- 1 Tbsp granulated sugar
- 2 tsp baking powder
- ¼ tsp salt

At Camp – Add:
- ¾ cup water (adjust for preferred batter consistency)

Optional: 1 Tbsp oil or melted butter for richness

Directions
1. **At home, combine all dry** ingredients in a sealable bag or container.
2. **At camp,** pour mix into a bowl, add water (and oil if using), and stir just until combined.
3. **Heat a pan** over your camp stove or fire, grease lightly, and cook pancakes until bubbles form and edges firm up; flip and cook until golden brown.

Huckleberry Syrup

Cook this up over the fire to enjoy the freshness of foraged berries—with the sweetness of a little added sugar (omit if your berries are already really sweet!)

Makes: 2 cups
Time to Make: 10 minutes

Ingredients
- 2 cups huckleberries, washed,
- ½ cup granulated sugar
- 4 Tbsp cornstarch
- 2 Tbsp lemon juice
- 1 dash salt

Directions
1. **Combine** washed huckleberries, sugar, and water in a saucepan.
2. **Bring** to a low simmer over medium-low heat.
3. **Simmer** for about 5 minutes, stirring occasionally.
4. **In a separate bowl**, mix together sugar, cornstarch, and lemon juice.
5. **Slowly add** the sugar mixture to the simmering huckleberries, stirring constantly.
6. **Continue stirring** until the mixture thickens—this should happen almost instantly.
7. **Remove from heat** and set aside to cool or use as needed.

Sockeye Salmon with Huckleberry–Fireweed Balsamic Sauce

Makes: 4 servings
Time to Make: 20 minutes

Ingredients

For the Salmon
- 4 sockeye salmon fillets (about 4–6 oz each)
- Dash of salt
- 1 tablespoon olive oil (for the pan)
- 1/2 teaspoon dried yarrow flowers
- 4 large fresh basil leaves, torn into small pieces

For the Huckleberry Sauce
- 1 cup fresh or frozen wild huckleberries
- 1 tablespoon brown sugar
- 1 tablespoon agave syrup (optional, reduce or omit if berries are very ripe)
- 1 teaspoon balsamic vinegar
- Pinch of fireweed flowers (plus extra for garnish, optional)
- Dash of salt
- 1 teaspoon (or more) all-purpose flour, for thickening

Directions

1. **Make the Huckleberry Sauce**
   o In a small saucepan over medium heat, combine huckleberries, brown sugar, agave (if using), balsamic vinegar, fireweed flowers, and a dash of salt.
   o Simmer gently for 2–3 minutes, stirring occasionally, until berries soften and release juice.
   o Sprinkle flour evenly over the surface and stir well to avoid lumps. Continue cooking 1–2 minutes, until sauce thickens to your liking.
   o Keep warm for serving.

2. **Season the Salmon**
   o Pat salmon fillets dry. Sprinkle with a dash of salt, dried yarrow, and torn basil leaves.

3. **Cook the Salmon**
   o Heat olive oil in a large skillet over medium-high heat.
   o Place salmon fillets skin-side down; cook 3–4 minutes until skin is crisp.
   o Flip and cook another 2–4 minutes, depending on thickness, until just cooked through.

4. **Serve**
   o Spoon warm huckleberry–fireweed balsamic sauce over salmon.
   o Garnish with a few fresh fireweed flowers if desired. Serve immediately.

Campfire Variety

To cook over a fire, build a bed of hot coals and place a cast iron skillet on a grate or directly on the coals. Prepare the sauce first in the skillet, then transfer it to a heat-safe bowl to keep warm near the fire. Add the olive oil, season salmon as above, and cook skin-side down 3–4 minutes before flipping for another 2–4 minutes, until just cooked through.

KELP GREENLING

Kelp Greenlings are small, tasty bottom-dwelling fish found in rocky coastal areas. The most common is the kelp greenling—speckled and colorful, with males often having bright blue spots. They're great for pan-frying and are common along Pacific coasts from California to Alaska. Kelp greenling is a nutritious fish rich in lean protein, omega-3 fatty acids, and essential vitamins and minerals that support heart health and brain function.

Did You Know?

The kelp greenling, found along the rocky Pacific coast, is one of the few fish that can *change color with age and sex*! Males are often brightly spotted while females are more camouflaged, helping them blend into kelp beds—making this delicious fish a true master of disguise in the underwater world.

Quick Guide to Cleaning Greenling Fish

What You'll Need:

- Sharp fillet knife
- Cutting board
- Bucket or container for waste
- Fresh water for rinsing

1. **Prepare Your Workspace:** Rinse the fish with fresh water to remove slime and debris.
2. **Scale the Fish:** Use the back of a knife or a fish scaler to remove scales, working from tail to head. Rinse again.
3. **Remove the Head (Optional):** Cut just behind the gills if you prefer to remove the head.
4. **Make an Incision:** With the knife tip, cut from the vent (anus) up toward the base of the head along the belly to open the body cavity.
5. **Gut the Fish:** Reach inside and remove the internal organs. Be careful to remove all entrails and the dark kidney line along the spine.
6. **Rinse Thoroughly:** Flush the cavity and the outside with clean, cold water.
7. **Fillet:** Lay the fish on its side and cut along the backbone to remove fillets if desired.

Flavor Profile

- White, flaky, and sweet
- Mild, almost crab-like flavor—great fried or baked

Where to Buy

As with the other seafood, checking coastal vendors is the best. The second best would be an Asian market. If you aren't in an area where these fish are native, you can substitute other white fish like cod or rockfish.

Greenling Tacos

These tacos are super easy to make over the fire, on the rocks at the jetty, or in a camp stove on the boat! Prepare your taco sauce ahead for easy prep.

Makes: 8 tacos

Time to Make: 8 minutes baking time plus assembly

Taco Sauce

Ingredients

- ¼ cup mayonnaise
- 2 Tbsp sour cream
- 2 Tbsp milk
- 1 tsp lemon juice
- Salt, to taste
- ½ tsp garlic powder
- 2 tsp cilantro

Directions

1. **Blend** all ingredients in a blender or food processor.

Ingredients For Baked Fish

- 4 greenling fillets, bones removed
- Chili powder
- Salt
- Butter for greasing the pan

Directions for Baking Fish

1. **Preheat** oven to 400°F.
2. **Grease** a cookie sheet with butter or oil.
3. **Lay** fish fillets skin-side down on the sheet.
4. **Sprinkle** chili powder and salt over the top of each fillet.
5. **Bake** for 8–10 minutes, until the fish flakes easily with a fork.
6. **Remove from oven**, peel the fillets away from the skin, and place the chunks in a bowl.
7. **Immediately assemble** tacos with your preferred toppings.

Camp Stove Variation:
Instead of baking, cook the fillets in a covered pot over a camp stove until fully cooked and flaky.

Toppings:

- 8 corn tortillas, warmed
- One recipe homemade salsa (see Pico de Gallo recipe in steelhead section)
- Grated cheddar cheese (optional)

Optional: Serve with Spanish rice (recipe below).

Spanish Rice

Makes: 4 Servings

Time to Make: 35 minutes

Ingredients

- 2 garlic cloves, minced
- ¼ purple onion, minced
- 1 tsp cumin
- 1 tsp chili powder
- ¼ tsp cayenne powder

- 1 tsp salt
- 2 Tbsp butter
- 1 cup rice, washed
- 2 cups water
- ½ cup pasta sauce

Directions

1. **Melt** butter in a saucepan over medium heat.
2. **Add** garlic cloves and optional minced purple onion.
3. **Stir in** your choice of spices.
4. **Cook** for about 5 minutes, until the garlic becomes fragrant.
5. **Add** rice and stir well.
6. **Cook** for an additional 2 minutes, allowing the rice to lightly toast.
7. **Pour in** water and pasta sauce.
8. **Stir** to combine, then **cover** the saucepan with a lid.
9. **Reduce heat** to just above low and **simmer** for 25 minutes, or until the liquid is absorbed and the rice is fully cooked.
10. **Fluff** with a fork and **serve** warm.

How to Bake Greenling in an Open Fire

Season with salt and pepper and, if desired, seafood seasoning. Wrap in aluminum foil. Place underneath a well-established fire, near the edge in the coals if the fire is large and hot. Cook for about 10 minutes, watching for steam coming from the packet. Remove with a stick or marshmallow roaster. Let cool for a couple of minutes before consuming!

Rendering Fish Oil from Greenling Skins

Even leaner fish like kelp greenling hold valuable oils in their skins and bellies. Rendering these oils was a traditional way to preserve calories and create a nutrient-rich cooking fat. While this recipe works with greenling, oilier fish such as salmon, black cod, or eulachon will produce far more oil and can be prepared in the same way.

Makes: Variable (small yield per fish)
Time to Make: 30–40 minutes

Ingredients

- Skins and fatty trimmings from greenling (or other fish)
- Small pot or cast iron pan

Directions

1. **Clean:** Scrape scales and excess flesh from the skins. Rinse well.
2. **Chop:** Cut skins into small strips or pieces.
3. **Heat:** Place skins in a pot or cast-iron pan over low, steady heat.
4. **Render:** Slowly cook until the oils release and skins turn crisp. Stir occasionally to prevent burning.
5. **Strain:** Pour liquid oil through a cloth or fine strainer into a jar. Allow to cool.

Pro Tip: Use rendered fish oil as a cooking fat for frying or as a drizzle over bannock or roots. Oils spoil quickly—store in a cool place and use within a few days, or seal tightly and keep chilled.

Kelp Greenling Curry

This is the perfect dish to prepare in advance and heat up over the camp stove after a long day of fishing the coast. You can make your sauce, then throw in freshly caught greenling when ready to heat up. See naan bread recipe in the chanterelle section.

Serves: 3-4
Time to Make: 45 minutes

Ingredients

- 1 lb kelp greenling fillets, cut into bite-sized pieces
- 2 Tbsp vegetable oil (or coconut oil)
- 1 medium onion, finely chopped
- 3 garlic cloves, minced
- 1 Tbsp fresh ginger, grated
- 1-2 green chilies, sliced (optional, adjust for heat)
- 2 tsp curry powder (or a blend of turmeric, coriander, cumin)
- 1 tsp ground cumin
- 1 tsp ground coriander
- ½ tsp turmeric powder
- ½ tsp paprika (optional for color)
- 2 tsp sugar
- 1 can (14 oz) coconut milk
- 1 medium tomato, chopped (or ½ cup canned diced tomatoes)
- 1 cup water or fish stock
- Salt to taste
- Fresh cilantro leaves for garnish
- Juice of half a lime

Directions

1. **Prep the fish:** Rinse the kelp greenling fillets and pat dry. Cut into bite-sized chunks. Set aside.
2. **Cook the aromatics:** Heat the oil in a large pan or skillet over medium heat. Add the chopped onion and sauté until soft and translucent, about 5 minutes.
3. **Add garlic, ginger, and chili:** Stir in the minced garlic, grated ginger, and sliced chilies. Cook for another 1-2 minutes until fragrant.
4. **Toast the spices:** Add the curry powder, cumin, coriander, turmeric, and paprika. Stir constantly for about 1 minute to toast the spices and release their aroma.
5. **Add tomato and liquids:** Toss in the chopped tomato and cook for 2 minutes. Pour in the coconut milk and water or fish stock. Stir well to combine. Bring to a gentle simmer.
6. **Simmer the curry:** Let the sauce simmer gently for about 10 minutes, allowing the flavors to meld.
7. **Cook the fish:** Add the kelp greenling pieces to the simmering curry. Cook gently for 5-7 minutes until the fish is opaque and cooked through. Avoid over-stirring to keep the fish intact.
8. **Finish and serve:** Season with salt to taste and squeeze in fresh lime juice. Garnish with chopped cilantro.

Serving suggestions:

Serve hot with steamed basmati rice, naan bread, or your favorite grain. A side of lightly sautéed greens or cucumber raita complements the curry well.

KOKANEE SALMON

Kokanee are landlocked sockeye salmon found in cold, freshwater lakes across the Pacific Northwest, Northern California, British Columbia, Alaska, and parts of the Rocky Mountains. Though smaller than their ocean-going relatives, they offer similar nutritional value—rich in omega-3 fatty acids, protein, vitamin D, and B vitamins, all of which support heart, brain, and immune health. Kokanee are most often caught by trolling or jigging in deeper, cooler waters during summer and early fall.

Note: The kokanee in this picture is a male during spawning season. Kokanee turn red during spawning season due to hormonal changes that trigger a shift in pigmentation, signaling maturity and readiness to reproduce. However, you wouldn't want to harvest a kokanee like this—harvest them instead in the spring, when they are bright silver. See picture near smoked kokanee recipe.

Filleting Kokanee:

To fillet a kokanee, make a clean cut behind the gill plate down to the backbone, then run your knife along the spine toward the tail in one smooth motion, keeping the blade flat to preserve as much meat as possible. Flip and repeat on the other side, then trim the rib bones and pin bones if desired. The skin can be left on for grilling or removed for pan-searing or stews.

Flavor Profile

Kokanee have a mild, clean flavor with a slightly sweet, rich flesh that's less oily than other salmon but still moist and satisfying. The texture is firm yet tender, making it ideal for grilling, smoking, or pan-searing with foraged herbs and wild greens.

Where to Buy/Substitutes

Substitute jack salmon or fresh sockeye or coho salmon.

Did You Know?

Kokanee populations can fluctuate dramatically every few years due to a natural boom-and-bust spawning cycle, which makes them an unpredictable but prized seasonal catch for foragers and anglers alike.

Easy Smoked Kokanee

Time to Make: 1 day
Makes: ¾ dry brine (can treat up to 1 lb fish)

- ¼ cup kosher salt
- ½ cup brown sugar
- 2 tsp garlic powder

Ingredients

- 4–6 kokanee fillets, cleaned and patted dry

Directions

1. **Make the dry brine:** Mix the salt, garlic powder, and brown sugar.
2. **Brine the fillets:** Lay the fillets skin-side down in a shallow dish. Coat evenly with the brine mixture. Cover and refrigerate for 4–6 hours.
3. **Rinse & dry:** Rinse fillets under cool water to remove excess brine. Pat dry and lay them on a rack to air-dry for 1–2 hours, until a tacky glaze forms.
4. **Smoke:** Preheat your smoker to 160–180°F. Use alder, apple, or cherry wood chips. Smoke the fillets skin-side down for 1.5 to 2.5 hours, depending on thickness, until firm and lightly golden.
5. **Cool & store:** Let cool completely. Eat warm, refrigerate for up to a week, or vacuum seal and freeze for later use.

Backwoods Smoker Method (Camp Version)

This rustic version delivers deep, earthy flavor and works well for preserving fish when refrigeration isn't an option.

If you're off grid or cooking in the wild:

- Build a **covered smoker** using a firepit with a grate, a lid or foil tent, and green alder or maple branches for smoke.
- Place fish on a grill rack over indirect heat, keeping the fire low and smoky (not hot and blazing).
- Maintain gentle smoke for 2–3 hours, checking often to avoid flare-ups or overcooking.
- Rotate the fish or shift the fire as needed to keep the heat consistent and low.

Pan-Seared Kokanee with Wild Herbs & Lemon

This is a rustic, forager's version of trout meunière—packed with bright flavor and minimal effort, whether cooked in a kitchen or beside a river.

Makes: 2 servings
Time to Make: 20 minutes

Ingredients
- 4 kokanee fillets, skin on
- 1 Tbsp butter or elk tallow

Optional: lemon zest or a sprinkle of dried wildflower petals for garnish

- 1 Tbsp olive oil
- 1 clove garlic, minced
- 1 tsp chopped wild herbs (like yarrow, wild thyme, or nettle)
- Juice of ½ lemon
- Salt and pepper to taste

Directions
1. **Heat butter** and oil in a cast iron skillet over medium heat—works just as well over a camp stove or fire grate.
2. **Season** kokanee fillets with salt, pepper, and your wild herbs.
3. **Place** fillets skin-side down and cook for 2–3 minutes until the skin crisps.
4. **Flip** and cook another 1–2 minutes, just until the fish flakes easily.
5. **Add** garlic and lemon juice to the pan, spooning the sizzling butter over the fish to glaze it.
6. **Serve** hot with crusty bread, roasted roots, or wilted wild greens.

Canning Kokanee Salmon (Pint Jars)

This is an easy way to convert an excess of kokanee to a shelf stable ingredient! You can also adapt this recipe to use with salmon if sliced thinly.

What You'll Need:
- Fresh kokanee fillets (skin-on or skinless)
- Salt (optional: ½ tsp per pint)
- Pint-size mason jars with lids and rings
- Pressure canner

Directions
1. **Clean & Cut the Fish:**
   Remove entrails and trim off fins. You can leave the skin on. Cut fish into jar-length pieces (about 3–3.5 inches) to fit inside the jar vertically.
2. **Sterilize Jars:**
   Wash jars, lids, and rings in hot, soapy water. Keep jars hot until ready to fill.

Packing the Jars:
3. **Pack the Fish:**
   Tightly pack raw fish into hot jars, leaving 1-inch headspace. The natural juices will release during processing.
4. **Add Salt (Optional):**
   Add ½ tsp of canning salt per pint for flavor (not for preservation).
5. **Clean & Seal:**
   Wipe rims with a clean damp cloth. Place lids and screw bands on finger-tight.

Pressure Canning:
6. **Set Up the Pressure Canner:**
   Add water to the canner (usually 2–3 inches; follow manufacturer's instructions). Place jars inside.
7. **Process the Fish:**
   - Pints: Process for 100 minutes
   - Pressure:
     - 11 lbs pressure for dial-gauge canner (at sea level)
     - 10 lbs pressure for weighted-gauge canner (adjust for altitude)

(Check your altitude and adjust pressure if above 1000 ft.)
1. **Cool Safely:**
   Let the canner return to 0 pressure naturally. Wait 10 minutes, then open lid carefully. Remove jars and let cool for 12–24 hours on a towel.
2. **Check Seals:**
   Lids should be concave and not flex when pressed. Label with date and store in a cool, dark place for up to 1 year.

MORELS

When I first got into mushroom hunting, I didn't know what I was doing. I had begun finding chanterelles with little effort. Although the chanterelles seemed easy to find, I wanted to find morels (*Morchella* spp.). In spring 2018, the perfect opportunity presented. About six months after many acres of wildfires ravaged large areas of Oregon and Washington, I headed out to the newly burned areas, being careful to avoid hazards. Wildfires leave many dangerous obstacles, including ground that is more prone to landslides, and pockets of air underground, especially around the bases of trees, where one could easily fall and break an ankle. In addition to this, one must watch out for trees that are unstable and a hazard for falling on parked cars or even people.

Armed with the knowledge that I must take care, I packed up my two children, and we headed out. The first day we found only the tiny orange suction cup looking mushrooms that covered the burn areas everywhere. It was only April, and the snow was still on the ground in some spots. Although we found no mushrooms, the air, scented deliciously with high mountain pines, fir, and snow melt, offered a pleasant backdrop to beautiful areas. Later on, I noted that morels often pop within two to three weeks after the snow has melted, making them most likely to grow in May or June, depending on elevation. That year, once I found the first one, nestled at the root of a clump of sword ferns, the rest came easily. I would bend down, holding one arm around my seven-month-old daughter in the front pack, while I picked one, only to notice an entire flush of them spread out in front of my eyes.

When the baby got hungry, I would pull out the milk supply and feed her the natural way, as I slowly walked through the forest, scanning for more mushrooms. My partner carried the almost four-year-old, letting him walk at times and putting him back in the pack when he got tired. That spring will be one I always cherish. The memories we made will never be lost. We camped several weekends, guarded by the far-off magnificent Mount Jefferson, an ever-watching silent pillar that yielded her protection over us and the land. On Mondays, we packed five-gallon buckets full of morels, carefully drove home, and I weighed and packaged them, delivering them to my buyers, who would turn them into delectable meals. While I no longer harvest commercially, finding them each spring will always be a part of my seasonal DNA.

Did You Know?

Morels (*Morchella sp.*) contain natural compounds that stimulate digestion and may support immune function—making them not just a gourmet delicacy, but a nutritious one too! Their honeycomb-like shape also helps them soak up flavor like a sponge, making every bite rich and satisfying.

MORELS (MORCHELLA SPP.)

IDENTIFICATION GUIDE

Key ID Features:

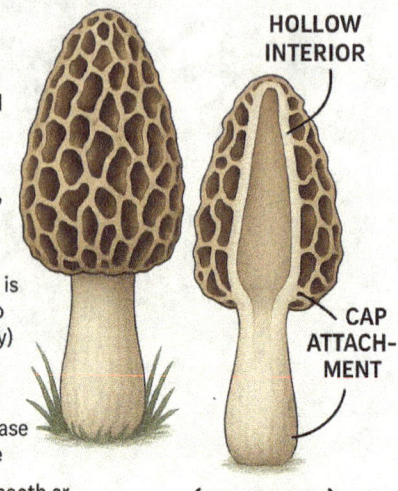

HOLLOW INTERIOR

- **Cap:** Sponge-like, pitted, and ridged (looks like a honeycomb)

- **Color:** Tan, yellow, gray, or black

- **Hollow Interior:** Entire mushroom is hollow from tip to stem (cut to verify)

- **Cap Attachment:** Fully attached to the stem at the base —not hanging free

- **Stem:** Whitish, smooth or slightly textured, also hollow

CAP ATTACH-MENT

2–6 in

Foraging Guide

Habitat

- Shady forest basins, coves, and moist depressions
- Burn sites the spring after a wildfire—especially 2–3 weeks after snowmelt
- Beneath cottonwood and ash trees in lower elevations, especially near rivers
- Logged or disturbed forests—look near fallen trees, leaf litter, and other fungi
- Light ground cover helps retain moisture—don't fixate on one spot, move around

Soil Temps & Timing

Morels tend to emerge when soil temperatures reach 50–55°F at a depth of 4–6 inches, with ideal daytime temps in the mid-60s to 70s°F. After a warm spring rain, it's time to grab your bucket and start hunting!

Season

- March to June

Toxic Look-Alikes and Cautions

1. **False Morel** (*Gyromitra spp.*)
   - Cap: Wrinkled or brain-like, not honeycombed
   - Color: Reddish-brown to dark brown
   - Interior: Often chambered or filled
   - Toxicity: Contains gyromitrin, **a potentially deadly toxin**

2. **Verpa** (*Verpa bohemica, "early morel"*)
   - Cap: Looks similar but is attached only at the top (like a thimble)
   - Stem: May be filled or cottony inside
   - Edibility: Sometimes eaten but can cause gastrointestinal distress

Cleaning

Gently brush off dirt and debris. Slice in half lengthwise to check for insects or grit. Briefly soak in cold salted water to flush out bugs, then air dry.

Drying

If you bring home more morels than you can use fresh, drying them on a screen with a box fan is an easy method—just lay them out unwashed and not overlapping, and circulate air until they're brittle and crack cleanly. Once fully dry, vacuum seal right away to keep them shelf-stable and prevent moisture reabsorption.

Freezing

Soak morels in a salt water bath (at least 2 Tbsp salt) for 30 minutes to overnight to draw out white worms. After draining, slice the morels lengthwise, remove any worms, and cut into bite-sized pieces. Cook over medium-low heat until liquid evaporates, then add butter or oil and sauté briefly. Let cool completely, then vacuum seal and freeze for later use.

Flavor Profile

Morels have a rich, earthy, nutty flavor with umami depth and a hint of smokiness. Their texture is tender but slightly chewy, ideal for absorbing sauces and fats. Cooking enhances their complex flavor dramatically.
Texture: Meaty, sponge-like
Pairs Well With: Butter, garlic, cream, eggs, pasta, wild greens, asparagus
Best Cooking Methods: Sautéed, stuffed, added to creamy dishes or soups

Where to Buy

Farmers markets, some specialty grocery stores in the spring, Facebook foraging groups, or dried on Amazon.
Note: Morels are not edible until cooked. Also avoid consuming morels with alcohol.

Morel and Spring Veggie Kabobs

This recipe combines several different springtime vegetables and fungi with red wine vinegar and thyme to create the perfect marinade for these grilled or baked vegetables. Also included is the option to add either wild turkey, grouse, or chicken breast for some extra protein. Or, if you prefer a lighter, vegetarian-based meal, you can trade out the chicken for tofu chunks.

Makes: 15-20 skewers (3-4 per serving)
Time to Make: 5 hours including marinating time

Step 1: Make the Marinade

In a medium bowl or large zip-top bag, whisk together:

- 1 cup red wine vinegar
- ¼ cup white wine vinegar
- ½ tsp thyme
- ½ cup Bragg's Liquid Aminos (or soy sauce)
- 8-10 wild chives, chopped into small pieces
- ½ cup olive oil
- Fresh basil leaves (roughly torn)

Step 2: Prep the following vegetables:

½ red pepper
½ white or purple onion
5-10 morels, washed and soaked
2 chicken or grouse breasts (optional, can use tofu instead)

- Slice red pepper and onion into large chunks.
- Drain morels.
- Cube the chicken, grouse, turkey, or tofu into bite-sized chunks.

Add all the vegetables and protein to the marinade. Cover and marinate for 1–4 hours in the fridge, turning occasionally for even coating. If using tofu, don't marinate with the rest of the veggies—it will fall apart. Instead, add this when you assemble your vegetables.

Step 3: Assemble the Kabobs

Thread veggies and mushrooms alternately with meat or tofu onto skewers.
(If using wooden skewers, soak them in water for 30 minutes to prevent burning.)

Step 4: Cook the Kabobs

Grill or Campfire:
Grill over medium-high heat, turning every few minutes, for 10–15 minutes or until meat is cooked through and veggies are lightly charred and tender.

Oven Method:
Bake at 425°F on a foil-lined baking sheet for 15–20 minutes, turning once halfway through.

Pro Tip:
Baste the kabobs with leftover marinade during cooking for extra flavor—but don't use raw meat marinade as a finishing sauce unless it's boiled first.

Morels With Cream Sauce served over Pan-fried Kokanee

Last year, while camping with my dad and the kids at Odell Lake, I came up with this recipe. Because we had only a few supplies and me, being the slightly disorganized Gemini that I am, forgot some of my ingredients, I decided to keep this simple. Now, I want you to just close your eyes and envision what I am about to describe. The camp stove was setup on a roughhewn wooden picnic table facing the lake, where I could see the blood orange sun, an even deeper orange than normal, due to close by forest fires, sinking towards the horizon at the other end of the long lake. The mosquitos, due to the wind, had decided not to join us this evening. The air was a perfect 75 degrees, and smelled faintly of forest fire, but strongly of pine trees and fir needles. It was one of those evenings that could almost make one forget that they lived in the city, or had a stressful job, or an annoying spouse. I called the kids and my dad over, gesturing to paper plates filled with tender pan-fried kokanee fillets drizzled with morel and cream sauce served with freshly cooked kale greens. We settled into our camp chairs to eat a (mostly) wild harvested dinner in nature.

Makes: 4 servings
Time to Make: 35 minutes

Ingredients

- 2 Tbsp Butter
- 8 Kokanee fillets
- 1 cup fresh morels (or cooked and frozen)
- 1 Tbsp butter
- ¾ cup half 'n' half
- ½ tsp salt
- 1/8 tsp pepper
- 2 cups chopped kale or greens of choice (optional)
- 1 Tbsp butter

Directions

Morel Cream Sauce

1. **Slice and prepare** morels.
   If using fresh morels, ensure they've been properly soaked and cleaned as described in the morel section.
2. **Cook** sliced morels in a saucepan over medium heat, stirring often.
3. **Continue cooking** until most of the moisture has evaporated.
4. **Add** butter and stir to coat the mushrooms.
5. **Cook** for about 2 minutes, until the butter is hot and the morels begin to sizzle.
6. **Pour in** half-and-half and stir well.
7. **Reduce heat** to a simmer and cook for about 10 minutes, or until the sauce thickens.
8. **Season** with salt and pepper to taste.
9. **Set aside** and keep warm until ready to serve over kokanee.

Kokanee Fillets

1. **Heat** butter in a cast iron skillet over medium-high heat.
2. **Place** kokanee fillets in a single layer, skin-side down if applicable.

If your burner is small, cook in batches to ensure even cooking.

3. **Cover the pan** with a lid if needed to retain heat.
4. **Cook** for about 3 minutes per side (adjust time based on fillet thickness).
5. **Flip** and repeat on the other side until fillets are fully cooked and flake easily.
6. **Serve** with morel cream sauce spooned over the top.

Optional: Fresh Greens

1. **Chop** your fresh greens of choice (such as spinach, wild nettles, or kale).
2. **Heat** 1 Tbsp of butter in a cast iron skillet.
3. **Add** the greens and **cover** the pan.
4. **Cook** for 3–5 minutes, until wilted to desired tenderness.
5. **Serve** as a side with the fish and sauce.

Foraged Green Substitutes

- **Stinging Nettle** – Mild, earthy flavor; rich in iron (must be cooked to remove sting).
- **Lamb's Quarters** – Tastes like spinach; tender and nutrient-dense.
- **Miner's Lettuce** – Mild, crisp, and slightly succulent; great wilted or raw.
- **Chickweed** – Mild and grassy; wilts quickly and works well in sautés.
- **Dandelion Greens** – Bitter and peppery; best when young or lightly cooked.
- **Wild Mustard Greens** – Spicy and bold; cook to mellow the bite.

Campfire Morel and Bear Sausage Pizza

This is the perfect pizza recipe for making while camping. If you do the preparation ahead of time, such as making the dough, or bringing pre-made dough, packing the pasta sauce, and frying up your sausage, it will cut preparation time and make an easy meal that you can cook with limited utensils. Depending on your camping setup, you may want to also slice your green pepper and onion beforehand. If you are foraging for morels, you can just prepare them right before putting on the pizza to cook, but if you are bringing frozen morels, then you have even less preparation.

Makes: one 10" round pizza
Time to Make: 30 minutes (not including time to rise pizza dough)

Ingredients
- 1 lb bear or pork sausage
- 1 recipe pizza dough (or enough for one crust of pre-packaged pizza dough)
- 1 green pepper
- ¼ purple onion
- 1 cup fresh or frozen sliced morels
- 4 Tbsp olive oil
- Salt
- Oregano
- 1 12 oz jar garlic pasta sauce
- 2 cups grated mozzarella cheese

Directions

Prepare the Toppings
1. **Slice** the peppers, onion, and morels into thin strips.
2. **Add** olive oil to a skillet and heat over a fire or camp stove.
3. **Add** the mushrooms, peppers, and onion to the skillet.
4. **Cook,** stirring frequently, until the onions are translucent and the peppers are just beginning to wilt.
5. **Season** with salt and oregano.
6. **Add** sausage and heat until warmed through.
If using unseasoned sausage, adjust salt to taste.
7. **Remove from heat** and cover with a lid to keep warm.

Cook the Pizza
1. **Add** enough olive oil to a large (pizza-sized) skillet to **thickly coat** the bottom and sides.
   You want enough oil so the dough doesn't stick—almost shallow-frying it.
2. **Spread** the prepared pizza dough evenly into the oiled skillet.
3. **Cook** over an open fire or camp stove for 5–10 minutes, until the bottom is golden and set.
4. **Flip** the dough carefully to cook the other side.
5. **Add toppings** in this order:
   o A thin layer of Alfredo sauce
   o The warm sausage and vegetable mixture
   o Shredded cheese of choice
6. **Cover the skillet** and cook until the cheese is fully melted.

Be cautious not to over-steam, as this can make the dough soggy.

Alternative Method:
You can also make this on a pizza stone over the fire or in a camp oven for crispier results.

Morels and Steak

Fine dining—survival style! You can impress your dinner guests with making this using elk steak, morels, and a side of wild chive mashed potatoes (see wild chive section).

Makes: 3-4 steaks

Time to Make: 25 minutes

Ingredients

- 16 oz Elk steak or Beef Top Sirloin or Ribeye steak (or whatever cut you prefer)
- 2 cups fresh morels, sliced lengthwise and pre-soaked to remove worms
- 1 small white onion, sliced into wedges

- ½ cup heavy cream
- 1/3 cup white wine
- Salt, to taste
- Steak seasoning

Directions

Make the Morel Cream Sauce

1. **Place** sliced morels in a cast iron skillet over medium-low heat.
2. **Cook** for about 6 minutes, stirring every couple of minutes, until most of the moisture has evaporated.
3. **Add** chopped onion and continue cooking, stirring to prevent sticking, until all remaining moisture is gone.

4. **Pour in** white wine and cook for about 5 minutes, or until most of the liquid has evaporated.
5. **Add** cream and reduce heat to very low. Stir occasionally to keep warm while preparing steaks.

Cook the Steaks

1. **Heat** another skillet to medium heat.
2. **Place** steaks in the skillet and **season** with your preferred steak seasoning.

3. **Sear** for 1 minute, then flip the steaks.
4. **Reduce heat** to medium-low and cook for 3–5 minutes per side, or until desired doneness is reached.

Alternatively, cook steaks on the grill, in an air fryer, or using your preferred method.

Serve

1. **Plate** steaks with a generous spoonful of morel cream sauce.
2. **Serve** with mashed potatoes and grilled or baked asparagus for a complete meal.

Morel Teriyaki

This is a wonderful recipe with a vegetarian twist—you can add meat if you prefer, but if you want to keep things plant based, just use tofu!

Makes: 3 servings

Time to Make: 25 minutes

Ingredients

- 2 oz Tofu, cut into bite-sized chunks (can change out for meat: venison or elk, sliced thinly works well)
- 2 large morels, cut into bite sized chunks, soaked and washed
- 1 cup broccoli, chopped
- 2 sprigs basil
- ¼ cup liquid aminos (can use soy sauce if needed)

- 2 Tbsp packed brown sugar
- 1 Tbsp honey
- 1 tsp fresh ginger, grated
- 2 garlic cloves, minced
- 2 Tbsp cornstarch
- ¼ cup cold water

Directions

1. **Prep ingredients:** Soak and wash the morels thoroughly. Cut tofu (or venison/elk) and morels into bite-sized pieces. Chop broccoli and mince garlic. Grate fresh ginger.
2. **Make the sauce:** In a bowl, whisk together the liquid aminos (or soy sauce), brown sugar, honey, and grated ginger until the sugar dissolves.
3. **Cook tofu and mushrooms:** Heat a Tbsp of oil in a skillet over medium-high heat. Add tofu (or meat) and cook until browned on all sides, about 5 minutes. Remove from pan and set aside.
4. **Sauté vegetables:** In the same pan, add morels. Cook until moisture evaporates, about 5 minutes. Add broccoli. Cook for 4-5 minutes until tender.

5. **Combine:** Return tofu (or meat) to the pan with the vegetables. Pour the teriyaki sauce over everything and stir to coat evenly.
6. **Thicken sauce:** In a small bowl, mix cornstarch with cold water to make a slurry. Pour slurry into the pan and stir constantly until the sauce thickens, about 1-2 minutes.
7. **Add basil and finish:** Tear basil leaves and stir into the teriyaki just before serving. Remove from heat.
8. **Serve:** Enjoy your mushroom teriyaki hot over rice or noodles.

Morel Gravy with Lemon Balm

This recipe combines wild ingredients and is easy to make either over a campfire, or on the stovetop!

Makes: 2 cups gravy

Time to Make: 15 minutes

Ingredients

- 5-7 morels, soaked, chopped finely
- ½ onion, chopped finely
- 1 clove garlic, minced
- 2 Tbsp fresh basil

- 4 Tbsp lemon balm infused butter
- 2 cups chicken broth (or grouse, pheasant, or wild turkey)
- 2-3 Tbsp cornstarch

Salt to taste

Directions

1. **Prepare ingredients:** Soak the morels thoroughly to remove wild critters. Wash and chop them finely. Chop the onion into small pieces and mince the garlic.
2. **Sauté aromatics:** In a saucepan, melt the lemon balm infused butter over medium heat. Add the chopped onion and garlic, and sauté until soft and fragrant, about 3-4 minutes.
3. **Cook morels:** Add the chopped morels and cook for 5-7 minutes, stirring occasionally until softened and fragrant.
4. **Add cornstarch:** Sprinkle the cornstarch over the morel mixture and stir well to coat evenly.
5. **Add broth slowly:** Gradually pour in the chicken broth, stirring constantly to prevent lumps, allowing the gravy to thicken as you add the liquid.
6. **Simmer and finish:** Bring the mixture to a gentle simmer, stirring occasionally until the gravy reaches your desired thickness. Add salt to taste.
7. **Add basil:** Stir in the fresh basil just before serving.
8. **Serve:** Perfect over roasted meats, mashed potatoes, or any dish that calls for rich mushroom gravy.

Stuffed Morels with Wild Chives

Spring of 2025 was one of the best years I have experienced for natural morels (as opposed to burn). After checking a spot that I had only ever found one or two natural morels at, in early April, I came home with over two pounds! Stoked with my finds, I immediately created this recipe for stuffed morels. It features freshly picked wild chives; the perfect addition to this appetizer!

Makes: 20 stuffed half mushrooms

Time to Make: 30 minutes including bake time

Ingredients
- 10 medium or large morels, sliced in half lengthwise
- 8 oz cream cheese, room temperature
- 1 cup grated cheddar cheese
- 1 dash salt (optional)
- 2 Tbsp fresh or dried wild chives
- 5-10 Doritos chips, crushed

Directions

Prep the Morels
1. **Place** morels in a bowl and **sprinkle** salt over the top.
2. **Cover** with water and **let soak** for at least 1 hour.
   Note: For natural morels (not burn morels), fewer white worms are usually present. If needed, you can shorten the soak time. The soak is optional, as the worms are harmless—but avoid oversoaking to prevent mushiness.
3. **Pat dry** gently with a paper towel.
4. **Lay** the cleaned morels on a baking sheet.
5. **Preheat** oven to 375°F.

Make the Filling
6. **Mix** cream cheese, chopped chives, and shredded cheddar cheese in a bowl.
7. **Spoon** the mixture into a piping bag or a plastic zip-top bag.
8. **If using a plastic bag**, seal it, then **cut a small hole** in one bottom corner to create a makeshift piping tool.

Stuff & Bake
9. **Fill** each half morel with the cream cheese mixture, using a spoon or piping bag to press the filling down into the mushroom.
10. **Sprinkle** crushed Doritos over the tops of the filled morels.
11. **Bake** in the preheated oven for 15 minutes, or until hot and golden on top.
12. **Serve warm** and enjoy!

Morel Breakfast Sandwiches

Makes: 3 sandwiches

Time to Make: 25 minutes

Ingredients

- 8 large morels, sliced in bite size pieces and presoaked in salt water to remove bugs
- 1 bunch fresh onion chives
- 2 eggs
- 1 steak, sliced thinly
- 1 oz goat cheese
- 1 oz cheddar cheese
- Butter, depending on the fat content in steak, for brushing in the pan
- 3 croissants

Directions

1. **Place** sliced morels in a skillet over medium-low heat.
2. **Cook** for about 5 minutes, or until most of the moisture has evaporated.
3. **Add** chopped chives and steak pieces to the skillet.
4. **Season** with a dash of salt if desired.
5. **Cook** for about 3 minutes, until the steak is browned.
6. **Add** eggs directly into the skillet and **scramble** into the steak mixture.
7. **Stir continuously** and cook until eggs are fully set, about 1 minute.
8. **Crumble** goat cheese over the top, then **sprinkle** with shredded cheddar cheese.
9. **Serve** warm over sliced or halved croissants.

NETTLES

Nettles (Urtica dioica) contain antihistamines and anti-inflammatory properties, which means they are a great tool to help combat allergies. They are also useful for hair growth because they encourage circulation to the scalp. They have been known to help with urinary tract infections as well. One wives' tale even claimed stinging nettles could help delay the onset of gray hair, due to the polyphenols in them. Adding them to recipes is a good way to enjoy not only some health benefits, but also the wild foraged flavor of nettles! See the bolete section for a mushroom and nettle dumpling soup recipe!

Did you know?

Some tribes used fresh nettle stings to treat arthritis, believing the sting stimulated healing and blood flow.

NETTLES
Urtica dioica

Key Features:

- **Leaves:** Deep green, heart- or lance-shaped with serrated edges
- **Surface:** Covered in fine stinging hairs, especially underneath and on stem
- **Arrangement:** Opposite pairs along a single stem
- **Stem:** Square-shaped also hairy
- **Height:** Typically 2–5 feet tall
- **Texture:** Slightly fuzzy but stings when touched raw

Flowers (Late Spring–Summer)

- Tiny, greenish-white Hang in drooping clusters from upper leaf nodes

Foraging Guide

Habitat

- Look in low-lying streambeds, creeks, and along riverbanks
- Often found along forest trails, especially where human disturbance is minimal
- Thrive in shaded areas beneath tall trees or forest canopy
- Favor rich, moist soil—especially in spots with leaf litter or organic decay
- Common near old homesteads, barnyards, or fence lines (due to nutrient-rich soil)
- Can grow along the edges of meadows or in clearings that receive partial sunlight
- Frequently spotted near springs, seeps, and seasonal runoffs

Season

- Harvest in spring and early summer as soon as the leaves are formed and while they are bright green
- **Do not harvest after flowering** – Once nettles flower, they begin producing cystoliths, which can irritate the kidneys and digestive system

Toxic Look-Alikes and Cautions

1. **Wood Nettle** (*Laportea canadensis*)
   - Has similar sting, but alternating leaves (not opposite)
   - Edible when cooked, but stings more severely than Urtica dioica
   - Not toxic, just more aggressive
2. **Horse Nettle** (*Solanum carolinense*)
   - **TOXIC**, unrelated to true nettles
   - Has spiny stems, not stinging hairs
   - Leaves resemble nightshade, with lobes or ruffled edges
   - Produces small, tomato-like berries—**do not eat**

Note: Hedge Nettle (*Stachys bullata*) looks very similar but won't sting you. While both are edible, true stinging nettle is more medicinally valued.

Key Differences:

- Opposite, toothed leaves
- Stinging hairs
- Square stems
- No berries

Note: Harvest without touching the stinging hairs on the bottom sides of the leaves, using gloves, long pants, and a long-sleeved shirt if possible.

Cleaning

Rinse well under cold water to remove grit and bugs. Snap off and discard any brown, withered, or tough lower segments. Use fresh or dry completely for later herbal use.

Drying

Tie a string or piece of yarn around the base of the harvested plants. Hang in a sunny part of the house or pantry. Dry for 2–3 days until the leaves crush easily to a powder. Store in a glass jar in a cool, dry place. Once dried, you can encapsulate them for health use.

Freezing

You can freeze nettles in oil depending on your intended use. Options include:

- **Extra virgin olive oil** – A safe, all-purpose choice
- **Sunflower oil** – Light, hypoallergenic, great for sensitive skin
- **Jojoba oil** – Technically a wax, very stable and excellent for skincare
- **Coconut oil** – Antimicrobial and solid at room temp; may overpower scent

Chop pre-wilted nettles and freeze in an ice cube tray with oil. Thaw one cube at a time for salves, balms, or topical use on joints and muscles.

Flavor Profile

When cooked, nettle leaves lose their sting and become tender and earthy. The flavor is similar to spinach or green tea, with a nutty, mineral-rich finish. Excellent in soups, teas, pastas, and savory pastries.

Where to Buy

Fresh or dried nettles are available at farmers' markets, herbal apothecaries, or online shops specializing in wild herbs and teas.

Simple Nettle Tea Recipe

Makes: 1 cup

Time to Make: 10 minutes

Ingredients
- 1 cup **fresh nettle leaves** (or 1 Tbsp **dried nettle**)
- 2 cups **water**

Directions
Harvest safely using gloves (if using fresh). Rinse the nettles gently. Bring 2 cups of water to a boil.

1. **Remove** from heat and add nettles.
2. **Cover** and **steep for 10–15 minutes**.
3. **Strain** out the leaves.
4. **Serve** hot, or chill for iced tea.
5. **Optional Add-ins:**
6. A squeeze of **lemon**
- A drizzle of **honey**
- A slice of **ginger** or **mint leaves** for extra flavor

Note: Once steeped, the sting is completely neutralized.

Wild Rice & Nettle Soup (Campfire or Stovetop)

Makes: 4 servings
Time to Make: 1 hour

Ingredients
- ½ cup wild rice, rinsed
- 1 small onion, chopped
- 2 Tbsp wild chives, chopped
- 2 Tbsp olive oil or butter
- 2 medium potatoes, diced
- 4–5 cups vegetable or chicken broth
- 2 cups young nettle leaves (rinsed, stems removed – use gloves!)
- Salt and pepper, to taste

Optional: Splash of cream or dollop of sour cream

Directions
1. **Cook the wild rice:**
In a pot over the campfire (or at home ahead of time), simmer wild rice in 2 cups water for 30–40 minutes, or until the grains split and are tender. Drain and set aside.
2. **Sauté aromatics:**
In a large pot, heat oil or butter. Add chopped onion and garlic; sauté until translucent and fragrant.
3. **Add potatoes and broth:**
Stir in potatoes and pour in 3 cups of broth. Simmer for 10–15 minutes, until potatoes are fork-tender.
4. **Add nettles and wild rice:**
Carefully stir in nettles and pre-cooked wild rice. Simmer another 5 minutes, until nettles are wilted.
5. **Season and finish:**
Add salt and pepper to taste. Optional: stir in a splash of cream or top each bowl with a dollop of sour cream for richness.

Serving Tip:
Serve hot with my easy overnight fry bread recipe in a skillet.

Note: You can use frozen nettles in place of fresh. Just throw in a couple of ice cubes of them and omit the oil in the recipe, putting them in at the step that says to heat oil and add chopped onions.

TROUT

Trout are freshwater fish found in cold, clear streams, rivers, and lakes across North America and beyond. They're especially common in mountain-fed waters and can often be spotted in shaded pools or near underwater structures like rocks and fallen trees. Popular species include rainbow and brook, each known for their beauty, fight on the line, and delicious flavor.

Trout is also a highly nutritious fish, rich in lean protein, omega-3 fatty acids, and B vitamins—supporting heart health, brain function, and reducing inflammation. It's lower in mercury compared to many other fish, making it a great choice for regular consumption.

Whether you catch them fly-fishing in alpine creeks or bring them home from a sustainable fishery, trout offers a clean, earthy flavor that works well grilled, pan-seared, or smoked. See references for fishing guidebook information.

Photo by Stockcake

Did You Know?

Trout have taste buds not only in their mouths—but also on the outside of their bodies! This allows them to "taste" their environment as they swim, helping them detect food, predators, and even chemical changes in the water.

Gutting and Cleaning a Trout

1. Rinse the Trout:

Rinse under cold water to remove slime and debris. Pat dry with a paper towel if needed.

2. Remove the Head and Tail:

- Cut behind the gills at an angle to remove the head
- Make a second cut at the other end to remove the tail (optional)

3. Make the Belly Cut:

- Lay the trout on its side with the belly facing you
- Insert the knife into the anus (small hole near the tail)
- Slice upward toward the gills in a shallow cut to avoid puncturing the intestines

4. Remove the Guts:

- Open the belly cavity
- Grab the entrails near the head and pull them out in one smooth motion

5. Clean the Kidney:

- Locate the dark red/brown kidney line along the backbone
- Use your thumb or the back of a spoon to gently scrape it out

6. Final Rinse:

- Rinse the inside cavity thoroughly under cold water
- Use your thumb or a soft brush to remove any remaining blood or tissue

Flavor Profile

Trout has a delicate, slightly nutty flavor with a clean, mildly earthy finish and tender, flaky flesh.

Where to Buy/Substitutes

Fresh steelhead is (in my opinion) much better than trout and a good substitute. Check Asian markets or ocean-side markets.

Classic Campfire Foil-Baked Trout

As the name implies...this is about as classic and easy as it gets!

Makes: 3 servings
Time to Make: 20 minutes

Ingredients
- 3 trout, cleaned
- 1 Tbsp butter
- 1 Tbsp mayonnaise
- 1 Tbsp lemon juice
- 2 Tbsp Parmesan cheese
- 1 dash salt
- 2 cloves garlic, sliced

- Foil

Directions
1. **Place** the trout on a sheet of foil. Season the inside with salt and pepper.
2. **Mix** the butter, mayo, lemon juice, and Parmesan together in a small bowl (alternatively, mix this ahead of time).
3. **Stuff** the cavity with the butter mixture.
4. **Drizzle** with more oil. Wrap tightly in foil.
5. **Cook** over hot coals or on a campfire grate for 6–8 minutes per side, depending on the size of the fish.
6. **Unwrap carefully** and enjoy right out of the foil.

Pan-Fried Shore Lunch Trout

Easy lunch recipe in the field (or in this case, the river!) serve with foraged mushrooms and acorn Bannocks for a completely foraged meal.

Makes: 2 servings

Time to Make: 25 minutes

Ingredients
- 1–2 trout fillets
- Salt, pepper, and paprika
- ¼ cup cornmeal or flour
- Butter or oil

Directions
1. **Mix** cornmeal with salt, pepper, and paprika.
2. **Dredge** trout fillets in the mixture.
3. **Heat butter** or oil in a campfire-safe skillet.
4. **Fry** fillets skin-side down first, about 3–4 minutes per side or until golden and flaky.
5. **Serve** with lemon wedges or wild greens.

SALMON

Salmon may be one of the hardest but most rewarding fish to catch in the Pacific Northwest and beyond. If you are lucky enough to catch one (or several) I have included a quick guide to filleting them. Salmon is a flavorful, nutrient-rich fish packed with omega-3 fatty acids, high-quality protein, and essential vitamins that support heart health, brain function, and overall well-being.

Did you know?

Many Pacific Northwest tribes hold **First Salmon Ceremonies**, returning the bones of the season's first fish to the river in gratitude.

How to Fillet a Salmon

What You'll Need:
- Sharp fillet knife
- Cutting board or flat surface
- Clean towel or gloves for grip
- Fresh whole salmon

Filleting Instructions

1. Lay the Salmon Flat
- Place the fish on its side, backbone facing you.
- Make sure it's stable and not slipping.

2. Make the First Cut (Behind the Gills)
- Slice downward just behind the gill plate, at an angle toward the head, stopping when you hit the spine.

3. Cut Along the Backbone
- Turn your blade flat and run it along the spine toward the tail in a smooth, shallow motion.
- Keep the blade just above the backbone to remove the full side fillet.
- You may feel the ribs—glide over or through them, depending on your technique.

4. Remove the Second Fillet
- Flip the fish and repeat the same steps on the other side.

5. Trim and Clean
- Cut away the belly fat, rib bones, and any ragged edges.
- Use tweezers to remove pin bones (the fine bones running down the center of each fillet).

6. Skin the Fillet (Optional)
- If desired, place the fillet skin-down.
- Starting at the tail, slip the knife between skin and meat and gently work it toward the head, pulling the skin tight as you go.

Flavor Profile

Salmon has a rich, buttery, and mildly sweet flavor with a moist, meaty texture. Wild Pacific salmon (like Chinook or Sockeye) tend to have a deeper umami flavor and firmer texture, while farmed varieties are milder and fattier.

Texture: Silky, tender, and flaky

Taste Notes: Buttery, ocean-fresh, slightly sweet, and savory

Pairs Well With: Lemon, dill, garlic, soy sauce, maple, mustard, herbs, and smoke

Best Cooking Methods: Grilled, pan-seared, smoked, baked, poached

Where to Buy

Local fish markets. Asian markets. Directly from fishermen at the docks or near the ocean.

Salmon Teriyaki Bowl with Wild Rice

I created this because I was tired of eating salmon every week...
it tastes more like takeout Japanese food—with a wild twist!

Makes: 3 bowls
Time to Make: 45 minutes including rice cooking time

Ingredients
- 2 salmon fillets, sliced into bite-sized chunks, skin removed
- 1 yellow squash, sliced
- ½ head broccoli, sliced into bite sized pieces
- 1 cup wild rice, for serving

Teriyaki Sauce
- ¼ cup liquid aminos (can use soy sauce if needed)
- 2 Tbsp packed brown sugar
- 1 Tbsp honey
- 1 tsp fresh ginger, grated
- 2 garlic cloves, minced
- 2 Tbsp cornstarch
- ¼ cup cold water

Directions
1. **Cook the Wild Rice:**
   - Prepare 1 cup of wild rice according to package instructions (usually about 45–50 minutes simmer time).
   - Once cooked, set aside and keep warm.
2. **Make the Teriyaki Sauce:**
   - In a small saucepan, combine ¼ cup liquid aminos, 2 Tbsp brown sugar, 1 Tbsp honey, 1 tsp grated ginger, and 2 minced garlic cloves.
   - In a separate cup, mix 2 Tbsp cornstarch with ¼ cup cold water until smooth.
   - Stir the cornstarch slurry into the sauce mixture.
   - Heat over medium heat, stirring constantly until thickened. Remove from heat and set aside.
3. **Sauté Everything:**
   - In a large skillet or wok over medium-high heat, add a small drizzle of oil.
   - Add chunked salmon fillets, skin removed. Next, mix in the sliced yellow squash and broccoli florets; sauté everything for 4–6 minutes, or until tender-crisp and fish is flaky.

Mix Sauce into Vegetables:
   - Pour the teriyaki sauce over the salmon and stir gently to coat.
4. **Assemble the Bowls:**
   - Spoon wild rice into each bowl.
   - Top with sautéed vegetables and teriyaki-glazed salmon.

Optional: Garnish with sesame seeds, chopped green onions, or a squeeze of lime.

Lemon Balm Balsamic Glazed Spring Chinook with Roasted Brussels Sprouts

Bright, fresh, and deeply flavorful, this recipe celebrates the best of spring. Spring Chinook, known for its rich texture and buttery flavor, is paired with a tangy-sweet balsamic glaze infused with lemon balm—an herb that brings a light citrus note and calming aroma. Roasted Brussels sprouts add a hearty, caramelized crunch, making this dish both elegant and nourishing. Perfect for a wild-caught dinner that feels gourmet but comes together with ease.

Makes: 2 servings
Time to Make: 1 ½ hours

Ingredients

- 2 pieces salmon (½-fillet each)
- ¼ cup balsamic vinegar
- 1 tsp brown sugar
- 1 Tbsp chopped lemon balm, freshly harvested
- 1 dash salt
- 2 Tbsp olive oil
- 1/8 tsp xanthan gum
- 8-12 Brussels sprouts, cut in half and washed

Directions

Make the Balsamic Vinaigrette

1. **Mix** all vinaigrette ingredients together in a bowl.
2. **Stir** until the sugar is fully dissolved.
3. **Set aside** and let rest for at least 30 minutes (or up to a few hours) to develop flavor.

Prepare the Salmon & Vegetables

4. **Place** salmon fillets in a baking dish.
5. **Drizzle** glaze over the salmon to coat, reserving some for later.
6. **In a separate baking dish**, toss Brussels sprouts with more of the glaze.
7. **Reserve** a small amount of glaze to brush over the salmon after baking.

Bake

8. **Preheat** oven to 375°F.
9. **Bake** both the salmon and Brussels sprouts for about 30 minutes, or until:
   - The salmon flakes easily with a fork
   - The Brussels sprouts are tender and caramelized
10. **Brush** the reserved glaze over the hot salmon before serving.

Serve

11. **Plate** the salmon with roasted Brussels sprouts and a scoop of chive mashed potatoes.

Foraged Variation:
Swap Brussels sprouts for **fiddleheads**—toss in glaze and roast the same way!

Oven Baked Salmon with Alfredo Sauce

If you've never made Alfredo sauce from scratch, you may be feeling overwhelmed right now. Completely understandable, however, without merit. This Alfredo sauce has five ingredients and is SO easy to make that you could have your child cook dinner for you! I like to serve this with either spaghetti or brown rice, and a side vegetable.

Makes: 2 servings
Time to Make: 25 minutes

Baked Salmon:

Ingredients
- 2 pieces of salmon (whatever size piece is a normal serving, maybe around 4 oz)
- Butter or olive oil

Directions
1. **Preheat** your oven to 400°F.
2. **Heat** oil or butter in a cast iron skillet over medium heat until hot—but not smoking.
3. **Place** the salmon in the skillet, skin side down.
4. **Fry** for 1 minute, then **flip** and sear the other side briefly (about 30 seconds to 1 minute).
5. **Remove** the skillet from the stove and **transfer** it directly to the preheated oven.
6. **Bake** for about 10 minutes, or until the internal temperature reaches 145°F.
7. **Remove** from oven and **serve immediately**.

Fire Cooked Variation:
Wrap salmon pieces in foil and place into the edge of an established fire. Cook until they are steaming, around 10 minutes.

Alfredo Sauce:

Ingredients
- 3 garlic cloves (I buy mine frozen and pre-peeled)
- 2 Tbsp Butter
- 1 ½ cup Half 'n' Half or heavy cream
- 1 cup Parmesan cheese
- Salt, to taste, around ¼ tsp
- Garlic and herb spice (optional)

Directions
1. **Chop** your garlic cloves.
2. **Warm** butter in a saucepan over medium heat.
3. **Add** the chopped garlic to the butter and **sizzle** for about 1 minute.
4. **Reduce heat** to low.
5. **Pour in** the half and half and **stir** to combine.
6. **Simmer** gently for about 2 minutes.
7. **Turn off the heat** and **stir in** the Parmesan cheese until melted and smooth.
8. **Season** with salt and garlic spice, if desired.
9. **Spoon** over salmon, pasta, or vegetables and **serve warm**.

Traditional-Style Smoked Salmon or Steelhead (Inspired by Native American Methods)

This method reflects the wisdom of Indigenous salmon smoking in the Pacific Northwest—built on patience, simplicity, and deep respect for the natural world. Smoke was their preservative, and the flavor still connects us to the land today.

Ingredients
- Fresh wild salmon (fillets or split whole fish, skin on)
- Non-iodized salt
- Alder, maple, or apple wood (green if possible)

Optional: brown sugar or wild herbs like sage, yarrow, or spruce tips

Directions
1. **Light Salt Cure:**
   Rub salmon with **non-iodized salt**—about 1 Tbsp per pound of fish. You can also add a small amount of brown sugar or crushed wild herbs if desired.
   Place in a shallow dish or container and place into the cooler or refrigerator (if off grid, an ice house) and keep cool for **8–12 hours**. This draws out moisture and starts preservation.
2. **Rinse and Dry Briefly:**
   Rinse off excess salt and gently pat the salmon dry. Instead of air-drying outdoors, **lay the fish on a clean rack in the fridge** (or a screened, shaded, fly-proof area in cooler climates) for **1–2 hours** until the surface becomes tacky. This "pellicle" helps smoke cling to the fish.
3. **Build a Low Fire:**
   Use **alder or maple wood**, green if available, for a slow-burning, fragrant smoke. Keep the fire **low and smoky**, ideally around **140–160°F** for hot smoking. Avoid direct flames.
4. **Smoke the Salmon:**
   Place salmon skin-side down on a rack in a smoker or improvised smoke box.
   Smoke for **6 to 12 hours**, depending on thickness and your desired texture—longer for firmer, drier fish. You can continue cold-smoking at lower temps (90–110°F) for multiple sessions if you're preserving it.
5. **Eat or Store:**
   Eat warm or cooled. Refrigerate or vacuum-seal and freeze for longer storage. For more traditional preservation, dry it fully until leathery, then store in paper or canvas in a cool, dry space.

West Coast Salmon Fish & Chips

Few meals feel more "classic" than fish and chips, but on the West Coast we give it a wild twist. Instead of cod, salmon takes the spotlight—rich, flavorful, and perfectly suited to frying in a light batter. And for the chips, you can stick with potatoes or go full survivalist with cattail rhizomes, peeled and fried into rustic, chewy sticks. Either way, this is comfort food with a forager's edge.

Makes: 4 servings
Time to Make: 35 minutes

Ingredients

- 1 lb. salmon fillet, skin removed and cut into strips
- 1 cup flour, plus extra for dredging
- 1 tsp salt
- ½ tsp pepper
- 1 tsp baking powder
- 1 cup cold beer (or sparkling water for non-alcoholic)
- Oil or rendered fat, for frying

For the "chips":

- 2–3 large potatoes, cut into fries

or

- 3–4 cattail rhizomes, peeled, cleaned, and cut into sticks

Directions

1. **Prepare the cattail rhizomes or potatoes:** If using cattails, peel thoroughly to remove the tough outer skin, then slice into fry-length sticks. Potatoes can be cut and soaked in water for 30 minutes to remove starch. Drain and pat dry either option.
2. **Heat oil:** In a deep pan or cast iron pot, heat 2–3 inches of oil or fat to 350°F.
3. **Make the batter:** In a bowl, whisk together flour, salt, pepper, and baking powder. Add cold beer and stir until smooth.
4. **Cook the fries:** Fry cattail sticks or potato fries in batches for 5–6 minutes until golden. Drain on paper or cloth. Keep warm.
5. **Batter the salmon:** Lightly dredge salmon strips in flour, then dip into the batter until coated.
6. **Fry the salmon:** Place salmon into hot oil and fry 3–4 minutes until golden brown and crisp. Remove and drain.
7. **Serve:** Pile salmon and fries together on a platter.

Pro Tip: Cattail fries will be more fibrous than potatoes, but they crisp well and carry the batter's flavor. Serve hot with a wild tartar sauce or spruce tip vinegar. For survival cooking without deep frying, cattail sticks can also be pan-fried in a thin layer of oil until crisp.

SORREL

Oregon Oxalis or wood sorrel (*Oxalis oregana*) is a tasty wild green found throughout the Pacific Northwest. I love picking a few leaves of this while mushroom hunting, and savoring the lemony flavor as I hike. Sorrel is rich in vitamin C, antioxidants, and fiber, which support immune function, aid digestion, and help reduce inflammation. It also contains potassium and iron, making it a nutritious wild green for heart and blood health and a good addition to your table especially if you are living off the land!

Did You Know?

Wild sorrel (Oxalis spp.) contains natural oxalic acid, which gives it a tart, lemony flavor—but that same compound also inspired its historical use as a natural cleaning agent and rust remover! Early settlers and Indigenous peoples often used sorrel both as food and medicine—for cooling fevers and aiding digestion.

OREGON OXALIS
(OXALIS OREGANA)

LEAVES

Clover-like trifoliate leaves (3 heart-shaped leaflets), often with a slight fold or crease down the center. Light green to deep green.

FLOWERS

O. oregana: Delicate pale pink to lavender, 5-petalled flowers with pusple veins

O. stricta: Bright yellow flowers, also 5-petalled

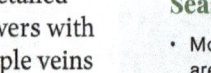

O. stricta

HEIGHT

Low-growing groundcover, usually 2-6 inches tall

2 – 6

TASTE/SMELL

Tangy, lemony flavor – instantly recognizable

Foraging Guide

Habitat

- Moist, shady forest floors, especially in coastal rainforests, under Douglas-fir, redwood, and hemlock
- Thrives in mossy, rich soil
- Grows best in partial to full shade, though some species tolerate dappled sun
- Found from lowland valleys to mid-elevation mountain forests in many temperate regions
- Widely found in the Pacific Northwest, across North America, Europe, and temperate parts of Asia

Season

- Most abundant in spring and early summer, though in moist areas it may grow well into fall

Toxic Look-Alikes and Cautions

1. **Creeping Buttercup** (*Ranunculus repens*):
   - Also grows in low clumps with yellow flowers, but leaves are deeply lobed, not heart-shaped
   - Toxic: Contains compounds that can irritate the digestive system and skin
2. **Shamrocks** (*Houseplants*):
   - Not typically found wild in Oregon, but look similar
   - Some species are mildly toxic if eaten in quantity

Key Test: Taste a small piece—oxalis has a bright, citrusy zing that's unmistakable. If it tastes bitter, bland, or unpleasant, don't eat it.

Safety Notes:

- Contains oxalic acid, the same compound in spinach and rhubarb
- Safe in small quantities for healthy individuals—best enjoyed as a trail nibble, salad accent, or garnish
- Avoid large amounts if you have kidney issues, gout, or are prone to kidney stones
- Always rotate foraged greens with other plant foods to minimize buildup of plant acids

Harvesting Tips

- Pinch or snip leaves at the base. Leave some to regrow
- Best gathered in the morning when leaves are crisp and cool
- Avoid leaves with spots or heavy bug damage

Cleaning

Rinse gently under cool water to remove forest debris. Soak briefly in water with a splash of vinegar if needed. Pat dry or spin in a salad spinner.

Storage

Wrap in a damp paper towel and store in a container or plastic bag in the refrigerator. Best if used within 2–3 days.

Freezing

Not recommended due to delicate consistency

Flavor Profile

- **Taste:** Bright, tangy, lemon-like sourness with a green, refreshing undertone
- **Aroma:** Light and grassy, with a hint of citrus when crushed
- **Texture:** Tender and delicate, melts on the tongue when fresh
- **Best Compared To:** A mix of lemon zest and green apple with a hint of spinach
- **Culinary Notes:** Perfect for garnishing salads, cooling summer soups, or balancing rich dishes like wild meats or creamy cheeses

Where to Buy/Substitutes

Arugula, spinach, or rhubarb are the closest commercially available plants to sorrel leaves

Vietnamese Pho with Wild Greens

This is a quick and easy version of traditional pho that only takes a few minutes to prepare. You can add any additional greens that you forage, in addition to the sorrel and chives. Pink purslane is a good wild plant that is often easily accessible to many foragers!

Makes: 3 bowls

Time to Make: 15 minutes

Ingredients

- 4 cups chicken broth (to make, boil chicken in water for 30 minutes, drain broth into a pan or bowl)
- 1–2 steaks, whatever cut you can afford, sliced very thinly (you can use venison or elk meat if you want this to be completely foraged!)
- ¼ cup fish sauce
- 1 Tbsp sugar
- 1 tsp salt
- Sorrel
- Wild chives or green onions
- Bean sprouts
- Basil
- Ginger, sliced
- 1 package rice noodles
- 1 lime, cut into rounds or wedges

Directions

1. **Add** fresh ginger slices to a pot of chicken broth.
2. **Stir in** fish sauce, sugar, and salt.
3. **Bring** the broth to a boil over medium-high heat.
4. **Add** rice noodles and **cook** for 3 minutes.
5. **Add** thinly sliced steak to the pot.
6. **Continue cooking** for another 4 minutes, or until the noodles are tender and the steak is cooked through.
7. **Squeeze** half a lime into the broth and **stir** to combine.
8. **Ladle** the hot soup into bowls.
9. **Top** with your choice of fresh herbs and greens, such as:
   - Fresh basil
   - Bean sprouts
   - Sorrel (*add at the last second to preserve color*)
   - Chives or green onions
   - Dandelion greens or other foraged greens
10. **Serve** with additional lime wedges on the side.

LOBSTER MUSHROOMS

Lobster mushrooms (*Hypomyces lactifluorum*) are a prized wild edible commonly found in late summer to early fall in coniferous and mixed forests across the Pacific Northwest, Northern California, the Rocky Mountains, and parts of the Northeastern U.S. and Canada. These mushrooms are a good source of antioxidants, fiber, and minerals like potassium and copper, supporting immune health and digestion when properly cooked and identified. While they aren't my personal favorite, I can't resist a good plate of lobster and venison stroganoff—especially when it's cooked over the camp stove while at fall salmon camp!

Did you know?

Lobster mushrooms aren't a species—they're a mold that transforms another mushroom into this bright, seafood-scented delicacy.

LOBSTER MUSHROOMS
(Hypomyces lactifluorum)

Color: Bright reddish-orange to burnt orange on the outside — often resembles cooked lobster shell.

Shape: Twisted, irregular, often lumpy or misshapen due to the host mushroom's distortion.

Surface: Dry, rough, sometimes pitted or cracked.

Interior Flesh: White, dense, and firm (not hollow or spongy)

Smell: Distinct seafood or crustacean-like aroma, especially when fresh

Foraging Guide

Habitat

- Grows in coniferous or mixed forests with fir, hemlock, and pine
- Found on the forest floor, often buried partially under duff or moss
- Usually solitary or in small groups—not clusters
- More common at sea level, in foothills and mountain forests
- Check for them as early as July along the coast in the Pacific Northwest

Tip: Check around the base of live or dying conifers. Look for orange "bumps" poking through moss and leaf litter.

Season

- Late summer to fall (typically August–October, after rains)

Toxic Look-Alikes and Cautions

1. **Jack-O'-Lantern Mushroom** *(Omphalotus spp.)*
   - Toxic
   - Glows faintly in the dark
   - Grows in clusters on wood
   - Sharp, non-forking gills—unlike lobster mushrooms, which often lack visible gills
2. **Moldy Lobsters**
   - Older specimens may grow white or gray mold
   - Avoid mushrooms that are soft, slimy, discolored, or have a fishy odor

General Rule: Only harvest firm, clean, orange specimens with a fresh scent and white flesh inside. Always cut them open to check for insects or rot.

Cleaning

Use a dry brush or knife to remove dirt and debris. Wipe clean—avoid soaking, as they absorb water easily. Slice open to check for bugs or internal browning.

Storage

Store in a paper bag in the fridge for up to 5 days.
Note: Mushrooms need to breathe—paper allows for air circulation and prevents spoilage. Never store wet mushrooms in plastic.

Drying

Follow drying instructions in the **Chanterelle** section for best results.

Freezing

Sauté first, then freeze in airtight containers or vacuum-sealed bags.

Flavor Profile

- **Taste:** Mild, nutty, and earthy with a hint of seafood or umami richness
- **Aroma:** Reminiscent of cooked lobster, shrimp stock, or shellfish bisque when fresh or sautéed
- **Texture:** Dense, meaty, with a pleasant chew—holds up well to cooking
- **Best Compared To:** A combination of firm tofu, shellfish, and porcini mushrooms
- **Culinary Uses:** Ideal for bisques, chowders, stir-fries, or as a wild mushroom substitute in seafood dishes

Where to Buy

You can often find lobster mushrooms at farmers markets during the season or from local foragers through Facebook Marketplace or wild mushroom groups.

Vegetable Barley Soup with Lobster Mushrooms and Wild Chives

This soup recipe will always bring me back to winter time as an 8-year-old, growing up in the Washington Cascade Range, surrounded by fir and maple trees. My mother's cooking will always be a pleasant memory from my childhood. She had a way of making comfort food, extra comforting. The dishes she made were simple yet delicious, warm and hearty. She often made this soup on cold, rainy days in mid-winter when the only thing we had to look forward to was a far-off spring time (which included more rain by the way), and of course her cooking! This is a great recipe for an off-grid type living situation as everything in it can be grown or harvested (and the barley is shelf stable).

Time to Make: 2 hours
Serves: 10-12 (freezes well!)

Ingredients

- ½ onion, chopped
- 3 carrots, diced
- 2 stalks celery, diced
- 2 parsnips or turnips, diced
- ¾ cup olive oil
- 2 quarts hot vegetable stock or hot water
- 1 cup whole barley
- 2 tsp salt
- 1/8 tsp pepper
- ½ tsp marjoram
- ½ tsp thyme
- If making a big batch to freeze, omit following items and add only to the portion you want to serve immediately:
- 2 Tbsp chopped parsley
- ¼ cup dried lobster mushrooms, chopped
- ½ cup chard or kale
- ½ cup wild chives, chopped
- Cheddar cheese, cut into squares, for garnish (optional)

Directions

1. **Cook** onions, carrots, celery, and any other desired vegetables in oil in a large pot.
   Cover the pot and cook over medium heat for about 10 minutes, stirring occasionally.
2. **Add** stock and **bring to a boil**.
3. **Stir in** the barley and **bring to a boil** again.
4. **Cover**, reduce heat to low, and **simmer** for about 45 minutes.
5. **Add** your desired seasonings (such as salt, pepper, thyme, or bay leaf).
6. **Continue simmering** for another 35 minutes.
7. **Add** dried lobster mushrooms and **simmer** for an additional 10 minutes.
8. **Chop** kale and **stir it in**.
9. **Cook** for another 10 minutes, or until the kale reaches your preferred doneness.
   For more nutrients, cook the kale for a shorter time.
10. **Serve** hot and **garnish** each bowl with:
    - Fresh chopped parsley
    - Chopped green onions
    - Generous chunks of sharp cheddar cheese

Lobster mushroom stroganoff

This is a delicious and easy way to introduce people to wild mushrooms if they are skeptics regarding foraged foods. It is one of the only ways that I personally will eat lobster mushrooms.

Makes: 4 servings
Time to Make: 35 minutes

Ingredients

- 1 lb steak, sliced into 2" strips (can use venison or elk, or even ground beef or venison!)
- 1 onion, chopped
- 2 garlic cloves, minced
- 1 large lobster mushroom, cleaned and sliced thinly (bite sized)
- 1 tsp thyme
- 1 tsp salt, or to taste
- 1 cup sour cream
- Pasta, for serving

Directions

1. **Heat** a cast iron skillet over medium-high heat.
2. **Add** steak, onions, and garlic to the skillet.
3. **Fry** for about 4 minutes, until the steak is browned and the onions are soft.
4. **Add** chopped lobster mushrooms and fresh thyme.
5. **Cook** for 5–10 minutes, depending on the moisture content of the mushrooms:
   Early-season mushrooms are often dry and cook faster. Rain-soaked fall mushrooms will release more water and take longer to cook down.
6. **Continue cooking** until all the water has evaporated and the mushrooms are fully cooked.
7. **Stir in** sour cream and heat just until everything is hot—Do not boil.
8. **Remove from heat** and **season** with salt to taste.
9. **Serve immediately** over al dente pasta.

Lobster Mushroom Vegetable Sauté

Serves: 2
Time to Make: 15 minutes

Ingredients

- Bacon fat or 2 Tbsp olive oil
- 1 large lobster mushroom, cleaned, sliced (can use dried and rehydrated)
- ½ purple onion, sliced thinly
- ½ summer squash, sliced thinly
- 2 cherry tomatoes, sliced
- 1 cup spinach
- 3 sprigs basil, leaves only, washed
- Salt, to taste
- Parmesan cheese, to taste

Directions

1. **Heat** olive oil in a cast iron skillet over medium heat.
2. **Add** lobster mushrooms, chopped onion, and sliced summer squash.
3. **Sauté** for about 5 minutes, stirring frequently to prevent sticking.
4. **Stir in** spinach and fresh basil.
5. **Cook** until the greens are wilted.
6. **Sprinkle** with salt and Parmesan cheese to taste.
7. **Serve** warm over pasta, on burgers, or as a side dish.

Optional Omelet Variation

8. **Whisk** 4 eggs in a bowl.
9. **Pour** over the cooked vegetables in the skillet.
10. **Stir gently** for about 1 minute, then **cook** until the eggs are fully set.
11. **Remove from heat** and serve immediately.

End of Summer Salmon Lobster Garden Pasta

This is an easy thrown together style meal that exemplifies not only the wild foraged harvest available in the PNW, but also combines ingredients harvested from a traditional vegetable garden!

Makes: 7 servings
Time to Make: 35 minutes

Ingredients

- 15 oz salmon (one can if not using fresh)
- 1 zucchini, thickly sliced
- 1 cup green pepper, chopped
- ½ white onion, chopped
- ½ cup wild chives, thinly sliced
- 1 clove garlic, minced
- 2 Tbsp olive oil
- 2 large lobster mushrooms, brushed, cleaned, and sliced
- 2 tsp fresh basil leaves
- ¼ cup parsley, chopped
- 14 oz cooked fettuccine, drained
- 1 cup heavy cream
- Salt and pepper

Directions

1. **Roast** salmon in the oven at 400°F for 15 minutes, or until flaky.
   If using canned salmon, skip this step.
2. **Break** the salmon into chunks and set aside.
3. **Sauté** lobster mushrooms in a skillet over medium heat for about 5 minutes, until their moisture has evaporated.
4. **Add** olive oil, then stir in zucchini, green pepper, onion, and garlic.
5. **Sauté** for about 3 minutes, until vegetables are crisp-tender.
6. **Add** the salmon chunks, along with chopped parsley, basil, and salt and pepper to taste.
7. **Heat thoroughly,** stirring gently to combine.
8. **Pour in** cream and stir to coat.
9. **Toss with cooked pasta** or **serve over pasta**, topped with grated cheese.

Vegetarian Variation

Use a spiralizer or pasta maker to turn zucchini into veggie "pasta."

Sauté briefly, then serve with the sauce for a light, low-carb version.

Lobster and Artichoke-Spinach Dip

If you dry or freeze some lobster mushrooms in the late summer, you can pull them out of the freezer to make this easy snacking dip anytime! The only thing better than a good dip for tortilla chips—a foraged dip!

Makes: 4 servings
Time to Make: 35 minutes

Ingredients

- 4 oz artichoke hearts, canned
- 4 oz cream cheese
- 1 clove garlic, minced
- One lobster mushroom (about ½ cup uncooked, fresh mushroom) *
- 1 ½ cup spinach
- ½ cup sour cream
- ¾ cup grated Parmesan cheese, plus more for sprinkling over the top

Directions

* Substituting dried mushrooms is fine; soak in water for 5-15 minutes before using.

1. **Chop** lobster mushrooms into small pieces.
2. **Chop** spinach (or your foraged greens).
3. **In a skillet**, combine lobster mushrooms, spinach, and garlic.
4. **Cook** over medium heat for about 5 minutes, until the spinach wilts and the mushrooms release their juices.
5. **Add** artichokes and cream cheese.
6. **Turn off the heat** and stir until the cream cheese softens and blends in.
7. **Stir in** sour cream and grated Parmesan cheese.
8. **Transfer** the mixture to a small baking dish.
9. **Bake** at 375°F for 15 minutes, or until bubbling.
10. **Serve** warm with chips, crackers, or pita bread.

Foraged Variation

Swap spinach for fresh **nettles** or **sorrel** for a wild twist.

ROCKFISH

Rockfish are an assorted group of marine fish commonly found along the Pacific Coast of North America, from California up through Alaska, thriving around rocky reefs and kelp forests. Known for their firm texture and mild flavor, rockfish are a popular catch among anglers and commercial fisheries alike. Nutritionally, rockfish offer a lean source of high-quality protein and are rich in omega-3 fatty acids, which support heart health and brain function among other things.

Rockfish Cleaning Guide

Step 1: Rinse the Fish
Rinse the rockfish under cold water to remove any slime and debris.

Step 2: Make the First Cut
Lay the fish flat. Cut behind the gills down to the spine using a sharp fillet knife.

Step 3: Fillet Along the Backbone
Turn the knife and run it along the backbone toward the tail, slicing cleanly to remove the fillet.

Step 4: Repeat on the Other Side
Flip the fish and repeat the same motion to remove the second fillet.

Step 5: Trim and Skin (Optional)
Remove the rib bones and skin if desired, depending on your preferred cooking method.

Flavor Profile

Rockfish has a mild, sweet, and slightly nutty flavor, making it extremely versatile and appealing even to those who aren't big fish lovers. The flesh is white, flaky, and lean, holding up well to frying, baking, and grilling.

Did You Know?

Along the Pacific Northwest coast, Indigenous peoples like the Tlingit, Haida, and Salish have long harvested rockfish using hook-and-line fishing from canoes. Rockfish were often smoked or dried for winter storage and used in feasts and potlatches. Their bones and spines were sometimes repurposed as tools or ornaments.

Kombucha Battered Rockfish with Homemade Tartar Sauce

This recipe will beat anything you could order from a bar or oceanside diner, by a long shot!

Makes: 4 servings
Time to Make: 25 minutes

Ingredients
- 2 rockfish fillets, cleaned and cut in half lengthwise
- 2 cups vegetable oil, for frying
- ¾ cup flour
- 1 Tbsp Parmesan cheese
- ½ tsp salt
- ½ tsp paprika
- 1 tsp garlic powder
- ¼ tsp pepper (optional)
- 1 egg, beaten
- ½ can (12 oz) Kombucha

Directions

Prepare the Oil
1. **Heat** oil in a deep pan or pot until it reaches about 350°F.

If you don't have a thermometer, test by flicking a drop of water into the oil—if it sizzles, it's ready.

Make the Batter
2. **Mix** flour and seasonings together in a bowl.
3. **Add** the beaten egg to the flour mixture.
4. **Quickly whisk in** kombucha just until the batter is smooth—do not overmix.

Fry the Fish
5. **Dip** rockfish fillets into the batter, coating well.
6. **Carefully place** fillets into the hot oil.
7. **Fry** for about 4 minutes on the first side.
8. **Flip** the fillets and fry for another 4 minutes, or 1 minute longer for extra crispiness.
9. **Remove** from the oil and **drain** on paper towels.

Serve
10. **Plate** with homemade tartar sauce, fries, coleslaw, or homemade sauerkraut.

Over-the-Fire Tip
- **Control the heat** by letting the fire burn down or placing your pot to the side if it's too hot.
- **Use a deep-frying basket** or long-handled tongs to safely lower and remove fish without splashing or breaking them.

Tartar Sauce

Ingredients
- 1 Tbsp sweet relish
- 1 Tbsp lemon juice
- 1/3 cup mayonnaise
- 2 Tbsp sour cream
- ½ tsp yellow mustard
- ½ tsp dill weed, optional

Directions
1. **Mix** all ingredients together in a jar.
2. **Chill** at least an hour before serving for optimal flavor.

Pickled Rockfish with Wild Lobster Mushrooms

I recently learned how to make my own sauerkraut after studying about the health benefits related to pickling and fermenting. I decided to do some research and find out how to safely pickle fish; while I was at it, I threw in some lobster mushrooms! If you like pickled mushrooms, but want some seafood flavor, this recipe is great! You could also add an optional seaweed component.

Makes 8-pint jars
Time to Make: 1-2 days

Ingredients

- 1 lb rockfish fillets, par-frozen and cut into 1-inch chunks
- 1 cup fresh lobster mushrooms, cleaned, sliced into bite-sized pieces
- 1 ½ cups white vinegar (5% acidity)
- ½ cup water
- ¼ cup granulated sugar
- 2 Tbsp sea salt
- 1 small red onion, thinly sliced
- 2 garlic cloves, smashed
- 1 tsp mustard seeds
- 1 tsp black peppercorns
- ½ tsp crushed red pepper (optional)
- 2 bay leaves

Optional: fresh dill, fennel fronds, or spruce tips for flavor nuance

Preparing the Mushrooms:

1. **Clean thoroughly:**
   Use a soft brush or damp towel to clean lobster mushrooms. Trim off dirty or tough ends.
2. **Blanch to preserve texture and safety:**
   Bring a pot of lightly salted water to a boil. Blanch the sliced lobster mushrooms for 2–3 minutes. Drain and let cool before adding to the jars.

Directions

1. **Salt-cure fish:**
   Toss rockfish chunks with 1 Tbsp salt and refrigerate for 1–2 hours. Rinse gently and pat dry.
2. **Make the brine:**
   In a saucepan, combine vinegar, water, sugar, and remaining salt with garlic, mustard seeds, peppercorns, red pepper, and bay leaves. Bring to a boil, then let cool fully.
3. **Pack jars:**
   Layer rockfish, lobster mushrooms, and onion slices in clean pint jars. Add herbs like dill or spruce tips if using.
4. **Add brine:**
   Pour cooled brine over ingredients to fully submerge. Tap jars gently to release air bubbles and seal.
5. **Refrigerate:**
   Let sit in the fridge for at least 48 hours. Flavors deepen over 3–5 days. Eat within 10–14 days for best texture and safety.

Bonus Tips:

- Add a few slices of raw jalapeño or horseradish if you want heat.
- Serve chilled with crusty bread, pickled greens, or as part of a camp-style charcuterie board.

Optional Add on:

Edible PNW Seaweeds You Can Add to Pickled Rockfish:

1. Bladderwrack (*Fucus distichus*)

- **Flavor:** Mildly salty, slightly briny.
- **Texture:** Chewy but tender after a quick blanch.
- **Use:** Slice into strips and blanch briefly before adding to the jar.
- **Health benefits:** High in iodine, calcium, and antioxidants.

2. Sea Lettuce (*Ulva spp.*)

- **Flavor:** Light, grassy, oceanic.
- **Texture:** Soft and delicate.
- **Use:** No blanching needed if used fresh and clean. Tear into small pieces.
- **Health benefits:** Rich in protein, iron, and vitamins A and C.

3. Sugar Kelp (*Saccharina latissima*)

- **Flavor:** Slightly sweet and umami-rich.
- **Texture:** Silky and firm when blanched.
- **Use:** Cut into thin ribbons and blanch for 1–2 minutes before pickling.
- **Health benefits:** Excellent source of iodine, magnesium, and fiber.

Note:

- Only harvest **in clean, non-industrial waters** and **below the high tide line**.
- Avoid **blue-green algae lookalikes** or heavily fouled seaweed.
- Always harvest sustainably—cut, don't rip, and take only what you need.

How to Add Seaweed to Pickled Rockfish:

- **Blanch** firmer seaweeds like kelp or bladderwrack in boiling water for 1–2 minutes.
- **Drain,** cool, and add to jars in thin strips or chopped pieces.
- **Layer with fish,** mushrooms, and onions before adding the brine.

The seaweed will infuse the brine with minerals and a subtle oceanic depth, while also soaking up the vinegar flavors for a nutrient-packed addition.

Off Grid Rockfish Ramen

A shelf-stable, wild-crafted noodle soup featuring dehydrated rockfish for protein and umami-packed broth—perfect for backcountry cooking.

Makes: 3 packets
Time to Make: 15 minutes (putting it together) and 1 day for dehydrating fish

Ingredients
- 1 small fillet rockfish (about 4 oz), cooked and dehydrated
- 1 Tbsp soy sauce powder or sea salt
- 1 tsp dried garlic
- 1 tsp dried wild mushrooms (optional)
- 1 tsp dried wild chives or green onion
- Pinch of dried seaweed (kelp or nori, optional)

Optional: Crushed dried chili, powdered ginger

Directions

1. Cook & Dry the Fish:
- Bake, pan-fry, or steam your rockfish fillet until fully cooked.
- Remove all bones and skin.
- Break it into small flakes and dehydrate at a low temp (125–135°F) for several hours until brittle and dry.

2. Grind Into Powder:
- Use a mortar & pestle or a clean spice/coffee grinder.
- Pulse into a fine powder (or leave it coarser for texture).

Mix
1. Mix fish powder with remaining dried seasonings.
2. Store in a sealed wax wrap, pouch, or mini jar—this is your flavor packet. To make individual packets, divide into 1 ½ Tbsp individual servings.

Great for trail meals, bug-out kits, or cooking over a fire with minimal gear.

Noodle Assembly (At Camp or Off Grid)

What You'll Need:
- 2–3 cups water
- 1 serving ramen noodles (store-bought dry or homemade)
- 1 rockfish flavor packet with rockfish powder

To Prepare:
1. Bring water to a boil over fire or camp stove.
2. Add noodles and cook until soft.
3. Stir in your rockfish flavor packet. Let simmer 1–2 minutes to dissolve and infuse.
4. Serve hot with optional wild greens, dried veggies, or poached egg.

Foraged Variation: Add dried seaweed to each packet or crush and add to flavor packet.

Clay-Baked Rockfish

Baking fish in clay is one of the oldest cooking techniques in the world. The clay seals in moisture, steams the fish inside, and hardens into a crust that peels the skin away when cracked open. In Oregon, riverbank or creek-bed clay works best, but any dense, sticky clay that holds together when pressed can be used.

Makes: 2–3 servings
Time to Make: 1 hour (plus clay gathering if in the wild)

Ingredients
- 1 whole rockfish (about 2 lbs), cleaned and scaled
- 1 handful wild herbs (spruce tips, yarrow, wild onion, or nettle tops)
- 1 tsp salt
- ½ tsp pepper
- Fresh clay from riverbank or creek bed (enough to fully encase the fish, about 2–3 cups)

Directions
1. **Prepare the clay:** Gather dense, sticky clay. Remove pebbles or debris. Mix with a little water if needed until it forms a smooth, pliable paste.
2. **Season the fish:** Rub salt and pepper inside and out. Stuff the cavity with wild herbs.
3. **Wrap in clay:** Pat clay around the entire fish in a thick layer, at least ½ inch, sealing edges well.
4. **Build fire bed:** Create a bed of hot coals in a firepit. Place the clay-wrapped fish directly onto the coals. Shovel additional coals over the top.
5. **Bake:** Cook for 30–40 minutes, depending on fish size. The clay will harden and may crack slightly.
6. **Unwrap:** Use a stick or rock to break the clay shell. The skin will peel away with the clay, leaving tender, aromatic fish beneath.
7. **Serve:** Pull chunks of fish straight from the bone and enjoy hot.

Pro Tip
- Firmer clays from riverbanks seal better and peel away more cleanly.
- This same method works with salmon, trout, or other whole fish.
- If the clay is crumbly, mix in a bit of ash or sand to help it bind.

WILD STRAWBERRIES

Wild strawberries (*Fragaria vesca* and *Fragaria virginiana*) are a beloved wild edible found across North America, Europe, and parts of Asia, often thriving in sunny meadows, forest edges, and disturbed soil. Though much smaller than cultivated varieties, their intense, concentrated sweetness makes them a prized seasonal treat for foragers. These tiny berries are rich in vitamin C, antioxidants, and fiber, supporting immune health, skin regeneration, and digestion. Their leaves also have a long history in traditional herbal medicine for soothing sore throats and aiding inflammation.

Did you know?

According to Native legend, wild strawberries were the **first fruit**, symbolizing peace and the healing of broken relationships.

Wild Strawberry
Identification Guide

Fragaria vesca (also Fragaria virginiana)

Key Features:

Leaves: Three leaflets with toothed edges; bright green; slightly fuzzy; grow in a rosette

Flowers: Small white five-petaled flowers with yellow centers (bloom in spring)

Fruit: Tiny red berries (¼–½ inch), cone-shaped, with seeds on the outside

Aroma: Sweet, unmistakably strawberry-like when crushed

Pro Tip: If it looks like a miniature version of a store-bought strawberry and smells sweet, it's likely the real thing.

Foraging Guide

Habitat

- Open woodlands and forest edges
- Grassy meadows and fields
- Hillsides and road embankments
- Garden edges and trails
- Low elevation mountain regions

Wild strawberries prefer moist, well-drained soil and partial sun. They spread by runners and often form small colonies in undisturbed areas. Look low to the ground for their characteristic three-part leaves and tiny red fruit.

Season

- Late May through early July

Toxic Look-Alikes and Cautions

- **Mock Strawberry** (*Duchesnea indica*):
  – Looks similar but has yellow flowers (not white)
  – Fruit sits upright rather than drooping
  – Not toxic, but bland and mealy

Safety Note: Avoid areas near heavy pesticide use or polluted roadsides. Always rinse berries thoroughly before eating.

Cleaning

Place berries in a colander and rinse gently under cool water. Because they're small and delicate, avoid vigorous handling. Pat dry with a paper towel or air dry on a clean cloth.

Storage

Wild strawberries are highly perishable and best eaten fresh. Store unwashed in a breathable container in the refrigerator for 1–2 days. For longer storage, freeze or dry.

Freezing

Lay berries in a single layer on a parchment-lined baking sheet. Freeze for 3–4 hours until solid. Transfer to a labeled freezer bag. Frozen wild strawberries will keep up to a year and are excellent in smoothies or sauces.

Flavor Profile

Tiny but intensely flavorful, wild strawberries offer a sweet, floral burst with notes of rose, honey, and tart apple. They're juicier and more aromatic than cultivated strawberries, making them a prized treat in desserts, jams, or eaten straight off the vine.

Where to Buy/Substitutes

Wild strawberries are rarely available in grocery stores due to their fragile nature and short shelf life. Your best chance is to forage them yourself or visit a specialty market or farmers' market during their short growing season. Some local farms grow alpine or wild varieties that can be purchased fresh or as starter plants for your garden.

Strawberry Protein Pancakes with Whipped Cream

I created this as a way to have a nutritionally balanced meal, while still enjoying the sweetness of pancakes. Due to the added collagen, your hair, skin, and nails enjoy a boost too! You can easily mix the dry ingredients in advance for easy preparation at camp or as a nutrition packed pancake mix that is shelf stable.

Makes: 3-4 pancakes
Time to Make: 15 minutes

Ingredients

- ¼ cup + 2 Tbsp all-purpose (or wild foraged) flour
- ¼ cup Vital Protein Collagen Powder
- 1 tsp granulated sugar
- 1 Tbsp melted butter
- 1 egg
- ¼ cup milk
- 1½ tsp baking powder
- 1/8 tsp salt
- 1 tsp vanilla extract
- ½ cup whipped cream
- 1 Tbsp agave nectar
- 1 tsp vanilla extract
- 1 cup freshly picked wild strawberries (or farmers market or homegrown as in this picture)

Directions

Make the Pancake Batter

1. **In a bowl**, combine:
   - ← flours
   - ○ Baking powder
   - ○ Salt
   - ○ Sugar
   - ○ Protein powder

   Mix well.
2. **Make a well** in the center of the dry ingredients.
3. **Add** milk, melted butter, and vanilla extract to the well.
4. **Crack in** the egg.
5. **Beat the egg**, then mix everything together until well combined.

Cook the Pancakes

6. **Heat** a cast iron skillet over low to medium heat.
7. **Add butter** to the skillet and tilt the pan to coat the bottom evenly.
8. **Pour** about ¼ cup of batter onto the skillet for each pancake.
9. **Cook** until bubbles form across the surface but before it begins to smoke.
   Gluten-free pancakes need slightly more time before flipping to avoid breakage.
10. **Flip** and cook for an additional 30 seconds to 1 minute, until golden and cooked through.

Make the Whipped Cream Topping

Option 1: Blender or Mixer Method

1. **Add** whipping cream to a blender or stand mixer.
2. **Blend** on medium speed for 1–2 minutes, or until it becomes too thick to blend.
3. **Add** agave nectar and vanilla.
4. **Blend briefly**, just until mixed—do not overwhip.

Option 2: Off Grid Jar Method

1. **Pour** cold whipping cream into a **chilled jar** with a tight-fitting lid.
2. **Add** a little sugar and vanilla.
3. **Shake** vigorously for 5–7 minutes, checking every minute or two.
4. **Stop shaking** once soft peaks form.

Pro Tip: I started making whipped cream this way at age 12—if a kid can do it, so can you!

Serve

5. **Top** warm pancakes with fresh whipped cream and sliced strawberries.
6. **Enjoy** your hearty, protein-rich breakfast—whether at home or off grid!

Wild Strawberry Ice Cream

While many of the recipes in here are geared towards off grid type situations, I have several different ice-cream recipes featuring a traditional ice cream maker. However, one way to remedy that is to get an old-fashioned hand crank ice cream maker. Another option is the shaking method. See bonus section at the end for an ice cream making method that involves only ice, a bag, and a strong arm!

Makes: 8 cups
Time to Make: 2 hours

Ingredients
- 3 cups heavy cream
- 3 cups whole milk
- 1 1/3 cup sugar (may need less if strawberries are really sweet and ripe)
- 1/8 tsp salt
- 1½ Tbsp vanilla extract
- 2 cups fresh wild strawberries

Directions
1. **Combine** cream, milk, sugar, and a pinch of salt in the ice cream maker's canister.
2. **Stir** with a wooden spoon until the sugar is fully dissolved.
3. **In a food processor**, pulse strawberries until chopped but not fully pureed—leave some texture.
4. **Add** the strawberries and vanilla extract to the cream mixture and stir to combine.
5. **Place** the canister into your ice cream maker.
6. **Layer** ice and rock salt around the outside of the canister, following your machine's guidelines.
7. **Plug in** the ice cream maker and **churn** according to the manufacturer's instructions, usually about 20–40 minutes.
8. **Serve immediately** for soft-serve texture, or **freeze** for firmer scoops.

Strawberry Lemon Frozen Yogurt

This is not only delicious, but high protein and high collagen,
with 20 grams collagen and 25 grams protein!

Makes: 1 serving
Time to Make: 5 minutes

Ingredients
- ¼ cup Vital Protein Lemon Collagen Powder
- 1 cup Wild or locally grown strawberries, frozen
- ¼ cup Zoi Strawberry Greek Yogurt
- 1/3 cup milk
- ½ tsp vanilla Extract

Directions
1. **Put frozen** strawberries into blender.
2. **Add** in the protein powder, Greek yogurt, milk, and vanilla extract.
3. **Blend** till it becomes a thick frozen yogurt like consistency.
4. **Serve** immediately.

Wild Strawberry and Lemon Crumble

This is the perfect summer treat to make and share with family—whether you foraged your berries or got them from a U-pick!

Makes: 8" x 8" pan
Time to Make: 35 minutes

Ingredients

Strawberry Filling
- 2 cups strawberries, washed
- ½ cup granulated sugar
- 4 Tbsp cornstarch
- ¼ cup lemon juice
- 1 Tbsp Lemon zest
- 1 dash salt

Crust
- 1 cup flour
- ¼ tsp salt
- 1 tsp baking soda
- ¼ cup granulated sugar
- 1/3 cup butter
- 1 Tbsp milk
- **Topping**
- ¾ cup rolled oats
- ½ cup granulated sugar
- 1/3 cup butter
- ¼ tsp salt
- 2 Tbsp flour

Directions

Make the Strawberry Filling
1. **Combine** washed strawberries, sugar, and water in a saucepan.
2. **Bring** to a low simmer over medium-low heat and **simmer** for about 5 minutes.
3. **In a separate bowl**, mix sugar, cornstarch, and lemon juice.
4. **Slowly add** the cornstarch mixture to the simmering strawberries, stirring constantly.
5. **Cook** until the mixture thickens—this should happen almost instantly.
6. **Add** lemon zest, then **remove from heat** and set aside.

Prepare the Crust
7. **In a bowl**, mix flour, salt, sugar, and baking soda.
8. **Cut in** butter using a pastry cutter or your hands, mixing until a soft, pliable, and sticky dough forms.
9. **Press** the dough evenly into the bottom of an 8x8-inch glass baking dish.

Make the Topping
10. **In another bowl**, combine sugar, rolled oats, and salt.
11. **Cut in** butter and mix until small crumbles or balls form. Set aside.

Assemble and Bake
12. **Preheat** oven to 375°F.
13. **Spread** the strawberry filling evenly over the prepared crust.
14. **Sprinkle** the crumble topping over the filling by hand.
15. **Bake** in the preheated oven for about 25 minutes, or until the strawberry filling is bubbling and the topping is golden brown.

STEELHEAD TROUT

Steelhead are a sea-run form of rainbow trout, native to North America's West Coast, especially abundant in the Pacific Northwest, Alaska, and along rivers from California to British Columbia. Unlike rainbow trout, steelhead migrate between freshwater and the ocean, developing firmer, richer flesh and a more complex flavor profile.

This prized fish is rich in lean protein, omega-3 fatty acids, and vitamin D, supporting heart health, brain function, and anti-inflammatory processes. Wild-caught steelhead is a nutrient-dense food that fuels endurance and recovery—ideal for those living close to the land or eating for strength. See reference guide at the end of this book for information on related fishing guidebooks. See salmon section for a detailed fillet guide.

Flavor Profile

Steelhead trout has a flavor and texture that's somewhere between salmon and rainbow trout. It's mild, clean, and slightly sweet, with a soft, flaky texture and a subtle richness from its moderate fat content.

Where to Buy

Grocery stores like Safeway sometimes have steelhead in the frozen section. Check docks or oceanside markets specifically in the winter.

Did You Know?

In many Indigenous cultures of the Pacific Northwest, steelhead symbolize strength, perseverance, and renewal. Their epic upstream migrations—often against harsh currents and through treacherous terrain—are seen as a metaphor for overcoming adversity and returning to one's true purpose. Traditionally, their arrival signaled a time of abundance and connection to ancestral lands and waterways.

Summer Steelhead with Pico De Gallo

This is a light, easy way to prepare summer steelhead—catch them, fillet them, and prepare this on the river—as an early morning breakfast, or as dinner while you watch the sun set.

Makes: 4 servings
Time to Make: 25 minutes

Ingredients
- 1 steelhead fillet, cut into four portions
- 1 clove garlic, minced
- 1 Tbsp butter, room temperature

Directions
1. **Mix** garlic and butter.
2. **Spread** over steelhead fillets.
3. **Put** the steelhead fillets in foil, or paper bags and wrap shut.
4. **Bake** for 12-15 minutes until flaky.

For campfire, wrap in foil and cook about 5-10 minutes.

For Pico De Gallo
- ¼ purple onion, chopped into tiny pieces
- 1 tomato, chopped into small pieces
- ½ bunch cilantro, chopped finely
- ½ avocado, chopped
- ½ tsp cumin
- ½ tsp chili powder
- ½ to 1 lemon, cut in half
- Salt to taste

Optional:
- 1 jalapeno pepper, chopped finely

Directions
1. **Mix** all chopped vegetables, stirring gently to avoid crushing the tomatoes.
2. **Juice** desired amount of lemon on top, mix in cumin and chili, and salt to taste.
3. **Add** in jalapeno, if using.
4. **Serve** over the baked or grilled steelhead.

Baked Steelhead with Basil Feta Pesto

This recipe pairs the tender, flaky meat with a bold basil feta pesto that's earthy, salty, and fresh all at once. It's simple enough for weeknight dinners, but elevated enough to serve around the campfire or for guests. Using basil and garlic means you can truly grow or harvest everything in this dish—even the feta, if you have a goat or raise sheep!

Makes: 4 servings
Time to Make: 35 minutes

Ingredients
- 4 pieces steelhead
- 1½ cloves garlic
- 1½ cups fresh basil
- 1/3 cup block feta cheese
- 1 lemon
- 2 Tbsp olive oil

Directions

Prepare the Steelhead
1. **Wrap** the steelhead fillet in tin foil.
2. **Place** it directly in the fire embers **or** preheat your oven to 400°F.

Make the Basil Feta Pesto
3. **Add** fresh basil leaves to a blender.
4. **Add** garlic cloves and **crumble** feta cheese into the blender.
5. **Pour in** olive oil and **squeeze** in the juice of one lemon.
6. **Blend** until everything is combined but still slightly chunky in texture.

Note: Without a blender, you can use a mortar and pestle to crush everything—start by chopping it into small bits.

Cook the Steelhead
7. **Spread** the pesto evenly over the top of the steelhead.
8. **Wrap tightly** in foil if not already done.
9. **Bake or roast** for 15–20 minutes, or until the fish flakes easily with a fork.

Serve
10. **Unwrap carefully** and plate the steelhead.
11. **Serve with** steamed broccoli and cooked rice for a complete meal.

Smoked Steelhead Wild Chive Dip

This recipe is a perfect foraged addition to your holiday snack table! Impress your angler friends by serving this delicious dip—which features not only your catch, but also freshly foraged herbs!

Makes: 4 servings

Time to Make: 5 minutes

Ingredients

- 2 oz smoked salmon, steelhead, or trout (see Molasses Steelhead Jerky or salmon section for traditional smoked fish)
- ¼ cup cream cheese, room temperature
- 2 Tbsp sour cream
- ½ tsp garlic powder (can use fresh garlic for a stronger taste)
- 2 Tbsp chopped wild chives
- Triscuit or Almond Thin crackers, for serving

Directions

1. **Flake** fish into bowl with cream cheese.
2. **Mix** together with a fork, until incorporated.
3. **Add** sour cream, garlic powder, and chives, saving some for garnish.
4. **Serve** on crackers of your choice!

Molasses Steelhead Jerky

This jerky is sweet, smoky, and perfect for trail snacks or storing in camp — just like the old way. This recipe also offers the perfect opportunity to make steelhead jerky without a smoker. You can do this over the fire; see alternate instructions at the end.

Makes: 2 lbs of dehydrated fish
Time to Make: about one day

Ingredients
- 3 lbs Steelhead or salmon, sliced into strips
- 2 tsp garlic powder
- ¾ cup brown sugar
- 1 cup iodized salt
- ¼ cup molasses, plus more for drizzle

Directions
1. **Trim the Fish:**
   Cut steelhead into strips and trim off any freezer-burned or tough edges. Leave the skin on to help hold the strips together while they dry.
2. **Layer & Season:**
   Lay the strips in a single layer in a dish. Sprinkle with salt to cover. Then add a thicker layer of brown sugar, a dusting of garlic powder, and a light drizzle of molasses.
3. **Repeat:**
   Add another layer of fish and repeat the seasoning steps until all strips are coated.
4. **Brine:**
   Pour filtered water over the fish until just covered. Let sit in the fridge or a cool place for 6 hours or overnight.
5. **Dry the Fish:**
   Drain the fish and pat dry with paper towels.
6. **Arrange on Rack:**
   Place the strips in a single layer on a smoker rack or oven rack. If using the oven, line the bottom with parchment paper to catch drips.
7. **Smoke or Bake:**
   Heat your oven to **200°F**. Place the fish on the middle rack.
8. **Molasses Drizzle:**
   After the first hour, drizzle a thin line of molasses over the fish every 30 minutes.
9. **Finish:**
   Bake for about **5 hours**, or until the strips are dry and leathery like soft jerky.

Campfire Smoking Directions
1. **Set Up a Rack or Frame:**
   Use a campfire-safe grill grate, smoker box, or DIY wooden A-frame with racks. Keep the fish **at least 2–3 feet above the coals** to avoid cooking it too quickly.
2. **Build the Fire:**
   Use alder, maple, or fruitwood (preferably green) for the fire—avoid resinous woods like pine. Build a small, steady fire and let it burn down to hot coals. Add green wood chunks, for smoke.
3. **Smoke the Fish:**
   Place strips skin-side down on the grate in a single layer. Cover loosely with foil, bark, or a canvas tarp propped with sticks to trap smoke but still allow airflow.
4. **Drizzle Molasses:**
   After the first hour, drizzle each piece with a thin line of molasses. Repeat every 30–60 minutes.
5. **Maintain Temperature:**
   Try to keep the smoking temp around 180–200°F. Add coals or wood as needed to maintain heat and smoke.
6. **Cook Time:**
   Smoke for 4–6 hours, or until the fish reaches a soft jerky texture—leathery, slightly pliable, but dry to the touch. Thicker pieces may need longer.

SALAL BERRY

A staple wild fruit of the Pacific Northwest, salal berries (*Gaultheria shallon*) grow in thick, evergreen thickets along coastal forests, hillsides, and shady trails. These deep purple berries are mildly sweet with an earthy, black-tea finish—often likened to a cross between blueberries and huckleberries. Once a key food source for Indigenous communities, salal was dried into cakes for winter or eaten fresh off the bush. Today, it's a prized forager's find, perfect for jams, fruit leather, and backcountry snacking.

Did You Know?

Indigenous peoples of the Pacific Northwest used salal leaves as a medicinal tea to treat inflammation, stomach issues, and sore throats, thanks to their astringent and antibacterial properties.

Salal Berry
(Gaultheria shallon)

Leaves
Thick, leathery,
egg-shaped with
fine serrations;
dark green and glossy

Stems
Woody and branched,
often reddish
or brown

Flowers
Pink to white, urn-shaped,
clustered near the tips
(late spring to early summer)

Berries
Dark blue to purple-black;
round to oblong;
soft, seedy, slightly hairy

Taste
Mildly sweet, earthy, slightly dry
(like blueberry meets black tea)

Foraging Guide

Habitat
- Coastal forests, especially under coniferous trees like Douglas-fir and Sitka spruce
- Partial shade to full shade environments
- Acidic, well-drained soils, often in mossy or fern-filled understories
- Elevations from sea level to about 3,000 feet
- Common in clearcuts, forest edges, and coastal bluffs

Season
- Berries ripen mid to late summer (July–September); they can persist into fall.

Harvesting Tips
- Choose fully dark, soft berries for best flavor.
- Berries are easily stripped from stems; avoid underripe reddish ones—they're bland and astringent.
- Leaves can also be harvested for tea (astringent and mildly antiseptic).

Toxic Look–Alikes and Cautions
Oregon Grape (Mahonia spp.)

- Grows in similar forested areas as salal.
- Leaves are spiny and holly-like, not smooth and leathery.
- Berries are dark blue and grow in upright clusters, often with a dusty coating.
- **Only the berries are edible** (and quite sour); **the leaves and stems are not edible and may cause digestive upset if consumed in quantity.**

Note: Salal berries are high in tannins, which give them a slightly dry mouthfeel—great for mixing with juicier fruits like huckleberries or thimbleberries.

Drying
Dry whole berries for 12 hours at 130 ▯ in the dehydrator. See **Elderberry** section for additional drying tips.

Freezing
See **Huckleberry** section for freezing instructions.

Flavor Profile
Salal berries have a mildly sweet, earthy flavor with a dry finish—like a cross between blueberries and black tea.

Where to Buy/Substitutes
Use blueberries or huckleberries.

Salal Berry Tin Can Cake (Campfire Boil-Bake Method)

I created this recipe on the spot when I found an abundance of salal berries at a campground near Florence, Oregon. The boiling in a coffee pot method is simple and can be used for many kinds of baked goods when a traditional oven isn't available.

Makes: Two 12 oz tins full of cake
Time to Make: 45 minutes including cooking time

Ingredients
- ½ cup salal berries (fresh or rehydrated dried)
- 1 egg
- 2 Tbsp oil, butter, or rendered tallow
- ¼ cup sugar (or honey/maple syrup)
- ½ cup flour (acorn or all-purpose)
- ¼ tsp baking powder

- Pinch of salt

Optional: A dash of cinnamon or vanilla

Directions
1. **Grease** a clean, food-safe tin can (12–15 oz) with oil or fat.
2. **Beat** egg, oil, and sugar in a small bowl. Stir in flour, baking powder, salt, and salal berries until just combined.
3. **Pour** batter into the can, filling it no more than halfway to allow room for rising.
4. **Set** the can inside a large cast iron pot or enamel coffee pot. **Add water** around it so it reaches only halfway up the sides of the can.
   Avoid letting water touch the top of the can—it can seep in and make the cake soggy.
5. **Cover** the pot with a tight-fitting lid or foil to keep ash and debris out.
6. **Place** the pot over hot coals on a rack, or hang over the fire using a tripod or sturdy branch.
7. **Simmer** gently for 35–45 minutes, maintaining a low, steady boil. The cake is done when a stick or knife inserted comes out clean.
8. **Cool** slightly, then run a knife around the edge to release the cake. **Enjoy warm by the fire!**

Salal Fruit Leather (Dehydrator Method)

This leather is earthy-sweet with a hint of tartness from the apple and a whisper of vanilla—perfect for wild snack packs or kid-friendly foraging treats.

Makes: 3 trays or cookie sheets
Time to Make: 8-15 hours

Ingredients
- 1 cup salal berries (fresh or thawed from frozen)
- ½ cup blueberries (optional, for added brightness)
- 1 green summer apple, peeled and chopped
- 1–2 Tbsp agave syrup (to taste)
- ¼ tsp vanilla extract *or* a pinch of ground vanilla bean

Directions
1. **Blend** salal berries, optional blueberries, and chopped apple until smooth.
2. **Transfer** to a saucepan, then stir in agave and vanilla. Cook gently over low heat for about 5 minutes, until it bubbles and is heated through.
3. **Taste** and adjust sweetness as needed.
4. **Line** dehydrator tray with wax or parchment paper, and lightly grease with oil or fat to prevent sticking.
5. **Spread** the fruit purée evenly into a thin, uniform layer (about ⅛ inch thick).
6. **Dehydrate** at 135°F for 6–8 hours, or until dry to the touch but still slightly flexible.
7. **Cool**, peel off, cut into strips, and roll up if desired. Store in a cool, dry place or wrap for trail use.

Venison and Salal Stew

A rich, slow-simmered stew that brings together the wild flavors of venison, sweet salal berries, and earthy roots. This dish balances the deep game flavor with the subtle fruitiness of salal, a traditional Northwest staple.

Makes: 4 servings
Time to Make: 1 ½–2 hours

Ingredients
- 1 lb. venison stew meat, cubed
- 2 Tbsp oil, fat, or butter
- 1 wild onion (or ½ cup garden onion), diced
- 2 cloves garlic, minced
- 2 wild carrots (or 2 garden carrots), sliced
- 2 medium potatoes (optional for bulk), cubed
- 1 cup fresh salal berries (or ½ cup dried, rehydrated)
- 1 tsp salt
- ½ tsp cracked black pepper
- 1 tsp wild thyme, yarrow, or oregano
- 4 cups water, broth, or bone stock

Directions
1. **Brown the meat:** Heat oil in a cast iron pot over the fire. Add venison cubes and brown on all sides. Remove and set aside.
2. **Cook aromatics:** Add onion, garlic, and carrots to the pot. Cook until softened and fragrant.
3. **Simmer:** Return venison to the pot. Add potatoes (if using), salal berries, salt, pepper, herbs, and stock. Stir well.
4. **Cook slow:** Cover and simmer 1–1 ½ hours, stirring occasionally, until venison is tender and stew has thickened.
5. **Serve:** Ladle into bowls and enjoy hot with bannock or flatbread.

Pro Tip: This recipe works equally well with elk or bear meat.

Note of Caution on Wild Carrots
Wild carrot (Daucus carota, also known as Queen Anne's Lace) is edible, but it is easily confused with poison hemlock, which is deadly. Always verify identification with certainty before harvesting. If unsure, substitute with garden carrots.

SALMONBERRIES

Salmonberries *(Rubus spectabilis)* are one of the first berries to ripen in the Pacific Northwest, often appearing in early spring along coastal forests, stream banks, and clearings. Ranging in color from golden-orange to deep red, they resemble raspberries in shape and texture but offer a unique, lightly tart flavor that's sometimes compared to apricots or rhubarb.

These vibrant berries are rich in vitamin C, antioxidants, and hydration, making them a refreshing wild food and a gentle immune booster. Indigenous communities have long valued salmonberries for their early-season nourishment and traditionally paired them with dried fish or oolichan grease for added richness.

Did You Know?

Salmonberries were traditionally eaten by Indigenous peoples alongside salmon—often dipped right into oil from eulachon or candlefish for added richness. These jewel-toned berries are found in moist coastal forests of the Pacific Northwest. Their name comes from both their pink-orange hue and their historical pairing with salmon meals.

SALMONBERRIES
(Rubus spectabilis)

Fruit
Raspberry-like, made up of small drupelets; colors range from yellow to red

Shape
Cone-shaped or round, about the size of a raspberry

Taste
Mild and slightly sweet when ripe; tart or bland if underripe

Leaves
Three-parted (trifioliate) with serrated edges; soft and green

Stems
Thorny but not as aggressively as blackberries; green to reddish in color

Flowers
Five-petaled, bright magenta-pink; bloom in early spring

Foraging Tip
Ripe berries pull off easily. If they resist, let them ripen a bit more.

Foraging Guide

Habitat
- Along gravel roads, especially near water or lining rivers
- Along streambanks, forest edges, and wet trails
- In coastal rainforests and foothills, often near red alder, Sitka spruce, or salmon-spawning streams
- At low to mid elevations from Northern California through Alaska
- In areas with disturbed soil, such as old logging roads or landslides, where they quickly colonize and form dense thickets
- Campgrounds with a lot of tree cover often have salmonberry bushes lining the road in the PNW

Season
- Late-spring to early summer (typically May–July)

Toxic Look-Alikes and Cautions
Salmonberries are fairly distinct, but a few other native berries might confuse beginners. Fortunately, their leaves are quite different, helping you tell them apart.

Red Elderberry (Sambucus racemosa)
- **Berry:** Small, shiny red berries in tight clusters, not solitary
- **Leaves:** Compound leaves with 5–7 narrow, pointed leaflets
- **Toxicity:** Toxic when raw—can cause nausea, vomiting, and diarrhea
- **Growth Habit:** Grows on large shrubs or small trees with woody stems (not canes)

Key ID Tip: If the berries look like raspberries and grow singly on thorny, cane-like stems with trifoliate leaves, you're likely looking at salmonberries.

Cleaning
Rinse gently under cold water in a colander immediately before use. Do not soak—berries are delicate and absorb water. Store in the fridge and use within a day; they spoil quickly.

Drying
Not recommended—they become all seeds.

Freezing
Not recommended due to the fact that they become mushy. Instead, make into jam and freeze.

Flavor Profile
Salmonberries are mild, juicy, and lightly sweet, with a flavor that varies by ripeness and color. Red ones tend to be tarter, while orange ones are softer and sweeter.

Texture: Tender and juicy, with fine seeds

Taste Notes: Mildly sweet, fruity, lightly tangy, sometimes bland

Pairs Well With: Honey, yogurt, citrus, wild mint, seafood (especially salmon)

Best Uses: Fresh snacking, jam, jelly, syrup, desserts, shrub, or wine

Where to Buy/Substitutes
Due to their delicate nature, they don't keep long enough to sell. Substitute white raspberries.

Camping Salmonberry Sauce for Fry Bread

This salmonberry sauce reflects the simplicity with which the Native Americans cooked and used these wild foraged berries—making it the perfect camping recipe to try!

Makes: 4 servings
Time to Make: 10 minutes

Ingredients

- 1 cup salmonberries, freshly harvested (they fall apart fast when stored)
- 2 Tbsp honey
- 3 Tbsp water

Directions

1. **Combine** all three ingredients (fruit, sweetener, and water) in a **stainless-steel pot**.
2. **Cook** over medium heat on a **camp stove** or **open fire** until the sauce begins to bubble.
3. **Stir often** as the mixture thickens to prevent sticking or burning.
4. **Continue cooking** for about 10 minutes, or until most of the water has evaporated and the mixture reaches a thick, sauce-like consistency.
5. **Remove from heat** and let cool slightly.
   Note: A stainless-steel pot works best—cast iron can impart a metallic flavor to the sauce.
6. **Serve warm** with hot frybread for a rustic, foraged breakfast in the wild.

See also:

- *Acorn section* for a **Bannock recipe**
- *Truffle section* for **Frybread instructions**

Salmonberries with Smoked Fish

This dish reflects the traditional pairing of sweet, tart salmonberries with rich, oily preserved fish, used by many coastal Indigenous peoples as a nourishing and seasonal food. It's earthy, simple, and deeply satisfying.

Makes: 3 servings

Time to Make: 10 minutes

Ingredients

- 1 cup fresh salmonberries (or substitute with wild raspberries)
- 2–4 oz smoked salmon, steelhead, or dried/smoked oolichan
  Optional: A drizzle of rendered tallow, oolichan grease, or a few crushed hazelnuts or acorns for richness
- Pinch of salt

Directions

1. **Gently** mash the salmonberries in a wooden bowl or with a spoon to release their juices. Leave them mostly whole.
2. **Flake** or crumble the smoked fish into bite-sized pieces and stir into the berries.
3. **Add** a small pinch of salt and a light drizzle of fat (optional) to bring the flavors together.
4. **Let** sit for 5–10 minutes, then serve at room temperature—alone or with an acorn Bannock.

Rustic Salmonberry Bars (Fig Bar Style)

If you enjoy traditional fig bars, you will like these more. Inspired by a classic hiking or road trip snack, salmonberry bars offer the flavors of the forest—without the preservatives and dyes that come in many commercially available fig bars.

Makes: 12–16 bars

Time to Make: 50 minutes (20 minutes baking)

Filling Ingredients

- 2 cups fresh or frozen **salmonberries (or thimbleberries)**
- 2–4 Tbsp honey or maple syrup (adjust to taste)
- 1 Tbsp lemon juice

- 1 tsp lemon zest (optional)
- 1 Tbsp cornstarch or arrowroot powder
- Pinch of salt

Dough Ingredients

- 1½ cups all-purpose flour (or sub half with acorn flour)
- ½ tsp baking soda
- ¼ tsp salt
- ½ tsp cinnamon (optional)
- ½ cup unsalted butter, softened (or coconut oil)
- ½ cup brown sugar or coconut sugar
- 1 egg
- 1 tsp vanilla extract

Directions

1. Make the Filling:

- **In a saucepan** over medium heat, combine salmonberries, sweetener, lemon juice, zest, and salt.
- **Simmer** until berries break down, about 10–15 minutes.
- **Stir in cornstarch** and cook until thickened, another 2–3 minutes.
- **Remove** from heat and let cool completely. It should be jammy and spreadable.

2. Prepare the Dough:

- **Preheat** oven to 350°F.
- **In a bowl,** whisk flour, baking soda, salt, and cinnamon.
- **In another bowl,** cream butter and sugar until fluffy.
- **Mix in egg and vanilla,** then slowly stir in dry ingredients until a soft dough forms.
- **Chill dough** for 15–20 minutes if too sticky.

3. Assemble the Bars:

- **Divide** dough in half. Roll each half into a rectangle about 4 inches wide and 12 inches long on parchment.
- **Spread** a line of filling down the center (about 2 Tbsp per strip).
- **Fold** both sides over the filling like a log and seal edges.
- **Carefully** flip seam-side down and press gently to flatten.

4. Bake:

- **Transfer** parchment with logs to a baking sheet.
- **Bake** 20–25 minutes until lightly golden.
- **Let cool,** then slice into bars with a sharp knife.

Tips:

- **These** freeze beautifully—wrap individually for trail snacks.
- **Add** a spoonful of chia seeds to the filling to help thicken without cornstarch.
- **Want** more texture? Stir in chopped toasted hazelnuts or oats to the dough.

TRUFFLES

Truffles (*Tuber melanosporum* and *Tuber aestivum*) are rare, aromatic fungi that grow underground near certain trees, prized worldwide for their rich, earthy flavor and found mainly in Europe, North America, and Australia. Besides their gourmet appeal, truffles offer antioxidants, essential minerals, and anti-inflammatory benefits, making them a nutritious, low-calorie delicacy.

Back in 2020, my Catahoula Leopard pup and I found black truffles by accident in a secluded area of a tree farm in western Oregon! I found her digging at the base of a fir, and thought that she must be finding bits of an old charred log. Surprised, since it wasn't a burn area, I investigated more closely. The distinct fruity scent of truffles, combined with breaking one in half to see a white, marbled interior, was a dead giveaway. My smart girl had discovered black truffles, without even trying! Turns out, she loved them.

Did You Know?

Truffles aren't just gourmet delicacies—they're a hidden survival food rich in protein, fat, and minerals. Found just beneath the forest floor near fir, oak, or hazel trees, these underground fungi form a symbiotic bond with tree roots and often grow where few other food sources thrive. In a pinch, they can provide dense nutrition and are far easier to preserve than meat.

Cleaning

Cleaning truffle mushrooms properly is essential to preserve their unique flavor and aroma. Follow these easy steps to ensure your truffles are clean and ready for use. It's best to clean truffles just before you add them to your dish to ensure they are fresh and flavorful.

Remove Loose Dirt

Begin by using a soft brush, such as a toothbrush or pastry brush, to gently brush off any loose dirt or soil from the surface of the truffle.

Avoid Water and Soap

Truffles are delicate and sensitive to water. Rinsing or soaking them can wash away their volatile aroma and impact their flavor. Therefore, it's crucial to keep them dry during the cleaning process—never soak or rinse truffles under water.

Persistent Dirt

If you encounter stubborn dirt or soil particles that don't come off with brushing, take the tip of a small, sharp knife and carefully remove them. Be gentle to avoid damaging the truffle's surface.

Dry Thoroughly

After cleaning, it's essential to dry the truffle immediately. Use a paper towel or a clean cloth to absorb any moisture. This step prevents any excess moisture from affecting the truffle's flavor and aroma.

Additional Tips

White vs. Black Truffles
- White truffles are more delicate and should be cleaned with an extra soft brush.
- Black truffles can be cleaned more robustly, but regardless, it is best to avoid soaking them in water.

Storage

After cleaning your truffles, store them in a paper bag, wrapped in paper towels, in the refrigerator, to maintain their flavor and aroma. Use within 7 days of harvesting, or if purchased, find out how long ago they were harvested and adjust their shelf life based on this.

Drying

Drying truffles is simple if you have a food dehydrator. With that being said, I would recommend freezing them instead, ideally in an oil infusion, because truffles are nothing without their aroma, and a lot of that will be lost during the drying process.

To dry truffles, slice them into about 4 or 5 slices per truffle, around ¼-inch thick. Lay them on a dehydrator tray in single layers. Turn the dehydrator to 110F and set a timer for about 10 hours. They are done when they snap in half. You want to make sure they are completely dry or they can mold. After they are dried, let them cool completely and then vacuum pack.

Flavor Profile

Black truffles have a deep, earthy, musky aroma and a rich, savory flavor that's often described as intensely umami and slightly nutty, with hints of garlic, chocolate, and forest floor. The taste is subtle when raw but blooms with gentle heat or fat-based dishes.

Texture: Firm, slightly spongy when fresh; shaved or grated

Taste Notes: Earthy, musky, nutty, garlicky, with hints of cocoa and aged cheese

Aroma: Pungent and complex—more powerful than the taste itself

Pairs Well With: Butter, eggs, pasta, cream, potatoes, mushrooms, Parmesan, beef, and foie gras

Best Uses: Infused into oil or butter, folded into creamy sauces or risottos

Where to Buy

Truffles are hard to find without a trained truffle dog. However, they are widely known as a prized edible—making them fairly easy to find when in season. Here in the PNW, the season goes from about October to February. Check farmers markets, marketplace, and, if all else fails, dried Truffles can suffice—but don't skimp on the price or quality!

Black Truffle-Infused Oil

Note: While some recipes use raw truffle oil, I recommend using this oil only in cooked dishes. Raw truffles can be a potential source of bacteria, especially if not washed properly. As with other wild mushrooms, cooking is always best.

This oil is the base to many recipes that use truffle oil! Armed with this knowledge, you can easily preserve your truffle harvests and enjoy the full flavor of these aromatic fungi!

Makes: 1 cup

Time to Make: 48 hours

Ingredients
- 1 cup neutral oil
  (grapeseed or light olive oil work best—avoid extra virgin olive oil for a cleaner infusion)
- 1 Tbsp finely grated or chopped fresh black truffle
  (or 1–2 tsp high-quality dried black truffle)
  Optional: pinch of sea salt to enhance flavor

Directions
1. **Gently warm** the oil in a small saucepan over low heat—do not let it simmer or bubble.
   (Aim for about 120°F. Overheating can dull the truffle flavor.)
2. **Add the truffle** to the warm oil and stir gently. Let it steep on low heat for 5–10 minutes, then remove from heat.
3. **Let the oil cool** to room temperature, then pour it (truffle bits and all) into a clean glass bottle or jar.
4. **Seal tightly** and store in the refrigerator. Let it infuse for at least 24–48 hours before using. The flavor gets stronger with time.

Shelf Life: 2-3 days in the fridge for fresh truffle oil. Use it quickly for best flavor.
- For longer storage, strain out the truffle after 48 hours and freeze immediately. Thaw when ready to use.

Truffle Oil Fry Bread

This is the easiest bread recipe I have ever tried! We make this the day before camping and it rises beautifully in the cooler overnight! If you pack it in a plastic Ziploc bag that has been lined with oil, you don't need to even touch it. Just squeeze it out of the bag into the heated skillet and fry it up! For an after-dinner treat, drizzle a little bit of local wildflower honey on top!

Makes: 2 frybread (the size of a medium cast iron skillet)
Time to Make: 1 hour to overnight (rising time)

Ingredients
- 2 ¼ cups all-purpose flour
- 1 cup whole wheat bread flour
- 1 ½ tsp salt
- 1 ¾ tsp active dry yeast
- 1 ½ cups warm water
- 1 Tbsp olive oil + more for greasing the bag
- 2 Tbsp truffle oil, for frying

Directions

Make the Dough
1. **Mix** together all dry ingredients in a bowl until well combined.
2. **Pour in** water and oil.
3. **Stir** until a dough forms and everything is fully incorporated.
4. **Knead** the dough gently for about 1 minute—just enough to bring it together.
5. **Grease** a gallon-size Ziploc (or two quart-size bags) by drizzling olive oil inside and spreading it around.
6. **Place** the dough in the bag and **store** in a refrigerator or cooler until ready to cook.

When Ready to Cook
7. **Heat** a cast iron skillet over a fire or camp stove.
8. **Add** about 2 Tbsp of the *truffle oil recipe* (referenced in this book).
9. **Wait** for the oil to bubble, indicating it's hot enough.
10. **Add** a portion of dough (about half the ball) to the skillet. *You want a very thin layer so it cooks through—use the bag as a glove to help spread the dough evenly across the pan.*
11. **Cook** for about 2 minutes, monitoring closely to avoid burning.
12. **Check** the underside by carefully lifting an edge—it should be golden brown.
13. **Flip** using a spatula, two forks, or even a couple of sticks!
14. **Cook** the second side for another 2 minutes or until golden.
15. **Remove** from the pan and **serve immediately**.

Parsnips Baked in Truffle Butter

Parsnips are naturally sweet. Combined with the slight sweetness of butter and the fruity, earthy taste of truffles, this recipe will blow your mind—and your taste buds! You can adjust this for cooking over an open fire—simply by putting everything into foil and leaving it on the coals for about 10 minutes!

Makes: 4 servings

Time to Make: 55 minutes

Ingredients

- 4 parsnips
- 2 Tbsp truffle oil

- 1 Tbsp butter

Directions

1. **Preheat** your oven to 350°F.
2. **Place** a baking dish with both the truffle butter and regular butter into the oven while it preheats.
   This allows the butter to melt and infuse together.
3. **Cut** parsnips into crosswise slices of even thickness.
4. **Remove** the hot dish from the oven and **toss** the sliced parsnips in the melted truffle butter, stirring to coat thoroughly.
5. **Return** the dish to the oven and **roast** for 40–50 minutes, or until the parsnips are tender and golden brown.
   If they start browning too quickly, flip them halfway through to ensure even cooking.
6. **Remove** from the oven and **let rest** for a few minutes before serving.

Tip: This method works well with many vegetables! Try it with carrots, sweet potatoes, or rutabagas—just adjust the bake time based on thickness.

Truffle Cheesecake

This cheesecake is so good that even non-mushroom lovers will love it! My son, who won't touch mushrooms in any capacity, ate two slices of this before it had even cooled. The rich creaminess of cheesecake is combined with the unique rich flavor of truffles to make the perfect baked dessert sourced locally (or foraged) and representing natural food sources.

Makes: 1-8(inch) round cake pan
Time to Make: 1½ hours

Ingredients

Crust
- 2 packages graham crackers, crushed
- ½ cup butter
- ¾ cup granulated sugar
- Filling
- 1½ grated or crushed fresh truffle (can substitute dried)
- 2 packages cream cheese, softened
- ½ cup sour cream
- 1½ cup granulated sugar
- 4 eggs
- 2 tsp vanilla extract

Directions

Make the Crust
1. **In a small bowl**, combine graham cracker crumbs, softened butter, and granulated sugar.
2. **Mix or knead** until the mixture is evenly combined.
   If the butter is too firm, knead it by hand to prevent mess.
3. **Press** the mixture firmly into the bottom of an 8x8-inch baking dish or a round springform pan to form the crust.

Prepare the Filling
4. **In a bowl**, combine grated truffle and cream cheese. Mix until smooth.
5. **Add** sour cream and sugar, then beat in the eggs.
6. **Mix** until most cream cheese lumps are gone.
7. **Stir in** vanilla extract.
   Alternatively, combine all filling ingredients in a blender for a smoother consistency.
8. **Pour** the filling into the prepared crust.

Bake
9. **Preheat** oven to 325°F.
10. **Bake** for about 1 hour, or until the center reaches 165°F.
    The center may still be slightly wobbly—that's normal.
11. **Check periodically** to ensure the edges aren't browning too much and the top isn't cracking.

Cool and Serve
12. **If using a springform pan**, allow the cheesecake to **cool for at least 1 hour** before removing the outer ring.
13. **Chill** in the refrigerator before serving for best texture.

Truffle Scalloped Potatoes

Out in the wild, comfort food isn't about convenience—it's about making the most of what the land gives you. Potatoes store well through winter and truffles, if you're lucky enough to find them, are a rare treasure of the forest floor. This dish is simple, hearty, and rich with flavor pulled straight from the soil.

Makes: 4 servings
Time to Make: 1 hour

Ingredients
- 1 purple onion, sliced
- 3 red potatoes, thinly sliced (peel optional)
- 2 Tbsp truffle oil
- 2 Tbsp flour
- 1½ cups milk
- Salt and pepper, to taste
- 2 cups cheddar cheese, grated

Directions

Prepare the Layers
1. **Grease** an 8x8-inch baking dish.
2. **Layer** potato slices and purple onion rounds alternately in the dish.

Make the Sauce
3. **Heat** truffle oil in a medium pan over medium-low heat.
4. **When warm** (but not sizzling), **sprinkle** flour over the oil.
5. **Whisk** quickly to combine.
6. **Slowly pour** in the milk in a steady stream while whisking.
7. **Continue stirring** until the sauce thickens to a gravy-like consistency.
8. **Season** with salt and pepper to taste.
9. **Remove** from heat.

Assemble and Bake
10. **Pour** the sauce evenly over the potato and onion mixture.
11. **Sprinkle** the grated cheddar cheese on top.
12. **Cover tightly** with greased tin foil (or parchment paper plus foil to prevent sticking).
13. **Bake** at 350°F for 30–40 minutes, or until bubbly and the potatoes are fork-tender.
14. **Let sit** for 5 minutes before serving, leaving the foil covering on during resting time.

Truffle-Infused Goat Cheese

This is an easy way to infuse the flavors of truffle into soft cheese to be used in various dishes.

Makes: 4 oz
Time to Make: 5 minutes

Ingredients
- 1 (4 oz) package goat cheese
- ½–1 whole fresh truffle, sliced

Directions

Infuse the Cheese
1. **Cut** the goat cheese block in half horizontally.
2. **Insert** fresh truffle slices between the two halves.
3. **Press** the cheese back together gently.
4. **Wrap** tightly in plastic wrap, then place in a sealed plastic bag.
5. **Refrigerate** for 2–3 days to allow the flavors to infuse.
6. **Unwrap** and use in baked recipes, pasta, or as a spread.

Wild Mushroom & Truffle Pasta

A rustic pasta dish that brings out the earthy depth of wild mushrooms and the aromatic punch of fresh truffle. It's simple, hearty, and luxurious all at once—a way to turn a humble camp meal into something extraordinary.

Makes: 4 servings
Time to Make: 30 minutes

Ingredients

- 8 oz. dried pasta (or homemade egg noodles)
- 2 Tbsp butter, oil, or rendered fat
- 1 cup mixed wild mushrooms (chanterelle, morel, bolete, or lobster), sliced
- 2 cloves garlic, minced
- ½ cup cream (or evaporated milk for camp cooking)
- ¼ cup grated hard cheese (Parmesan or aged cheddar)
- 1–2 tsp finely shaved truffle
- Salt and pepper, to taste
- Handful of wild greens (nettles, lamb's quarters, or dandelion), optional

Directions

1. **Cook the pasta:** Boil noodles in salted water until al dente. Drain, reserving ½ cup of the cooking water.
2. **Sauté mushrooms:** Heat butter or oil in a cast iron skillet. Add mushrooms and garlic. Cook until mushrooms release their juices and edges are golden.
3. **Make the sauce:** Stir in cream and cheese. Simmer gently until slightly thickened.
4. **Combine:** Add cooked pasta and toss, loosening with a splash of reserved pasta water if needed.
5. **Finish with truffle:** Remove from heat and shave truffle over the pasta. Toss lightly to release its aroma.
6. **Serve:** Sprinkle with salt, pepper, and wild greens if using.

Pro Tip: Truffles are best added at the end—heat dulls their aroma.

LEMON BALM

Lemon balm (Melissa officinalis) is a fragrant herb in the mint family, known for its calming citrus scent and mild, soothing flavor. Native to Europe and the Mediterranean, it now grows widely across North America in gardens, fields, and along roadsides, and is valued for its ability to ease stress, support sleep, aid digestion, and gently lift mood.

Did You Know?

Lemon balm was once known as the "elixir of life" in medieval herbal medicine. Beloved by beekeepers for attracting bees (its name *Melissa* means "honeybee" in Greek), this calming herb was used by early homesteaders and survivalists to ease anxiety, aid digestion, and even repel insects. It's easy to grow, wild in some regions, and makes a refreshing tea that soothes the nerves and lifts the spirits—making it a must-have in any off grid medicine chest.

LEMON BALM
(*Melissa officinalis*)

Lemon balm is a member of the mint family (*Lamiaceae*) and shares many traits with its relatives.

Key Features:

- **Leaves:** Soft, wrinkled, oval to heart-shaped with deeply serrated edges
  - Lght to medium green when crushed
- **Stem:** Square (four-sided), branching, and slightly hairy
- **Height:** 1–3 feet tall in the wild
- **Flowers:** Small, pale yellow to whitish tubular and grow in clusters at leaf axils
  - Bloom mid to late summer
- **Growth Habit:** Forms bushy clumps, spreads by underground rhizomes and seed

Pro Tip: The lemony smell is your best field ID – crush a leaf and sniff. If it doesn't smell lemony, it's not lemon balm.

FLOWERS

SQUARE STEM

Foraging Guide

Habitat

- Sunny or partially shaded areas
- Gardens, abandoned homesteads, forest edges, and roadsides
- Often naturalized in the Pacific Northwest, especially near human disturbance
- Grows best in moist, well-drained soil but tolerates a range of conditions

Season

- Late-spring through early fall (best harvested before flowering)

Toxic Look–Alikes and Cautions

1. **Catnip** (*Nepeta cataria*)
   - Also in the mint family, with similar square stems and fuzzy, toothed leaves
   - Smells minty or skunky, not lemony
   - Flowers: Lavender-purple, not pale white or yellow

2. **Ground Ivy** (*Glechoma hederacea*)
   - Low-growing, creeping mint with rounded leaves and scalloped edges
   - Smells earthy, not lemony
   - Common in lawns and ground cover, not upright like lemon balm

3. **Poisonous mint relatives** (*rare*)
   - Some exotic ornamental mints may resemble lemon balm in shape
   - Always rely on the distinct lemony smell and soft serrated leaves for a positive ID

Key Differences:

Lemon balm has:
- Strong lemon scent
- Serrated, wrinkled leaves
- Square stems
- Upright growth habit (not creeping)

Cleaning

Rinse leaves gently in cold water to remove dust, insects, or dirt. Pat dry with a towel or air-dry on a clean cloth or mesh screen. Discard any yellowed, wilted, or bug-eaten leaves.

Drying

Air Dry: Bundle small stems and hang upside-down in a cool, dark, well-ventilated area

Dehydrator: Use a dehydrator on low heat (~95–105°F) until leaves are crisp

Storage: Store in airtight containers away from sunlight and moisture,

Flavor Profile

Lemon balm has a mild, lemony flavor with hints of mint and grass, making it a soothing addition to teas, desserts, and savory dishes.

Texture: Tender, soft leaves when fresh; brittle when dried

Taste Notes: Light citrus, herbaceous, slightly sweet, with a soft minty undertone

Aroma: Bright lemon zest with green herbal notes

Pairs Well With: Honey, chamomile, mint, berries, lemon, chicken, white fish, cucumbers

Best Uses: Herbal teas, infused water, desserts, jellies, vinegars, tinctures, and aromatherapy

Where to Buy

Lemon balm is a common garden herb in addition to growing wild. The best option would be to grow it yourself. If this isn't feasible, it can be purchased dried or in some stores in the herb section.

Lemon Balm Infused Butter

Makes: ½ cup infused butter
Time to Make: 2 hours

Ingredients
- ¼ cup fresh lemon balm leaves (about 3 small plants, leaves stripped, washed, and dried)
- 1 stick (½ cup or 8 oz) butter

Directions

Infuse the Butter
1. **Warm** the butter on very low heat in a small saucepan until it begins to melt.
2. **Remove** from heat once the butter is mostly liquid.
3. **Add** the lemon balm leaves to the melted butter.
4. **Transfer** the mixture to a glass jar, ensuring the leaves are fully submerged.
5. **Let sit** at room temperature for at least 2 hours to infuse.

Store and Use
6. **Use** it in baked recipes that call for lemon balm butter.

Note: This butter will remain in a melted or semi-liquid state and is intended for baking, not for spreading.
7. **Refrigerate** leftovers for up to 1 week, or **freeze** in an ice cube tray and store in a sealed bag for future use.

Lemon Balm Ginger Tea

This tea was inspired by a quiet moment in nature. Lemon balm, long used for emotional healing and intuition, pairs beautifully with ginger—a root symbolizing strength and spiritual protection. Let this brew be a companion in your healing journey, just as it was in mine.

Makes: 1–2 servings
Time to Make: 10 minutes

Ingredients
- 4–5 sprigs fresh lemon balm
- 2–3 thin slices fresh ginger
- Water

Directions

Brew the Tea
1. **Boil** water in a tea kettle or small pot.
2. **Place** lemon balm and ginger slices in a mug or teapot.
3. **Pour** hot water over the herbs.
4. **Steep** for 5–10 minutes.
5. **Remove** the herbs with a spoon or leave them in as you sip.

Mint & Lemon Balm Sun Tea

Makes: 3 cups
Time to Make: 1 day

Ingredients

- ½ cup fresh mint leaves
- ¼ cup fresh lemon balm leaves
- 3 cups water

Directions

Brew the Tea

1. **Wash** the mint and lemon balm leaves thoroughly.
2. **Stuff** the clean leaves into the bottom of a mason jar.
3. **Pour** in 3 cups of water, covering the leaves completely.
4. **Seal** the jar and **place** it in full sun for up to 24 hours.

Serve

5. **Pour** over ice to serve.
6. **Optional:** Stir in raw honey as the tea begins to cool if a sweeter flavor is desired.

Baked Chicken with Lemon Balm Butter

Make this with lemon balm morel gravy (see Morel section) for a completely foraged meal. Serve with mashed camas lily bulbs or mashed potatoes.

Makes: 3 servings
Time to Make: 1 hour

Ingredients

- 3 chicken breasts
- 3 Tbsp lemon balm–infused butter
- 1 tsp dried thyme

Directions

1. **Preheat** oven to 400°F.
2. **In** a small bowl, mix dried thyme and lemon balm butter.
3. **Rub** the mixture evenly under and over the chicken breasts.
4. **Place** chicken in a baking dish or cast-iron skillet, skin-side up.
5. **Bake** for 35–45 minutes, or until the skin is golden and the internal temperature reaches 165°F.
   To cook over an open fire: Wrap chicken in foil and place in hot coals. Cook for about 15 minutes, until the juices are running and it is steaming.
6. **Let** rest for 5 minutes before serving.

Lemon Balm Vanilla Cupcakes

This recipe is perfect for spring family gatherings—or just as a way
to enjoy the flavors of the wild in a delicate cupcake!

Makes: 1 dozen cupcakes
Time to Make: 1 hour

Ingredients

Cupcakes

- ½ cup lemon balm–infused butter (*see below*)
- 1 cup granulated sugar
- 3 eggs, separated
- 2 tsp vanilla extract
- ¾ cup milk, divided
- 15 sprigs fresh lemon balm (for milk infusion)
- 2 tsp baking powder
- 1¼ cups flour
- ½ tsp salt

Frosting

- 3 Tbsp lemon balm–infused milk (reserved from above)
- 2 cups powdered sugar
- ½ cup butter (room temperature)
- 2 tsp vanilla extract

Make the Cupcakes

1. **Infuse the Milk**:
   In a small saucepan, combine ¾ cup milk and 15 sprigs of lemon balm.
   Bring to a low boil, then remove from heat.
   Let sit for 1 hour. Strain and **reserve** the infused milk.

2. **Melt** the lemon balm–infused butter over low heat in a saucepan.
3. **In a large bowl**, combine sugar, melted butter, and egg yolks.
4. **Add** ½ cup of the reserved lemon balm milk and vanilla extract. Mix well.
5. **In a separate bowl**, whisk together flour, salt, and baking powder.
6. **In another bowl**, beat the egg whites until stiff peaks form (about 3–4 minutes).
   If you don't have a hand mixer, you can blend them in a blender for the same amount of time.
7. **Stir** the dry ingredients into the wet mixture until just combined.
8. **Fold** in the beaten egg whites gently.
9. **Spoon** batter evenly into a lined muffin tin.
10. **Bake** at 375°F for 15–18 minutes, or until a toothpick inserted in the center comes out clean.
11. **Cool** completely before frosting.

Make the Frosting

1. **In a bowl**, combine powdered sugar, 2 Tbsp lemon balm–infused butter, and 6 Tbsp regular butter.
2. **Beat** until smooth and creamy.
3. **Add** 3 Tbsp lemon balm–infused milk and vanilla extract.
4. **Beat again** until fluffy.

Frost and Serve

1. **Pipe** frosting onto cooled cupcakes in a circular motion.
2. **Garnish** with fresh sprigs of lemon balm, if desired.

PURPLE DEAD NETTLE

Purple Dead Nettle (*Lamium purpureum)* may look like a weed, but this non-native plant—introduced from Europe—has earned its place in the modern forager's toolkit. Herbalists have long turned to it for soothing wounds and easing seasonal allergies. Its tender young leaves are edible and often used in teas, salves, or added fresh to spring meals.

Did You Know?

Despite its name, purple dead nettle doesn't sting! The "dead" part refers to its lack of irritating hairs found on true nettles. This resilient little plant is one of the first wild edibles to pop up in early spring—and it's loaded with antioxidants, vitamin C, and anti-inflammatory properties. Foragers and herbalists alike use it in teas and tinctures to support the immune system.

PURPLE DEAD NETTLE
Lamium purpureum

Leaves: Triangular to heart-shaped, fuzzy with deep veins. Upper leaves often tinged purple.

Stem: square and slightly hairy, typical of the mint family.

Flowers: Small, tubular, pinkish-purple blooms clustered at top.

Height: 4–12 inches tall.

Scent: Mild, grassy or slightly minty when crushed

Foraging Guide

Habitat

- Found in disturbed soil, garden edges, roadsides, open fields, and forest edges
- Thrives in full sun to partial shade and moist but well-drained soil

Season

- One of the first greens to emerge in early spring (as early as February–April in the PNW)
- Can sometimes be found again in fall if conditions are mild

Toxic Look-Alikes & Cautions

1. **Henbit** (*Lamium amplexicaule*)
   - Similar appearance and also edible
   - Rounder, more scalloped leaves that hug the stem
2. **Ground Ivy** (*Glechoma hederacea*)
   - In the mint family
   - More sprawling growth habit and stronger scent
   - Edible in moderation

Caution: Always double-check for the square stem and fuzzy purple-tinged upper leaves to confirm ID. Avoid harvesting near roads or chemically treated areas.

Cleaning

Wash the leaves under running water or pull them off and rinse thoroughly in a colander.

Drying

Dry as you would nettles or mint. Remove flowering tops and tie several cut plants together with string (roots removed). Hang in a dry, well-ventilated space out of direct sunlight. The leaves are fully dry when they crumble easily between your fingers. Remove leaves from stems and store in a glass jar in a cool, dry place.

Freezing

See instructions for freezing nettles.

Flavor Profile

Purple dead nettle has a mild, slightly grassy flavor with subtle hints of sweetness and a faint herbal aftertaste.

Where to Buy

You can occasionally find dried purple dead nettle in herbal apothecaries, farmers markets, or online from foraging-focused suppliers. If unavailable, suitable substitutes include dried red clover, chickweed, or fresh young (non-stinging) nettle—all with similarly mild, earthy flavors and gentle herbal benefits.

Purple Dead Nettle Pesto (Survivalist Style)

Serve this over pasta, or cauliflower mushroom steamed to resemble
pasta. Or use it in the salmon pesto recipe (see salmon section).

Makes: ~1 cup
Time to Make: 10 minutes

Ingredients
- 1 cup purple dead nettle leaves and tops (rinsed and patted dry)
- ½ cup sunflower (or pumpkin) seeds
- 1–2 cloves garlic
- ¼–½ cup olive oil (or other oil available)
- 2 Tbsp lemon juice (or a dash of crabapple cider vinegar—see crabapple section!)
- Salt to taste

Optional: 2 Tbsp grated hard cheese (if available) or nutritional yeast for a shelf-stable option

Directions
1. **In** a mortar and pestle or food processor, combine nettle leaves, garlic, and nuts or seeds. Pulse or grind until coarse.
2. **Add** lemon juice (or vinegar) and slowly drizzle in olive oil while blending until smooth.
3. **Stir** in salt and optional cheese or nutritional yeast. Taste and adjust as needed.
4. **Store** in a small jar. Keeps for about 1 week in the refrigerator or freeze for long-term storage.

Purple Dead Nettle Allergy Support Tea

Purple dead nettle is rich in anti-inflammatory and antihistamine compounds, helping reduce
allergy symptoms like sneezing, sinus pressure, and itchy eyes. To make a simple tea with it,
brew a ratio of 2 Tbsp fresh purple dead nettle to 1 cup water. Let it steep for 10-15 minutes and
then add optional lemon balm or wild honey. Drink 1-2 cups daily during allergy season!

Purple Dead Nettle Chips

Purple dead nettle can be crisped into light, crunchy chips for a quick wild snack.
They don't store long but are a simple way to enjoy this common spring plant.

Makes: About 2 servings
Time to Make: 15 minutes

Ingredients
- 2 cups fresh purple dead nettle leaves
- 1–2 tsp oil or melted fat
- Pinch of salt

Directions
1. Prepare: Rinse nettle leaves and pat dry.
2. Coat: Toss gently with oil and a pinch of salt.
3. Cook: Spread in a single layer on a baking sheet or place on a flat pan over campfire coals. Heat until crisp, 5–7 minutes in an oven at 325°F or slightly longer over a fire.
4. Cool & eat: Let cool slightly—they'll crisp more as they cool. Enjoy immediately.

Pro Tip: These are best with tender spring leaves. For trail use, dehydrate instead of baking for longer storage.

Purple Dead Nettle Honey Infusion

Purple dead nettle has been used for centuries as an aid to seasonal allergies—as someone who struggles with them myself, I can attest to the benefits that this recipe has provided in helping me manage my allergy related asthma. Raw honey, when harvested or purchased locally, can help build tolerance to seasonal allergies—making this the perfect way to benefit from not only the plant, but also the benefits incurred by ingesting wild, raw honey!

Makes: 1 cup
Time to Make: 1-2 weeks

Ingredients
- 1 cup fresh purple dead nettle tops (or ½ cup dried)
- Raw local honey (enough to cover herbs fully)
- Clean, dry glass jar with lid (4–8 oz recommended)

Directions
1. **Harvest & prep:** Gently rinse fresh purple dead nettle leaves. Pat dry and let air-dry for an hour to remove surface moisture (prevents spoilage).
2. **Jar it:** Lightly pack the nettle into your jar—don't smash it down.
3. **Pour honey:** Slowly pour raw honey over the nettle until completely submerged. Use a chopstick or spoon to stir and release air bubbles.
4. **Infuse:** Seal the jar and store in a sunny windowsill or warm spot for 1–2 weeks, shaking gently every day.
5. **Strain (optional):** After 1–2 weeks, you can strain out the plant matter—or leave it in and scoop as needed.

How to Use:
- Take 1 spoonful daily during allergy season
- Stir into herbal tea or warm water
- Use on minor cuts and scrapes (nettles + honey = gentle antiseptic)

Wild Arthritis Relief Salve

- **Purple dead nettle:** Anti-inflammatory and isoothing to irritated tissue.

Pine resin: Natural analgesic and anti-inflammatory; also helps draw out soreness.

Cayenne (capsaicin): Stimulates circulation and desensitizes pain receptors.

Carrier oil (olive or grapeseed): Penetrates the skin and carries the herbal benefits deep into joints.

- **Beeswax:** Firms up the salve and provides a protective barrier.

Makes: 1 cup
Time to Make: 2 hours

Ingredients
- ½ cup dried purple dead nettle (or 1 cup fresh, lightly wilted)
- 1 Tbsp pine resin (optional, but great for deeper relief)
- 1 tsp cayenne powder (optional – omit for sensitive skin)
- ¾ cup olive oil or grapeseed oil
- 1 oz beeswax (about 2 Tbsp grated)
- 10 drops wintergreen or peppermint essential oil (optional for cooling effect)

Directions
1. **Infuse the oil:**
   - In a double boiler or heat-safe jar, combine dead nettle, pine resin, and cayenne with oil.
   - Gently heat on low for 1–2 hours, stirring occasionally. Avoid frying the herbs.
   - Strain the oil through cheesecloth or a fine mesh strainer.
2. **Make the salve:**
   - Return strained oil to the pot and add beeswax.
   - Stir until fully melted and combined.
   - Remove from heat and add essential oils if using.
3. **Pour into tins or jars** and let cool completely before sealing.

Use:
Massage a small amount onto arthritic joints 2–3 times daily. Always do a patch test first—cayenne can irritate sensitive skin.

How to Harvest Pine Resin for Salves

What It Is:

Pine resin (also called sap or pitch) is the sticky substance that oozes from conifer trees—especially pines—when the bark is damaged. It protects the tree by sealing wounds and repelling insects. That same protective power can be used in natural medicine for humans.

Best Trees to Harvest From:
- Ponderosa Pine
- Lodgepole Pine
- Douglas Fir
- Spruce or Larch (less common but usable)

Look for mature trees in forests or off-trail areas. These trees often leak resin naturally due to weather, animal damage, or old breaks.

How to Harvest:
1. **Locate naturally exuding resin**—Look for dried, amber-colored globs or fresh sticky patches on bark wounds.
2. **Use a knife or stick** to scrape the resin off gently. Avoid cutting into the tree or wounding it intentionally—harvest only what's already oozing.
3. **Collect in a jar** or waxed paper. Resin is sticky and messy, so keep it separate from your gear.
4. **Store in a cool place**—it will harden and keep for years.

Note: Never harvest too much from a single tree. Take only a small amount to avoid weakening the tree's natural defense system.

How to Use:

To use in salves, gently melt the resin in oil or strain it after infusing. It adds antimicrobial and pain-relieving properties to any herbal preparation. Since resin also burns well, add this to the tallow fire starter (see elk section) for added benefits to an all-natural, wild-harvested fire starter.

REISHI

Reishi mushrooms (*Ganoderma lucidum*) are a woody, medicinal fungus long revered in traditional Chinese and Indigenous medicine for their immune-boosting and adaptogenic properties. Commonly found on decaying hardwood trees in temperate forests across North America, Asia, and Europe, reishi is valued for its ability to reduce stress, support sleep, and promote overall vitality.

Did you know?

Called the "Mushroom of Immortality" in ancient China, reishi was believed to grow only for those with good intentions or spiritual purity.

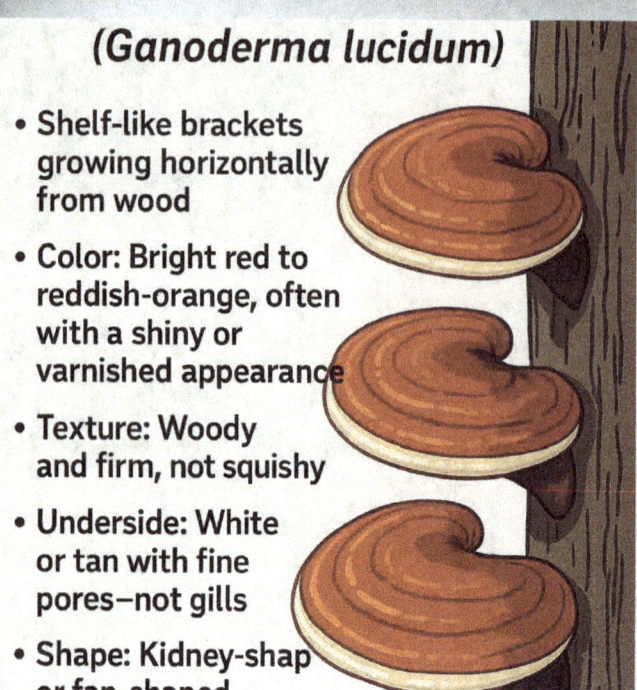

(Ganoderma lucidum)

- Shelf-like brackets growing horizontally from wood

- Color: Bright red to reddish-orange, often with a shiny or varnished appearance

- Texture: Woody and firm, not squishy

- Underside: White or tan with fine pores—not gills

- Shape: Kidney-shap or fan-shaped

Foraging Guide

Habitat

- Grows on dead or dying hardwood trees—especially oak, hemlock, and maple
- Often found on decaying stumps or logs
- Prefers humid, temperate forests with plenty of shade
- Common in low- to mid-elevation woodlands, especially along moist forest trails
- Sometimes spotted near riverbanks or damp ravines where deadwood accumulates

Season

- Late-spring through fall; occasionally into early winter depending on climate

Toxic Look-Alikes and Cautions

1. **Ganoderma curtisii** (*not toxic, but sometimes confused*):
   - Similar in shape and color, but less glossy
2. **Red-Belted Polypore** (*Fomitopsis pinicola*)
   - More common on conifers
   - Has a thick red or orange band, but lacks Reishi's lacquered shine
   - Not poisonous, but not medicinal either
3. **Artist's Conk** (*Ganoderma applanatum*)
   - Brownish-gray, not shiny, and grows in similar environments
   - Not toxic but lacks the medicinal benefits of Reishi

Avoid mushrooms with gills, slime, or that grow on the ground—these are **NOT** Reishi.

How to Harvest Reishi

Use a knife or saw to cut the mushroom at the base where it attaches to the tree.
Choose younger, fresh specimens—older ones become too woody and lose potency.
Avoid specimens that are moldy, cracked, or bug-infested.

Cleaning

Brush off debris and dirt with a soft brush. Rinse lightly with cold water if needed—do not soak. Pat dry immediately with a clean towel. Slice into thin pieces for drying or tincturing.

Drying

Place thin slices on a dehydrator tray. Set to 110 ▯ and dry for about 10 hours, or until pieces snap when bent.

Flavor Profile

Reishi mushrooms have a bitter, woody, and earthy flavor with a tough, leathery texture—best suited for teas, tinctures, or broths rather than direct consumption.

Where to Buy

Available dried on online marketplaces like Amazon, and sometimes in herbal apothecaries or health food stores.

How to Make a Reishi Tincture

Making a **Reishi mushroom tincture** is a powerful way to extract both the water-soluble (polysaccharides) and alcohol-soluble (triterpenes) compounds. This is known as a **double extraction tincture** and is one of the best ways to use reishi medicinally.

Time to Make: 1-2 months

Materials:
- Dried reishi mushroom (sliced or chopped)
- 80–100 proof vodka or grain alcohol (40–50% alcohol)
- Distilled water
- Glass jars with lids
- Fine mesh strainer or cheesecloth
- Dark glass dropper bottles (for storage)
- Labels and marker

Directions

Step 1: Alcohol Extraction
1. Fill a jar halfway with dried, chopped reishi mushroom.
2. Cover completely with alcohol, at least 1 inch above the mushrooms.
3. Seal and let sit for 4–6 weeks, shaking occasionally. Use a food safe rock or cooking weight to make sure the mushroom stays submerged.
4. After 4–6 weeks, strain out the mushrooms and set aside the alcohol extract.

Step 2: Water Extraction (Decoction)
1. Take the strained mushrooms and simmer in distilled water (2:1 ratio of water to mushrooms) for 1–2 hours with the lid slightly ajar.
2. Simmer until the volume reduces by about half.
3. Cool and strain.

Step 3: Combine the Extracts
1. Mix the alcohol extract and water decoction in a 1:1 ratio by volume.
   - Example: 1 cup alcohol + 1 cup water extract
2. **Optional:** Use a hydrometer to ensure final alcohol content is at least 25% for shelf stability.

Step 4: Bottle and Store
- Pour into **dark glass tincture bottles**.
- Label with date and contents.
- Store in a **cool, dark place** for up to 1–2 years.

Dosage (General Guidance)
- 1–2 dropperfuls (about 30–60 drops), 1–2 times daily.
- Always consult a qualified herbalist or healthcare provider.

Reishi Mushroom Coffee

Reishi mushroom coffee blends the energizing effects of coffee with the calming, adaptogenic properties of reishi, helping to reduce stress and support immune health. It offers a focused, jitter-free boost with added antioxidant and anti-inflammatory benefits.

How to Make:

Grind dried reishi in a coffee grinder or food processor until it is fine. If you are using older reishi it may look more like the consistency of wood chips or garden mulch. That should be fine.

Combine 3 parts coffee grounds with 1-part reishi mushroom. Place in the bottom of a French press coffee maker. Pour water over top. Let sit for 5-10 minutes. Press and serve as you normally would serve coffee.

Reishi Squash Soup

This soup brings together the earthy medicine of reishi and the sweetness of fall squash. Slow-simmered reishi creates the broth, while squash, wild roots, and greens turn it into a hearty, nourishing meal. Make the broth and freeze it for a medicinal punch later on—or make the whole recipe to enjoy the benefits all together!

Makes: 4–6 servings
Time to Make: 2 ½–3 hours

Ingredients

- ½ cup dried reishi slices (or 1 whole fresh conk, cleaned and chopped)
- 8 cups water
- 1 medium winter squash (butternut, acorn, or pumpkin), peeled and cubed
- 2 wild carrots (or garden carrots), sliced
- 1 wild onion (or 1 garden onion), diced
- 2 cloves garlic, minced
- 2 Tbsp oil, butter, or rendered fat
- 1 tsp salt
- ½ tsp pepper
- 1 tsp dried wild thyme, oregano, or yarrow
- 2 handfuls wild greens (nettles, dandelion, or lamb's quarters), chopped

Directions

1. **Make the reishi broth:** Place reishi slices and water in a large pot. Bring to a boil, then reduce heat to a very low simmer. Cover and cook 2 hours. Strain out and discard (or save for reuse) the reishi slices, keeping the broth.
2. **Cook vegetables:** In the same pot, heat oil. Add onion, garlic, and carrots. Cook until softened.
3. **Simmer soup:** Add squash cubes, salt, pepper, herbs, and prepared reishi broth. Simmer 30–40 minutes, until squash is tender.
4. **Blend or mash:** For a creamy soup, mash squash with a spoon or blend until smooth. For a rustic version, leave chunky.
5. **Finish with greens:** Stir in wild greens during the last 5 minutes of cooking. Serve hot.

Pro Tip: This soup is excellent with wild game—stir in shredded venison or duck for extra protein. Reishi can be reused 2–3 times; dry the strained slices and save for another pot of broth.

WILD ROSE

Wild roses (*Rosa nutkana* (Nootka rose), *Rosa woodsii*, *Rosa gymnocarpa*, and others) grow along forest edges, meadows, and roadsides across North America, Europe, and Asia, offering more than just beauty. From the fragrant petals to the vitamin C–rich hips that follow, nearly every part of the plant has been used in traditional healing and nourishment.

Wild rose petals and hips support immune health, digestion, and skin repair, while also offering gentle anti-inflammatory and calming effects. Their delicate floral flavor adds softness to teas, syrups, and even wild desserts.

Did You Know?

Wild roses (especially *Rosa nutkana* and *Rosa woodsii*) aren't just beautiful—they're survival powerhouses. Rose petals are rich in antioxidants and vitamin C, while rose hips—those red fruits that appear after the bloom—were traditionally used by Indigenous peoples as a winter source of nourishment and immune support. Some tribes even used wild rose root for treating colds and sore throats. Plus, the petals can be steeped into calming teas or infused into healing salves. In tough times, this humble flower can soothe, nourish, and heal.

WILD ROSES

Identification: *Rosa nutxana, R. woodsii, c. d. gymdcäj,* and others

FLOWERS
- Five broad petals, pink to pale pink or white
- Open, saucer shape with bright yellow stamens
- Mild, sweet fragrance; 1–3 inches wide

LEAVES
- 5–9-toothed leaflets, oval with pointed tips
- Finely serrated, alternate along the stem

HIPS (FRUIT)
- Small, round to oval, red-orange after bloom
- Best picked after frost when slightly soft

STEMS
- Woody and thorny, often red-tinged at the base

> **Pro Tip.** True wild roses have a sweet scent and simple, open blooms—not layered like garden hybrids.

Foraging Guide

Habitat
- Open woods, meadows, roadsides, streambanks, and forest edges
- Sunny, well-drained areas with minimal tree cover
- Common throughout the Pacific Northwest, often forming thickets

Season
- Flowers: Late-spring to early summer (May–July)
- Hips (fruit): Late summer to fall (August–October)

Toxic Look-Alikes and Cautions

1. **Multiflora Rose** (*Rosa multiflora*)
   - Invasive species, edible but considered a nuisance
   - Tiny white flowers in dense clusters, not solitary pink blooms
   - Leaves: Have a distinct fringe at the base (stipules)
   - Still a rose, but not ideal for harvesting—stick to native species like *Rosa nutkana*
2. **Hawthorn** (*Crataegus spp.*)
   - Flowers: White or pink, small, in dense clusters, with unpleasant smell
   - Leaves: Deeply lobed, not rose-like
   - Thorns: Often large and stout
   - Toxicity: Fruit is edible when ripe, but leaves and seeds are mildly toxic
3. **Blackberry brambles** (*Rubus spp.*)
   - Can resemble rose thickets at a glance due to thorns
   - Leaves: Usually 3–5 leaflets, coarser and fuzzier
   - Flowers: White to pink but smaller and more delicate

Key Difference: No rose scent, and leaves are not finely serrated

Cleaning

For Flowers:
Harvest only fully open, fragrant petals—avoid wilted or browning ones. Gently shake or blow off bugs, then rinse lightly in cool water. Pat dry and use fresh, or dry flat on a towel or screen.

For Rose Hips:

Remove stems and blossom ends. Rinse thoroughly in cool water. For tea or jelly use, cut open and remove seeds and fine hairs (they can irritate the throat). Dry whole or sliced hips in a dehydrator or warm dry room until leathery or brittle.

Drying

Petals: Lay flat on a screen or berry flat. Air dry for about 2 days, until they feel like paper and tear cleanly.
Rose hips: Dehydrate at 125 ☐ for 12 hours.

Flavor Profile

Rose Petals
- **Taste Notes:** Delicate, floral, lightly sweet, with a soft herbal undertone
- **Best Uses:** Teas, syrups, jellies, floral sugars, baking, garnishes
- **Pairs Well With:** Honey, lemon, strawberries, cream, vanilla

Rose Hips
- **Taste Notes:** Tart, fruity, slightly floral with citrus and apple-like notes
- **Best Uses:** Teas, jams, syrups, jelly, tinctures, or dried for vitamin C-rich infusions
- **Pairs Well With:** Ginger, hibiscus, apple, cinnamon, orange

Where to Buy/Substitutes

Substitute commercially grown rose petals or hips, or grow them yourself. Some health food stores and herbal apothecaries also carry dried rose products.

Wild Rose Hip Syrup

This syrup is rich in **vitamin C**, antioxidants, and natural sweetness. It's excellent for **immune support**, soothing sore throats, or even as a flavorful addition to yogurt.

Makes: 2 ½ c

Time to Make: 45 minutes

Ingredients
- 2 cups fresh or 1 cup dried rose hips (halved and cleaned of seeds/hairs)
- 2½ cups water
- ½ cup honey or maple syrup (to taste)

Optional: a slice of ginger or a cinnamon stick for warmth

Directions
1. **Simmer the Rose Hips:**
   In a small pot, combine rose hips and water. Simmer gently for **30–40 minutes**, until the water is reddish and fragrant.
2. **Strain:**
   Use a fine mesh strainer or cheesecloth to strain the liquid. Discard solids.
3. **Sweeten:**
   While still warm, stir in honey or maple syrup. Add more to taste if desired.
4. **Store:**
   Pour into a clean jar and refrigerate. Use within 2–3 weeks, or water-bath can for longer storage.

Wild Rose Petal Jelly

This jelly is a jar of summer—floral, light, and wild—perfect for foragers who like a little elegance with their survival food.

Makes: 2 pints
Time to Make: 1 hour

Ingredients

- 1 cup fresh wild rose petals (unsprayed and rinsed)
- 2½ cups water
- 2 Tbsp lemon juice (for acidity and color)
- 1 package (1.75 oz) powdered fruit pectin
- 3 cups granulated sugar

Directions

1. **Make Rose Petal Infusion:**
   In a small pot, combine rose petals and water. Bring to a boil, then turn off heat and steep for **30–40 minutes**. Strain out petals—the liquid will be light pink or golden.
2. **Prepare the Jelly Base:**
   Pour the rose petal infusion (about 2 cups) into a clean pot. Add lemon juice and pectin. Bring to a full rolling boil over high heat, stirring constantly.
3. **Add Sugar:**
   Stir in the sugar all at once. Return to a rolling boil and boil **hard for 1–2 minutes**, stirring constantly. Skim off any foam.
4. **Jar It:**
   Pour into sterilized jars, leaving ¼-inch headspace. Wipe rims, seal with lids.
5. **Process (for shelf-stable storage):**
   Process in a **boiling water bath for 10 minutes**. Let cool. Check seals after 24 hours.

Wild Elderberry & Rose Hip Herbal Tea

A calming, immune-boosting herbal blend perfect for cold season or daily wellness.

Makes: About 8–10 servings of dry blend
Time to Make: 5 minutes

Ingredients

- 1 Tbsp dried elderberries – immune-boosting, antiviral
- 1 tsp crushed dried rose hips – rich in vitamin C, supports skin & immunity
- 1 tsp dried lemon balm – calming, antiviral
- 1 tsp dried nettle leaf – mineral-rich, energizing
- ½ tsp dried yarrow flowers – fever-reducing, supports immune response

Optional: A pinch of cinnamon chips or dried ginger – warming

Directions

1. **Combine** all herbs in a jar or tin and **shake** well to mix.
2. **To brew:** Use 1 Tbsp of the blend per 1 cup of boiling water.
3. **Cover and steep** for 15–20 minutes to fully extract the benefits.
4. **Strain well,** especially if using crushed rose hips with hairs.
5. **Sweeten** with honey or maple syrup if desired.

Notes

- You can **swap** rose hips for rose petals for a more floral, less tart tea.
- **Drink** 1–3 cups daily during cold season or as a gentle daily tonic.
- **Store** the dry blend in an airtight jar in a cool, dark place.

Bentonite Clay Detox Bath

Use this bath recipe when you are fighting illness. As you take your bath, envision the herbs and clay pulling toxins from your body—it really works!

Makes: Enough for 1 bath
Time to Make: 5 minutes

Ingredients
- 2 cups bentonite clay
- 1 cup Moroccan red clay
- 2 slices fresh ginger
- 2 Tbsp fresh lemon balm
- 2 cups Epsom salts
- 1 cup rose petals
- 5 drops lavender essential oil

Optional: Additional essential oils or healing stones such as rose quartz, black tourmaline, or smoky quartz (these can be added to the bath to enhance detoxification, grounding, and emotional healing).

Directions
1. **Add** the ginger, lemon balm, and rose petals to a mesh bag or muslin sachet.
2. **Place** the bag into the bathtub and **begin running** hot water.
3. **Add** Epsom salts and both clays to the bathwater.
4. **Drop in** essential oils, and optionally, any healing stones of your choice.
5. **Soak** for at least 30 minutes to allow the ingredients to draw out toxins.
6. **Rinse** off thoroughly after your bath.

Rose Water Facial Tonic

To make a facial tonic with wild rose petals and water, simply put two cups or about 10 wild roses (3-4 regular sized domestically grown roses) into a saucepan and add 4 cups of water. Bring to a boil, cover, and let sit for an hour. Remove rose petals. Combine ¼ cup rose water with 2 droppers full of hyaluronic acid. Rub onto face. Hyaluronic acid balances the facial pH, helping to bring out a radiant glow on the skin. Rose water hydrates.

For a complete facial skincare routine, begin with a facial ice bath. Soak your face in a bowl of ice water for 30 seconds to one minute. Towel dry and rub in rose water facial tonic.

THIMBLEBERRIES

Thimbleberries (*Rubus parviflorus*) are soft, red berries native to North America, especially abundant in the Pacific Northwest, the Great Lakes region, and parts of the Rocky Mountains. Found along forest edges, streambanks, and sunny clearings, these delicate berries resemble flattened raspberries and are known for their short shelf life and intensely tangy-sweet flavor.

Despite their fragility, thimbleberries are a powerful wild food, rich in vitamin C, fiber, and antioxidants. Indigenous peoples have long harvested them not only for nourishment but also for their leaves, which were used in teas to ease digestive discomfort and sore throats.

Did You Know?

Thimbleberries are one of the most fragile wild berries—and they never make it to the grocery store because they're too delicate to ship! Indigenous peoples used them not only as food, but also medicinally. The large, velvety leaves were used as poultices for wounds, and even as a wrap for smoked fish. They also make great toilet paper when nature calls! High in fiber and antioxidants, these fleeting berries are a forager's treasure— and a reminder to slow down and savor what's in season.

THIMBLEBERRIES
Rubus parviflorus

KEY FEATURES

FRUIT
- Flattened, hollow red berries shaped like a thimble
- Very soft, juicy, and easily crushed

LEAVES
- Large, fuzzy maple-like with 5 lobes and toothed edges

STEMS
- Thornless (unlike most wild brambles)
- Woody, often reddish or green

FLOWERS
- Large (1-2 inches), flat, white, five-petaled
- Bloom in late spring to early summer

PRO TIP
Soft maple-like leaves, white flowers, red thimble-shaped berries, and no thorns? You've found a thimbleberry.

Foraging Guide

Habitat
Thimbleberries are native to the Pacific Northwest and thrive in:
- Moist woodlands, clearings, forest edges, and roadsides
- Partial shade to dappled sunlight
- Often found in low to mid-elevation areas
- Grow in dense thickets, especially in disturbed soil

Season
Mid to late summer (July–August)

Toxic Look-Alikes and Cautions
1. **Red Baneberry** (*Actaea rubra*)
   - Berries: Shiny red, in tight upright clusters—not thimble-shaped
   - Leaves: Deeply lobed and fern-like, very different from thimbleberry
   - Toxicity: Highly toxic if ingested
2. **Unripe Salmonberries** (*Rubus spectabilis*)
   - Can resemble thimbleberries before fully ripening
   - Growth: On thorny canes with trifoliate leaves—not large maple-shaped leaves
   - Still edible, but not the same flavor or texture

Key Differences:
Thimbleberries have no thorns, fuzzy maple-like leaves, and flattened, soft red berries that grow alone or in small groups.

Cleaning
Pick gently—they're very delicate and crush easily. Do not soak. Rinse lightly with cool water in a colander. Use immediately or refrigerate briefly (they spoil fast).

Freezing
Freeze in a single layer on a cookie sheet, then transfer to a labeled freezer bag.

Drying
Dehydrate at 110 ☐ for 8 hours or until they break when bent.

Flavor Profile
Thimbleberries have a bold, sweet-tart, and intensely fruity flavor, more aromatic and complex than raspberries.
- **Texture:** Fragile, pulpy, and juicy with soft seeds
- **Taste Notes:** Tart, sweet, bright, and wild—like raspberry crossed with rhubarb and rose
- **Pairs Well With:** Honey, lemon, yogurt, vanilla, wild rose, and pastry
- **Best Uses:** Fresh snacking, jam, syrup, fruit leather, baked into muffins or cobbler, or mixed into wild berry blends

Where to Buy/Substitutes
Not typically sold fresh—best bet is to forage. Substitute with raspberries if needed.

Thimbleberry-Filled Donuts with White Chocolate

These donuts taste like bakery treats—only better, because they feature wild foraged berries!

Makes: 8 donuts
Time to Make: 2 hours

Ingredients

Dough

- 1 cup milk, warmed to about 110°F*
- 2¼ tsp instant or active dry yeast (1 standard packet)
- ⅓ cup granulated sugar
- 2 large eggs
- 6 Tbsp butter, melted and slightly cooled
- 1 tsp pure vanilla extract
- ½ tsp salt
- 4 cups flour, plus more as needed
- 1–2 quarts canola oil (for frying)

Berry Filling

- 1 cup thimbleberries or raspberries
- 2 Tbsp granulated sugar
- 1 Tbsp cornstarch

White Chocolate Topping

- ¼ cup baking white chocolate
- 1 Tbsp butter

Directions

1. **Start** by proofing the yeast in warm milk. Add milk to a mixing bowl, sprinkle yeast over the top, and add 1 Tbsp of the sugar. Let sit until foamy.
2. **Beat** in the melted butter, then add eggs, salt, and vanilla.
3. **Add** the flour and mix until a dough ball forms. Knead in additional flour as needed.
4. **Set** the dough in a warm spot to rise for 1 hour, or until doubled in size.
5. **Heat** oil in a saucepan over medium heat until a small piece of dough sizzles when dropped in.
6. **Shape** dough into donut rings.
7. **Place** gently into hot oil. Cook for about 1½ minutes per side, until lightly golden. Turn with a fork and **drain** on paper towels.
8. **In a saucepan**, combine thimbleberries, sugar, and cornstarch. Cook over low heat until bubbly and thickened, about 5 minutes. Remove from heat.
9. **Transfer** donuts to a parchment-lined cookie sheet. Fill each with berry filling using a piping bag or spoon.
10. **Melt** white chocolate in a double boiler. If too thick, stir in butter until spreadable.
11. **Pipe** the white chocolate over the donuts.
12. **Let cool** for at least 1 hour to prevent filling from leaking or eat warm and enjoy the messy, gooey goodness!

Campfire Thimbleberry Shortcake

Makes: 4–6 servings
Time to Make: 30 minutes (15–20 minutes bake time)

Ingredients

Shortcake
- 2 cups all-purpose flour
- 2 tsp baking powder
- ½ tsp salt
- 2 Tbsp sugar (optional)
- ½ cup cold butter (or coconut oil), cut into chunks
- ¾ cup milk or buttermilk

Toppings
- Fresh thimbleberries

Optional: sprinkle of sugar or drizzle of honey
- Whipped cream, yogurt, or a spoonful of foraged berry jam

1. Prep the Dough
- **Mix** flour, baking powder, salt, and sugar in a bowl.
- **Cut in** the butter until the mixture is crumbly.
- **Stir in** milk just until a soft dough forms—do not overmix.

2. Cook Over Fire

Option 1: Skillet Method
- **Grease** a cast iron skillet or Dutch oven.
- **Form** the dough into 6 rounds or one large biscuit-style round.
- **Cover** with foil or a lid and place over hot coals (not direct flame).
- **Cook** for 15–20 minutes, flipping once if possible.

Option 2: Foil Packets or Pie Iron
- **Wrap** flattened dough rounds in greased foil or place in a pie iron.
- **Cook** in hot coals for 10–12 minutes, turning occasionally.

3. Serve
- **Split** the shortcakes.
- **Top** with foraged berries and whipped cream, yogurt, or honey.

Thimbleberry Pecan Cake

Growing up, we often picked thimbleberries on hikes, but rarely did any excess make it home to go in a cake or pie! This recipe combines traditional ingredients like pecans and cream cheese frosting with freshly harvested wild berries to create a scrumptious foraged delight. You can also swap the pecans for wild-foraged nuts like roasted acorns or hazelnuts!

Makes: Two-layer 8" x 8" pan

Time to Make: 1 hour

Ingredients

- 2 cups all-purpose flour
- 1 tsp ground nutmeg
- ½ tsp baking soda
- ½ tsp baking powder
- ¼ tsp salt
- ½ cup butter, softened

- 1 cup packed brown sugar
- 2 eggs
- 1 cup thimbleberry preserves (*or raspberry preserves + fresh thimbleberries*)
- 1 tsp water
- ½ cup chopped pecans

Directions

1. **Preheat** oven to 350°F. Grease and flour two 8-inch cake pans.
2. **Sift** together flour, nutmeg, baking soda, baking powder, and salt. Set aside.
3. **In a small mixing bowl,** cream together butter and brown sugar until light and fluffy.
4. **Add** eggs one at a time, beating well after each addition.
5. **Beat in** the sifted flour mixture.
6. **Add** thimbleberry preserves, water, and chopped pecans. Mix until combined.
7. **Divide** batter between prepared pans.
8. **Bake** for 25–30 minutes, or until a toothpick inserted in the center comes out clean.
9. **Cool** on racks before assembling with frosting and filling.

Cream Cheese Icing & Thimbleberry Filling

Makes: Enough to frost 1 layered cake
Time to Make: 15 minutes

Ingredients

- 1 cup heavy cream
- ½ cup cream cheese, room temperature
- 1 cup powdered sugar
- 1 cup fresh thimbleberries (for filling)
- 1 cup frosting (reserve for mixing with berries)

Directions

1. **Beat** the heavy cream until small peaks form and it holds its shape.
2. **Gradually add** powdered sugar and continue beating until stiff—but do not overmix.
3. **Add** cream cheese while slightly warm and beat until smooth.
4. **Set aside** 1 cup of frosting.
5. **Mix** the reserved frosting with fresh thimbleberries just until combined.
6. **Assemble the Cake:**
   - Place one cooled cake layer on a serving platter.
   - Spread thimbleberry filling over the top.
   - Place the second cake layer on top.
   - Frost the top and sides with the remaining icing.
   - Garnish with additional fresh thimbleberries.

Thimbleberry Jam

If you can manage to have any leftover thimbleberries after enjoying them fresh off the bushes... this recipe is a great way to preserve their sweet and silky flavor for winter! Make a big batch to stock your survival kitchen—or to top acorn Bannocks!

Makes: 6 pints
Time to Make: 1 hour

Ingredients

- 8 cups fresh thimbleberries (to yield ~5 cups mashed)
- 3½ cups granulated sugar
- 1 box Ball low sugar pectin
- 3 Tbsp lemon juice (fresh or bottled)

Directions

1. **Sterilize your jars:** Wash in the dishwasher on sterilize setting or boil for 10 minutes. Set on a clean towel.
2. **Prepare the berries:** Rinse well and remove any leaves or debris. Mash or blend to desired texture.
3. **Mix the pectin:** In a small bowl, combine pectin, lemon juice, and ¼ cup of the measured sugar.
4. **Cook the jam:** Add mashed berries and pectin mixture to a large pot. Bring to a full boil, stirring constantly.
5. **Add** the remaining sugar and boil hard for 1 minute.
6. **Check for thickness:** If jam drips in thick sheets from a spoon, it's ready. If too thin, mix 1 Tbsp *additional* pectin with ¼ cup sugar and boil again for 1 minute.
7. **Fill the jars:** Soak lids in hot water. Use a funnel to fill jars, leaving ¼-inch headspace. Wipe rims, apply lids and rings, and tighten gently.
8. **Process in a water bath canner:**
   - 5 minutes at sea level
   - 10 minutes above 1,000 ft
   - 15 minutes above 6,000 ft
9. **Cool and seal:** Use jar lifters to remove jars and set on a towel. Let sit for several hours or overnight. Listen for the "pop" of sealing lids—press center to check.

Note: Always follow your pectin's instructions for sugar ratios and setting tips.

Thimbleberry Shrub

Shrubs, or drinking vinegars, were once a common way to preserve fruit and create a refreshing tonic. Thimbleberries make a particularly tangy, vibrant shrub that can be mixed with sparkling water for a summer drink—or taken by the spoonful as a traditional digestive aid.

Makes: About 2 cups syrup
Time to Make: 15 minutes active, plus 2–3 days infusing

Ingredients
- 2 cups fresh thimbleberries (or 1 cup frozen, thawed)
- 1 cup sugar or honey
- 1 cup crabapple cider vinegar (see recipe in this book)

Directions
1. **Macerate:** Combine thimbleberries and sugar in a clean jar. Mash lightly with a spoon. Cover and refrigerate 1–2 days, stirring occasionally, until juice is released.
2. **Strain:** Pour mixture through cheesecloth or a fine strainer into a clean jar. Discard seeds and pulp.
3. **Add vinegar:** Stir vinegar into the strained juice until well combined.
4. **Store:** Keep in the refrigerator for up to 2 months.

Pro Tip: Mix **2–3 tablespoons** shrub with sparkling water for a refreshing drink.

For a **digestive tonic**, take 1 tablespoon shrub diluted in a small glass of water before meals.

Flavor variations: Add a sprig of mint, yarrow, or ginger to the infusion for extra stomach-soothing power.

VENISON

I got my first blacktail deer back in 2017—when I was eight months pregnant with my daughter. Sitting in the forest on that November day, listening as rain drip-dripped among the leaves around me, I watched a doe walk quietly through the forest, stopping to sniff the wind. In Oregon, with a bow, you can harvest antlerless deer. An arrow nocked, I calmly pulled back on the release, letting it hit its mark. Sitting alone, I thanked her for her gift to our family.

Venison is a lean, flavorful red meat harvested from wild deer, long prized by hunters and traditional cultures across North America, Europe, and parts of Asia. Rich in protein, iron, and B vitamins, venison supports muscle strength, energy levels, and recovery—all while being naturally low in fat and free of additives.

Flavor Profile

Venison has a bold, earthy, and distinctly gamey flavor, often described as richer and more intense than beef. It's lean and slightly sweet, with a deep red color and a fine-grained texture. The flavor can vary based on diet, age, and processing—but well-prepared venison is savory, complex, and deeply satisfying.

Texture: Lean, dense, and tender when properly cooked

Taste Notes: Gamey, earthy, iron-rich, slightly sweet

Pairs Well With: Red wine, juniper, thyme, rosemary, garlic, wild berries, mushrooms, and smoky flavors

Best Cooking Methods: Grilled, seared, braised, roasted, or ground for burgers, sausages, and stews

Where to Buy/Substitutes

Lamb, elk, bison

Did You Know?

Venison isn't just about meat—the hide was a critical survival resource for Indigenous peoples and early settlers alike. Deer hides were tanned into soft, durable buckskin for clothing, moccasins, and bags. Unlike modern fabrics, buckskin breathes, insulates when wet, and can be crafted entirely off grid. For survivalists, learning to tan and use a deer hide means tapping into one of the oldest skills of self-sufficiency—turning every part of the harvest into something useful.

Venison Chili

This simple chili will hit the spot on a cold winter day! Try canning it using your pressure canner's instructions for chili—or freeze a large batch to take on your next hunting trip.

Makes: Enough for an 8"x 8" baking dish
Time to Make: 35 minutes

Ingredients
- 1 onion, chopped
- 2 garlic cloves, minced
- 1 lb venison or ground elk meat
- 2 Tbsp olive oil
- 1 Tbsp chili powder
- 1½ tsp cumin
- 2 tsp salt
- 2 cups canned kidney beans
- 1 cup tomato sauce or pasta sauce
- 1 cup water

Directions
1. **Chop** the onion and **add** to a cast iron skillet over medium heat.
2. **Add** chili powder and cumin to the skillet and stir to toast the spices.
3. **Add** the ground venison, minced garlic, and olive oil.
4. **Cook**, breaking up the meat with a spoon, until browned and evenly cooked.
5. **Stir** in tomato sauce and water until combined.
6. **Simmer** uncovered for about 20 minutes, until thickened but still saucy.
7. **Season** with salt to taste.
8. **Serve** with cornbread, grated cheese, chopped green onions, sour cream, or any other desired toppings.

This chili freezes well or can be pressure canned for future meals.

Cornbread

This cornbread can be mixed ahead of time—the dry ingredients, that is. To cook (in a cast iron over the fire or in the oven), just add the milk, egg, and oil!

Makes: 8"x 8" baking dish
Time to Make: 35 minutes (including baking time)

Ingredients
- 1 cup cornmeal
- 1 cup all-purpose flour (or ½ cup coconut flour + ½ cup almond flour for gluten-free)
- 1 tsp salt
- 1 Tbsp baking powder
- ¼ cup granulated sugar
- ⅓ cup olive oil or coconut oil
- 1 egg
- 1 cup milk

Directions
1. **Mix** together all dry ingredients in a bowl.
2. **Make** a well in the center and **add** the egg, oil, and milk.
3. **Beat** the egg gently, then stir everything together until just combined.
4. **Pour** batter into a greased 8"x 8" baking pan.
5. **Bake** at 375°F for 20–25 minutes, until the center springs back when touched.
6. **Serve** warm with local raw honey and butter—or **spoon** your venison chili right over the top!

Ground Venison and Feta Meatloaf

Ground game meat like venison can turn out dry because it doesn't have much natural fat. While many people add extra fat when they grind their own, this recipe uses feta cheese instead—keeping the meat moist and giving it a melt-in-your-mouth texture. And if you already added fat to your ground venison, this will still turn out amazing! Serve with chive smashed potatoes (see chive section).

Makes: 4 servings
Time to Make: 1½ hours

Ingredients
- 1 lb ground venison or elk burger
- ⅔ cup crumbled feta cheese
- 1 small white onion, chopped
- 2 garlic cloves, chopped
- 1½ tsp garlic and herb rub
- 1 egg

Directions
1. **Preheat** your oven to 350°F.
2. **Place** the ground meat in a stainless-steel mixing bowl.
3. **Add** feta cheese, crumbling it finer if the chunks are large.
4. **Add** the chopped onion, garlic, herb rub, and egg.
5. **Knead** gently by hand until just combined and evenly mixed—do not overwork.
6. **Transfer** to a baking dish or loaf pan and shape into a loaf.
7. **Bake** for 1 hour, or until the internal temperature reaches 165°F.
8. **Rest** for 5–10 minutes before slicing and serving.

Venison Fajitas (Perfect for Camping!)

This recipe is so easy, and a great way to incorporate some extra veggies into your diet! You can play around with which ones you add if there are foraged vegetables you prefer, or even wild herbs like chives!

Makes: 4 servings
Time to Make: 1 day for marinating and cooking

Ingredients

- ¼ cup lemon juice
- ¼ cup liquid aminos
- 1 tsp cumin
- ¾ tsp chili powder
- 1 onion, sliced
- 1 bell pepper, sliced
- 1 ½ lb venison, cut into 2" strips

Directions

- **Combine** all ingredients in a large Ziploc bag or glass jar.
- **Marinate** in the refrigerator for up to 24 hours.
- **When ready to cook,** pour the contents into a cast iron skillet over medium heat.
- **Cook** for about 10 minutes, stirring occasionally, until the meat is cooked through and the vegetables are tender.

Slow Cooker Venison Roast with Root Vegetables

This dish is an absolute favorite of mine in late fall when I'm either mushroom hunting or archery deer hunting. Coming home to dinner already made—after a long day in the Oregon Cascade rainforest—is one of the best feelings. Often, I walk in with a hat full of chanterelles, wash them up, and sauté them to serve with this roast. Life doesn't get much better!

Note: I like to soak my venison roasts in buttermilk for 12 hours before cooking to reduce the gamey flavor and improve tenderness. Simply cover the meat with buttermilk in a bowl, cover, and refrigerate overnight.

Makes: 4 servings
Time to Make: 8 hours

Ingredients
- 1 venison roast (approx. 1 lb)
- 4 red potatoes
- 4 carrots
- 1 onion (optional)
- 1 cup water
- Salt, to taste

Directions
1. **Chop** potatoes, carrots, and onion (if using) into bite-sized chunks.
2. **Drain** the roast if it was soaked in buttermilk, and rinse it off.
3. **Place** the roast in the bottom of the slow cooker.
4. **Layer** the chopped vegetables on top.
5. **Pour** 1 cup of water into the bottom of the slow cooker.
6. **Season** lightly with salt.
7. **Set** the slow cooker to LOW and cook for 8 hours.
8. **Serve** hot, optionally paired with sautéed chanterelles.

Pro tip: No buttermilk? Add 1–2 Tbsp vinegar to milk, stir, and let sit a few minutes to create your own.

Venison Cheddar Jerky Snack Sticks

If you are like me and want to avoid nitrates in your meat, give this recipe a try; celery powder acts as a natural nitrate preserving the meat while it smokes. With added cheddar cheese for flavor and a nice smokey finish, you can't go wrong!

Makes: about 20 jerky sticks

Time to Make: 8 hours

Ingredients

- 6.5 oz smoked cheddar cheese, grated
- 1 lb ground venison
- 1 lb ground pork
- ½ lb ground beef (85% lean)
- 2 tsp garlic powder
- 1½ tsp salt

- 2 tsp garlic and herb seasoning
- 1½ tsp dried fennel
- 1 tsp celery powder
- 1 tsp black pepper
- 2 Tbsp liquid aminos or soy sauce

Directions

1. **Mix** all meats, spices, and grated cheese thoroughly in a large bowl.
2. **Load** the mixture into a jerky gun fitted with a wide nozzle.
3. **Pipe** into edible collagen casings, moving slowly and carefully to avoid overfilling.
4. **Tie** the ends of each sausage with cooking string to secure.
5. **Place** sausages on a rack in your smoker or oven (use a wire rack over a baking sheet if using the oven).
6. **Set** smoker or oven to 180°F and cook for 1 hour.
7. **Increase** temperature to 190°F and continue cooking for 2 more hours.
8. **Raise** temperature to 200°F for the fourth hour.
9. **Finish** by increasing to 225°F and cook until internal temperature reaches 165°F.
10. **Cool** slightly before storing or serving.

BONUS Recipe!

Rustic Deer Hide Rug (Hair-On Buckskin)

Whether you're crafting a rustic cabin rug or making use of every part of a harvest, tanning a deer hide the old-fashioned way is a rewarding process. This method uses natural materials and simple tools—no harsh chemicals required.

Makes: 1 hide rug or throw
Time to Make: 3–5 days (including drying and curing time)

Materials
- 1 section of deer hide (preferably the back or flank)
- Sharp skinning knife
- Fleshing tool or spoon
- Scraper (bone, wood, or metal)
- Drying frame (a rectangle of wood and rope or nails)
- Twine or sinew
- Hardwood ash (or non-iodized salt)
- Water
- Brain or egg yolks (for softening – optional)

Directions
1. **Skin Carefully**
   Remove the hide from the deer as cleanly as possible. Choose a section with few holes or tears for the rug.
2. **Flesh the Hide**
   Place the hide hair-side down on a log or beam. Use your fleshing tool to remove all meat, fat, and connective tissue. This is important for preventing rot.
3. **Dry the Hide**
   Stretch the hide on a frame, securing it with twine or sinew. Let it dry in a shady, breezy place for a few days. Keep it off the ground and away from bugs.
4. **Preserve with Ash or Salt**
   Rub hardwood ash or non-iodized salt deeply into the flesh side of the hide. This prevents bacteria and helps preserve it for long-term use. Let it sit for 24–48 hours, then brush off excess.
5. **(Optional) Soften with Brain or Egg**
   Mix the brain of the deer or a couple of egg yolks with warm water. Rub into the hide and work it by hand or over a cable until it softens. This step isn't necessary for a stiff rug, but it adds flexibility if used as a throw or wall hanging.
6. **Finish & Trim**
   Cut your hide into the shape you want—circular, rectangular, or with a raw edge. You can sew backing on (like canvas) or leave it natural.

Survival Tip:
Hair-on buckskin keeps the ground warmer than woven mats and adds natural insulation to shelters—perfect for off grid living or winter camps.

Miscellaneous Survival Know-How Skills

Purifying Water in the Wild

When you're living off the land, harvesting wild greens, fish, and game—safe water is non-negotiable. Even the clearest mountain creek can hide bacteria, parasites, or runoff. Here's how to keep your water safe, wherever you roam.

1. BOIL IT

Bring water to a rolling boil for at least 1 minute (or 3 minutes if you're above 6,500 ft).
Kills bacteria, parasites, and most viruses. However, it doesn't remove other contaminants like heavy metals or sediment.
Best for camp cooking, tea, or filling your canteen.

2. FILTER IT

Use a portable water filter—pump or straw style.
Removes dirt, bacteria, and parasites (but not always viruses).
Light, reliable, and reusable—keep one in your pack.

3. TREAT IT CHEMICALLY

Purification tablets (iodine or chlorine dioxide) kill bacteria, viruses, and parasites.
Wait time: usually 30 minutes.
Great backup when you can't boil.

4. SOLAR IT (SODIS)

Emergency method: fill a clear plastic bottle, leave it in direct sun for 6–8 hours.
UV rays kill many germs if the water's clear.
Simple trick when you're stuck with no gear.

Safety Note: SODIS is a great survival or off grid method for killing pathogens in clear, safe-looking water, especially in tropical or sunny areas. However, it's not reliable in cloudy conditions, doesn't work on polluted water, and needs careful handling to avoid recontamination.

For best results, **combine SODIS with filtration** (cloth, sand, or biofilter) and **always use clean containers**.

5. BUSHCRAFT CHARCOAL FILTER

Layer cloth, charcoal, sand, and gravel inside a hollowed log or plastic bottle.
Strains out big debris—but always boil or treat afterward to kill microbes.
Good primitive skill to practice!

SURVIVAL TIP

Choose flowing water over stagnant.
Filter + boil = best combo if you can.
Avoid water near roads, mining, or animal waste.
Clean water keeps you alive—wild food keeps you strong. Use both wisely.

Off grid Ice Cream in a Bag (or Jar)

No electricity? No problem. This simple method lets you churn ice cream by hand using just a few household (or camp-ready) items. Perfect for wild berry mix-ins from the land.

Makes: About 1 serving
Time to Make: 10 minutes

What You'll Need:
- 1 pint-sized Ziplock bag (or small mason jar with a tight lid)
- 1 gallon-sized Ziplock bag
- Ice
- ½ cup rock salt (or coarse salt)
- Dish towel or gloves (optional—it gets cold!)

Directions
1. **Mix Your Base**
   In the small bag or jar, combine cream, sugar, and vanilla (plus any foraged flavor add-ins like wild strawberry or dandelion syrup).
2. **Seal Tightly**
   Make sure it's leakproof. If using a jar, wrap the lid in cloth and double-check the seal.
3. **Prep the Ice Bag**
   Fill the gallon-sized bag halfway with ice. Sprinkle rock salt over the ice.
4. **Combine & Shake**
   Place your small bag or jar inside the large bag with ice. Seal it. Shake vigorously for 5–10 minutes.
5. **Protect Your Hands**
   Use gloves or a towel to keep your hands warm while shaking—this gets *cold*.
6. **Check Consistency**
   Once the mixture feels like soft serve, it's ready. Serve right away or stash it in a cooler to firm up.

Why It Works
The salt lowers the freezing point of the ice, making it cold enough to freeze your cream mixture quickly—even without a freezer.

BONUS—Essential Off grid Survival Kit

A compact list of must-haves for wilderness survival, off grid living, or emergency readiness.

Fire & Warmth

- Ferro rod or waterproof matches
- Bic lighter (x2)
- Dryer lint, tallow fire starters, or waxed cotton
- Emergency blanket or wool blanket

Water & Purification

- Collapsible water bottle
- Portable water filter (e.g., Sawyer Mini)
- Purification tablets or tincture of iodine

Food & Cooking

- Lightweight stove or fire grate
- Metal pot/cup
- Long shelf-life food (jerky, oats, dehydrated meals)
- Fishing line/hooks or snare wire

Tools

- Fixed-blade knife
- Multitool
- Paracord (25–50 ft)
- Duct tape (flat-packed)

Navigation & Signaling

- Compass
- Reflective signal mirror
- Headlamp or mini flashlight (plus batteries)

Shelter

- Tarp
- 6–10 stakes or sturdy sticks
- Extra cordage

First Aid

- Basic kit with bandages, antiseptic, tweezers, pain reliever
- Electrolyte tablets
- Personal medications

Extras

- Bandana (multi-use)
- Small notebook & pencil
- Trash bag (can double as poncho or water catch)

Keep it packed, light, and waterproof. Test your gear before you need it.

If you enjoyed this book...

If *Eat Off the Land* helped you reconnect with nature, cook something incredible, or feel more confident living close to the land—I'd be honored if you'd leave a review on Amazon. Each individual review helps more like-minded individuals find my work, share it, and continues the education of these precious skills—living off grid, enjoying foraging, and eating well doing it!

Know someone who would love this book? Share it with a friend, your hunting buddy, or your local foraging group. Let's pass on this knowledge—just like our ancestors did.

When you cook these recipes, tag me with a stunning photo—

Instagram: @Outdoorsymomma

Facebook: Sharon Trammell

Website:

Amazon Reviews:

Thank you for being part of the wild food revival.
Stay grounded. Stay resilient. Stay wild.

— Sharon Trammell

YouTube Channel:

Also, be sure to check out my YouTube channel—
https://youtube.com/@outdoorsymomma where I share not only my adventures in the wild but also weekly information on preparing, cooking, and eating OFF THE LAND!

Reading Resources

I have compiled a list of books with the intent of further education on the part of my readers. These include dedicated plant ID guides and fishing guidebooks. See my Instagram or website for more specific resources on who to buy mushrooms from in the PNW.

Mushroom Foraging

All That the Rain Promises and More: A Hip Pocket Guide to Western Mushrooms
Arora, David
https://a.co/d/apnPTCz

Medicinal Plant Foraging

Pacific Northwest Medicinal Plants: Identify, Harvest, and Use 120 Wild Herbs for Health and Wellness (Medicinal Plants Series)
Kloos, Scott
https://a.co/d/8Qf2vgO

Hunting Guidebooks and Clam Digging Techniques

Any book by Scott Haugen
https://scotthaugen.com/
Amato Publishers—Many outdoor guidebooks, meat drying, wild game recipes, seafood harvest etc.
https://amatobooks.com/

Fishing Guidebooks

Any book by Gary Lewis. His work is thorough and includes locations as well as advice.
https://garylewisoutdoors.com/

Buying Links

Herbs and Plants, dried wild mushrooms
https://www.azurestandard.com/